SHORT WALKS
IN LAKELAND

D1460409

Falls in Dob Gill (Walks 34 & 36)

SHORT WALKS IN LAKELAND

Book 2:
NORTH LAKELAND

by

Aileen and Brian Evans

CICERONE PRESS
MILNTHORPE. CUMBRIA

6

ADVICE TO READERS

Readers are advised that whilst every effort is taken by the authors to ensure the accuracy of this guidebook, changes can occur which may affect the contents. A book of this nature with detailed descriptions and detailed maps is more prone to change than a more general guide. New fences and stiles appear, waymarking alters, there may be new buildings or eradication of old buildings. It is advisable to check locally on transport, accommodation, shops etc. but even rights-of-way can be altered, paths can be eradicated by landslip, forest clearances or changes of ownership. The publisher would welcome notes of any such changes.

WHEREVER YOU GO FOLLOW THE COUNTRY CODE

Enjoy the countryside and respect its life and work.
Guard against all risk of fire.
Fasten all gates.
Keep your dogs under close control.
Keep to public paths across farmland.
Use gates and stiles to cross fences, hedges and walls.
Leave livestock, crops and machinery alone.
Take your litter home.
Help to keep all water clean.
Protect wildlife, plants and trees.
Take special care on country roads.
Make no unnecessary noise.

Herdwick Ewes

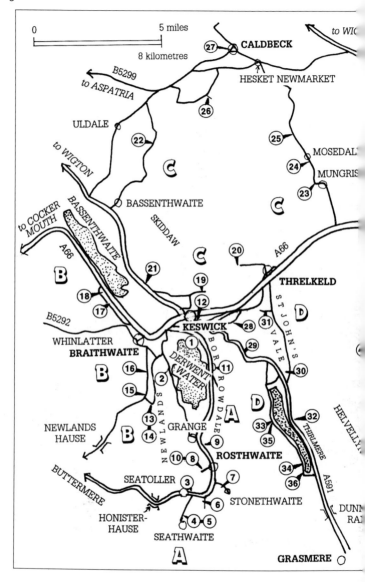

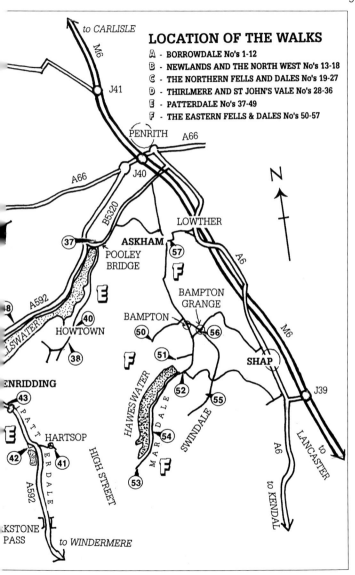

LOCATION OF THE WALKS

- Ⓐ - BORROWDALE No's 1-12
- Ⓑ - NEWLANDS AND THE NORTH WEST No's 13-18
- Ⓒ - THE NORTHERN FELLS AND DALES No's 19-27
- Ⓓ - THIRLMERE AND ST JOHN'S VALE No's 28-36
- Ⓔ - PATTERDALE No's 37-49
- Ⓕ - THE EASTERN FELLS & DALES No's 50-57

to CARLISLE

M6

J41

PENRITH   A66

A66   J40

B5320

LOWTHER

ASKHAM

Ⓔ 37

POOLEY BRIDGE

57

Ⓕ

A6

N

A592

Ⓔ

BAMPTON GRANGE

BAMPTON

40

HOWTOWN

50

38

Ⓕ

51

56

SHAP

M6

J39

ULLSWATER

HAWESWATER

52

55

to LANCASTER

ENRIDDING

43

MARDALE

54

SWINDALE

A6

Ⓔ

PATTERDALE

HARTSOP

42   41

Ⓕ

53

to KENDAL

A592

HIGH STREET

KSTONE PASS   to WINDERMERE

PREFACE

Our aim is to describe a wide variety of short walks, averaging between 4 and 8 miles, ideal for a half-day or a more leisurely full day, keeping mainly to the lower fells, valleys and woodlands. Whilst the classic walks of Borrowdale, the Keswick area and Patterdale are included, we also point out quieter walks which will appeal to those who seek less popular but equally beautiful places. Many of these use old green paths or hollow ways, once trodden by the feet of miners or shepherds, sometimes zig-zagging easily up extremely steep hillsides.

Although this is not primarily a high-fell walking guide, the nature of the area demands a degree of effort and most of the walks visit a summit. Priority is given to the lower fells, which our experience shows to be as rewarding as their higher brethren.

We have aimed to present a combination of comprehensive coverage, detailed route description and easy-to-follow maps in an interesting way. If you work your way through the walks you will, like us, retain many rich memories of some of England's most scenic countryside.

We hope you enjoy the walks as much as we have.

Aileen and Brian Evans
Preston, 1996

KEY TO MAPS

▬ ▬ ▬▬▬	THE WALK	LAKE
▬ ▬ ▬ ▬ ▬	OTHER IMPORTANT PATHS	
‐ ‐ ‐ ‐ ‐ ‐	ROUGH LANE	△ HILL SUMMIT
		INDICATION OF STEEP SLOPE
═══════	SURFACED ROAD OR LANE	
❶ ❷ ❸	DISTANCE WALKED IN MILES	WOODLAND OR FOREST
∿∿∿∿	STREAM	**P** CAR PARKING (NOT ALWAYS A CAR PARK)
≈≈≈≈	RIVER	LARGE AREAS OF BOG
╷ ╷ ╁ ╷	IMPORTANT WALLS	
─┼─┼─┼─	RAILWAY	LARGE AREAS OF MORAINES OR DRUMLINS

INTRODUCTION

This book is split into six sections: Borrowdale, Newlands and the North West, the Northern Fells, Thirlmere, Patterdale and Ullswater, and the Eastern Fells and Dales. Some of these are amongst the most visited beauty spots in Britain with consequent crowding in high season, yet even here we point out quieter ways. Our routes are carefully planned to incorporate interesting places with a minimum of walking on rough paths or surfaced lanes.

Maps
To locate your chosen walk there is a complete map on pages 8 & 9 which pinpoints the start of the walks and shows the approach roads. The individual sketch maps show each walk in detail and should be clear enough for you to follow the route. They have been specially drawn on the walks and incorporate relevant detail not shown on any commercial map. It is helpful to have the relevant Ordnance Survey map or the easy-to-read Harvey Superwalker 1:25,000 map which shows more of the surrounding area; these are specified in the route introductions with the following codes:

OL4	=	OS Outdoor Leisure No.4
		The English Lakes North Western Area 1:25,000
OL5	=	OS Outdoor Leisure No.5
		The English Lakes North Eastern Area 1:25,000
HSW-NL	=	Harvey Superwalker Lakeland North
HSW-WL	=	Harvey Superwalker Lakeland West
HSW-CL	=	Harvey Superwalker Lakeland Central
HSW-EL	=	Harvey Superwalker Lakeland East

Footwear and Clothing
Lightweight boots with a cleated rubber sole are the best footwear for almost all the walks, as there are usually some wet patches or rough ground to contend with. A wide range is available and as almost all the walks are on tracks or paths, there is no need to choose the most expensive boots. Comfort is the chief priority. In a dry spell in summer, trainers may be adequate for some of the lower walks, although make sure the soles still retain good tread - care is needed on steep slopes, particularly when descending wet grass.

Clothing needs to be sensible - bear in mind that even on a warm summer day it can be cold and windy on the fells. In winter, snow and ice may render the high fells dangerous. The high fells can be wintry until May. Every year unprepared walkers die of exposure in unexpected bad weather. There are plenty of low-level woodland walks in this book which are ideal for a day when conditions on the higher fells are dangerous or unpleasant.

The Lake District is notoriously wet and a wise walker never sets out without a waterproof/windproof, a jumper or pile jacket, warm trousers - seldom shorts.

A small daysack completes the gear, with a torch for short winter days, a compass (you need to practise how to use one!), some spare food and drink.

A recommended book which tells you all you need to know about walking in the hills is *The Hillwalker's Manual* by Bill Birkett (Cicerone).

Access

Almost all the walks are on rights of way or permissive paths, or over fell country with open access and a long history of use. On the higher fells the popular paths are stony and worn. These have had a considerable amount of repair work done on them in recent years, with great success. Please keep to paths instead of walking a parallel route which leads to ever-greater erosion. However, the majority of walks described in this book are on paths which are pleasant underfoot. Where the walk goes through farmland it is necessary to keep strictly to the paths and these are usually waymarked, often with yellow arrows. Away from the rough fells and forests, some of the paths cross pasture with grazing animals. Normally they do not bother walkers, although cows may be alarmingly interested in your dog, particularly if it is black and white. Occasionally they may have a bull with them - if in doubt as to your safety skirt the field to avoid problems.

Dogs should be under control at all times and on a lead, particularly during lambing time.

Parking

The walks start where possible from recognised car parks or places where parked cars can be tucked well out of the way of other road users. Please park sensibly. Remember that the Lake District is no different from most other places in Britain and Western Europe with regard to thieving from parked cars. Take everything of value with you and leave doors locked and windows closed.

Grades Used in this Book

Easy   -   A walk on good paths with modest ascents.
Moderate -   Some short steep ascents, or longer well graded ascents. Rough paths in parts.
Strenuous -   Longer steep ascents with rough paths.

Low Fell is generally below 400m, High Fell above 600m, Medium Fell in between.

Directional instructions
Left and right are abbreviated to L and R in the text.

Scheduled Sites
Several of the historical sites visited on the walks are scheduled. It is an offence to interfere with them. Please look, but do not disturb!

Useful Websites
Accommodation is easily found on the internet. Try the official Lake District Tourist Board website: www.golakes.co.uk

The specialist Mountain Weather Information Service forecast for the Lake District is available at: www.mwis.org.uk

Farm dogs guard a barn at Seathwaite

CHAPTER 1

Borrowdale

Borrowdale is a gem of a valley with Derwentwater the sparkling diamond, its coronet of surrounding peaks a joy for walkers of modest ambition.

Keswick is the gateway to this paradise, itself well worth a visit to sample the bustling main street.

Beyond Derwentwater the valley is squashed into the 'jaws', a narrow defile, where river, woods and hills create a perfect vision of Lakeland landscape. A little further the valley flattens and broadens, once a lake bed which reverts at times of incessant rain. The head of the valley is split by craggy fells backed by the dark half-dome of Great End: itself the northern bastion of England's highest peak, Scafell Pike.

Short walks abound in Borrowdale as the combination of modest peaks, attractive woods and lakeshore is ideally suited for this purpose. Most are well-trodden, indeed some over-trodden and uncomfortably stony, and in the summer season are used by a procession of people. The amount of car parking available in the valley is limited and the most popular soon fills at busy times.

Outside of the high season Borrowdale is at its best - visit in spring when the natural woodland is thrusting with fresh, green life; or in autumn for the riot of glorious colours. The lower walks are often sheltered in winter when a backdrop of snow-flecked fells add to the quality of the scene. You should have no trouble parking either!

WALK 1: Around Derwentwater by boat and shore

The launch at Brandlehow Landing

SUMMARY: A walk for any season, hugely popular in summer, it is the easiest in the book with no hills to climb. Children particularly enjoy this walk for they can paddle in the numerous bays, look for red squirrels, scamper along the narrow walkways (with passing places) and if they are tired, finish the day with another sail on the launch.

Distance:	Full round - 5¾ miles (9¼km)
	To Lodore Landing - 3 miles (4¾km)
Grade:	Easy
Height gain:	Negligible
Terrain:	Lakeshore and woodland on good paths.
Map:	OL4, HSW-NL

The Keswick launch runs a year-round service, at very reasonable cost, calling at various landing stages around the lake. The first sailing is around 10.30am.

Derwentwater is surrounded by lovely woods,

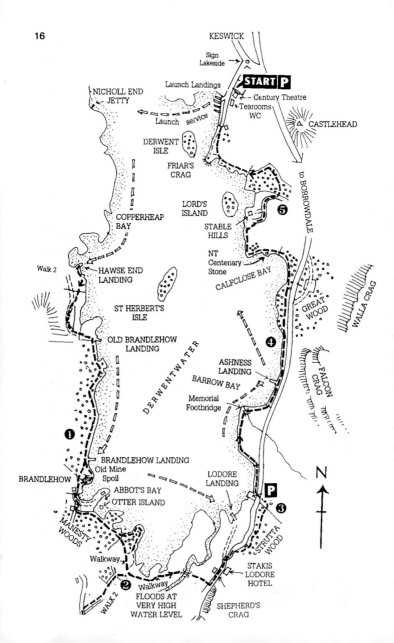

with particularly fine Scots pine gracing the edge of the lake. The finest part of the walk is the first half along the water's edge, but the return along the eastern shore only touches the busy road briefly and gets all the afternoon sun, with a lovely finish through National Trust woodlands past the world famous viewpoint of Friar's Crag.

HOW TO GET THERE AND PARKING: From the Keswick town centre bypass, towards Borrowdale turn R to park at the Lakeside pay & display parking.

THE WALK: Set off past the Theatre by the Lake (toilets) and go down to the landing stages. Booking office on the right. Take the launch to Hawse End, the second stop on the anti-clockwise circuit of the lake. The sail, with brilliant views of the dale, is all too short as you pass the first landing stage and Copper Heap Bay (where the mines of Newlands loaded their ore en route to the smelter at Keswick) and disembark at the foot of Cat Bells under the old pines lining the shore. Turn L on the shore path. Pass the outdoor centre and go over the stile by an old iron fence to merge with a path coming from the centre and the road. Keep ahead then bend L through a gate and field to return to the shore. Turn R through a kissing gate, passing Old Brandlehow landing stage, and through the variety of trees, mainly oak, larch and pine, in Brandlehow Woods and carry on until reaching the landing stage at High Brandlehow. *Across the lake the distinctive building of the Lodore Hotel stands amongst the trees just above lake level with Shepherds Crag to its right, and the valley of Ashness Gill backed by Bleaberry Fell above left. Between Bleaberry Fell and Falcon Crag steps of layered volcanic ash stand out on the fellside and Walla Crag lies at the end of the ridge.* There are many paths but stay by the shoreline where the ripples lap the spoil heaps of the Brandlehow Mine. Go over a stile and pass the white house, once the mine manager's residence. Cross the footbridge over the stream draining from the adit. *There was a large water-wheel hereabouts used to pump the mine below adit level. A photograph and old drawing of it still exist but its exact location is still a subject of debate.* Go through a kissing gate by Rupert's Wood, once coppiced, and ignoring the drive to Abbot's Bay house continue on the surfaced lane. Turn L at the National Trust sign Manesty Wood on the public footpath to Lodore. Pass Otter Island off Abbot's Bay which produces an exotic display of water lilies in summer and find the first of the many log bridges as you pass Myrtle Bay. The main pathway ahead is a short cut but don't be tempted, stay on the narrow shore path to a stile at the wall end and make your way round the headland to visit the splendid viewpoint seat on its promontory.

Continue to the edge of the wood and turn R to meet the main path then turn L to climb onto the raised walkway. *The walkway is wide, solid and kept in good repair so if you fall off while being charmed by the scenery of the mountains beyond the* *Jaws of Borrowdale and sink into the bog it is your own fault.* The walkways lead round the end of the lake, the water reflecting shapely Skiddaw to the north. *Little myrtle bushes grow and if you crush a leaf it releases a beautiful aromatic scent.* Go through a gate and along the next walkway, with passing places, which takes you safely across the lake end marsh to the footbridge over the River Derwent. Pause to look into the crystal water before crossing the pasture to the road gate.

Turn L to the public toilets and stay on this side of the road past the Lodore Hotel to the path on the left which leads to the Lodore landing stage.

TO CONTINUE the walk cross the Watendlath Beck, keep along the road for 100yds then cross into Strutta Wood. Turn L where the path through the old oak wood alleviates road walking. Go through a gate and hold the direction until weaving back through a gate again. Cross a footbridge over Cat Gill (not *the* Cat Gill which we cross later), cross the road and turn R along the footpath from Kettlewell car park to walk between the wall and the water enjoying a sweeping view down the lake to Barf and the Whinlatter forest. *From here a gash on Cat Bells shows clearly. It is a vein worked in the 16th century by the Elizabethan miners.*

Go over a stile to walk along the lakeside turf. Cross the memorial footbridge over Barrow Beck and progress round Barrow Bay. Negotiate another stile and along to the Ashness landing stage. Falcon Crag looms above, still frequented by falcons, and the shore is stony underfoot but the changing scene more than compensates as the 'beach' narrows into a strip of woodland. Cross a footbridge over Cat Gill, the one known by geologists for its succession of volcanic beds, and walk under the outlying pines of Great Wood (ignoring the many paths branching at all angles to the Great Wood car park). Pass a memorial seat (wood) and another (stone) and a National Trust contribution box then carry on round Calfclose Bay. Cross a footbridge and keep by the fence. *The field to the right contains green hillocks; the start of the rounded drumlims, deposited by the ice around Keswick. By the path is a sign erected to mark the centenary of the National Trust, December 1995, and on the left is the intricately carved boulder, placed to mark this special occasion.* Go ahead under the yew trees, listening for the variety of birdsong, and on through a gate into Strandshag Bay with Lord's Island lying close offshore. The path is lined with gorse, which seems to display a flower whatever the season, as it now bends away from the lake to go round Stable Hills House. Leave the field at the cattle-grid and go along the drive. Turn L through a gate into the 'everglades' and cross a bridge over Brockle Beck. The knoll to the right is Castlehead (see Walk 11) and as you go through the gate and over the bridge at the end of the wood there is a fine outlook west to Causey Pike and Cat Bells with the Newlands valley between. Ahead is beautiful pine-topped Friar's Crag, a scene well-known from countless chocolate boxes and calendars. Go through the gate (diversion left to the crag and monuments) and continue past the memorial tablet to Canon Rawnsley, founder of the National Trust, to arrive at the landings and start. (National Trust gift shop, sweets and drinks at the launch booking office, tea gardens, toilets 100yds.)

WALK 2: Cat Bells and Derwentwater Shore

SUMMARY: The walk over Cat Bells cannot be ignored. It is trodden by thousands every year, attracted by its fine little summit and excellent views. However, it is a victim of its own success, indeed the summit cone is completely bare of turf and some short sections have been eroded to mild rock scrambles where care is needed.

Distance:	4½ miles (7¼km)
Grade:	Moderate
Height gain:	1220ft (370m)
Terrain:	Medium fell and woodland. Some rough and stony paths.
Summit:	Cat Bells - 1479ft (451m)
Map:	OL4, HSW-WL

The return through the lovely woods by Derwentwater shore is a fine contrast to the bare fell. If you like company, this is the walk for you.

Cat Bells from the first summit

HOW TO GET THERE AND PARKING: From the A66 west of Keswick turn S to Portinscale then follow signs to Grange. In 1 mile the road climbs steeply up zig-zags with a cattle-grid beyond the second bend. Turn R to the parking area. Overflow parking is provided below the zig-zags.

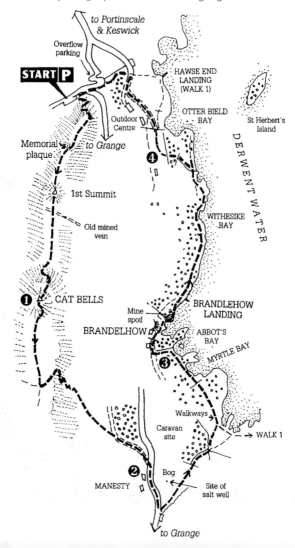

THE WALK: Set off from the east side of the parking area up the north spur of Cat Bells on a repaired path. *Due to the popularity of this peak, erosion is a major problem which is now being managed and walkers are asked to cooperate by using the assigned paths.* At a junction with the path from the road turn R. *There is already a good retrospective view of the lower Newlands valley, Derwentwater, Keswick and Skiddaw. As you climb you can see the motor boat launch making its way from landing stage to landing stage round the lake (see Walk 1). Notice the shards of rock, the Skiddaw Slates, underfoot as you walk on to gain the shoulder with a good view into the upper Newlands valley to the right and a wink of blue from the delicate harebells in the short-cropped grass.* Scramble up the rocks, choosing a way to suit, passing a plaque to Thomas Arthur Leonard, 'Father of the open-air movement in this country'. At the top don't get excited - this is not the summit but heralds an easing of gradient along a ridge which leads to the last steep pull up to the first summit with an extensive view to reward your efforts. Set off towards the main summit but as you go look out for a trench crossing the ridge at right angles. This is the remains of an old mining operation going back to the 16th century.

Make an attack on the main summit. There is no need for a description but do look back as you pause in the scramble up the final boss, for a better view of the mined vein.

The summit, its soil-covering worn away, shows white quartz stringers in the rock and a very meagre cairn. Continue over the summit and down the cairned path along Mart Bield to the saddle between Cat Bells and Maiden

View over the lower Newlands valley

Moor. Turn L (the path right leads to the old Yewthwaite Mine then down into the Newlands valley) and down the well-built stone pitched path, a vast improvement on the deeply eroded and dangerous gully which it replaced. The path makes its way easily down the steep bracken-covered slope with the tiny bright yellow flowers of the quatrefoil smiling on the verge. *About half way down, the outlook is to the Jaws of Borrowdale, the River Derwent forcing its way through the narrow wooded divide between Castle Crag and King's How and its neighbour, with the knobbly top, Brund Fell (Walk 9).* At a Y-junction above woodland keep R and down to join a wider mine track at the Cat Bells National Trust sign. Keep ahead to a gate by a permissive path sign, go through and R and to reach the road.

Turn R along the road passing Manesty Cottages and Youdale Knott. Now look on the left for a footpath to Lodore and a timetable for the launch. Go through the gate onto a broad path. *In the stream to the right is a water gauge where the National River Authority take readings to measure pollution from old mines.*

Go along the streamside path looking over the uninteresting, flat, rush-strewn marshland as you go. Yet this patch of land on the left holds secret memories of the Salt Well.

Ignore a track right to a gate and keep ahead over a two-plank bridge to a kissing gate at the wood corner. Go along with a view across the valley floor of Shepherd's Crag, its upper rocks protruding from a tight tree-top blanket, to a kissing gate in a fence. Mount the rock ahead to go L and parallel to the wall for 150yds then branch R heading for the lake. At the shore path turn L and balance along the wooden walkways. *It is worth stepping down onto the bog to smell the aromatic scent of the myrtle, examine the fly-trapping leaves of the butterwort and sundew and the array of delicate orchids which bloom in early summer. (Do not disturb the orchids, they need up to 14 years of growth before they produce seeds.)*

The main path runs through the trees with the beauty of the lake glinting alongside. Go through a gate in a wall and pass Myrtle Bay and Abbot's Bay with its little Otter Island and mat of water lilies to a cottage at Manesty Woods. Turn R on the surfaced track signed to Brandlehow. At a fork keep L (seat with view) to a kissing gate at Brandlehow. Pass the cottage, which was once the home of the mine manager, to the site of the Brandlehow Mine. Cross the bridge and to the left is the mine adit with other adits and spoil heaps on the hillside above. Cross the levelled spoil to the landing stage and along the beautiful shoreline of Withesike Bay and round a little knoll to the Victoria Bay landing stage. At the edge of the woodland go through a kissing gate then turn L along the woodside pasture (ignore a path right) over a stream to a gate with stile. Keep along the major path (ignoring a branch down right) and to an iron gate then up a gentle rise below an outdoor pursuits centre to a gate at a surfaced lane, turn R to Hawse End. Turn R along the drive for 100yds. At an iron fence end turn L into the wood and backtrack the signs from the parking to the jetty up the wallside beneath shady beeches to the main road at the zig-zags. Turn L to go over the cattle grid and ahead at the next bend into the parking area.

The Salt Well

A salt spring close to a copper vein was developed in the early 1800s by Major General Sir John Woodford. A well was dug, a bath house built over it and it was offered to the public free for medical purposes. It was unpopular and became derelict. Now only the site remains.

WALK 3:   Castle Crag from Seatoller

Seatoller

Distance:	5 miles (8km)
Grade:	Moderate
Height gain:	820ft (250m)
Terrain:	Valley and woodland with a short, steep climb onto Castle Crag. Good paths.
Summit:	Castle Crag - 951ft (290m)
Map:	OL4, HSW-WL

SUMMARY: This is the classic walk in the heart of Borrowdale with a rich variety of scene. Enjoy the enticing balcony path; don't miss the steep climb to the top of Castle Crag for it has a real miniature mountain atmosphere; linger at the quarries where Milican Dalton made his home; relish the beautiful woods which clothe the base of Castle Crag and enjoy the company of the river on your return to Seatoller.

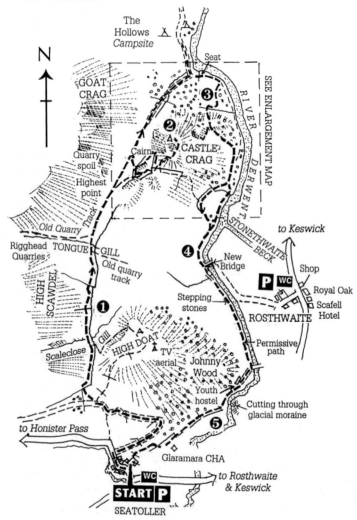

HOW TO GET THERE AND PARKING: Seatoller NT car park in upper Borrowdale. Toilets, bus terminus and timetables.

THE WALK: At the car park entrance turn R up the Honister road between the little cluster of cottages (*Yew Tree Cottage built* AD 1628 *is a country restaurant serving meals, refreshments and ice-cream*), a farm and a barn. M*assive gabions protect the hamlet from the waters of the Honister Beck which nearly swept the cottages away in the floods of* 1966. Opposite the old bridge and turning area turn R through a kissing gate onto the old Honister toll road. Go through a kissing gate in the intake wall and already there are pleasing views of Honister and upper Borrowdale until you go through the next gate where a magnificent stand of aged oaks and pines shade the view and frame a picture of the rooftops now receding below. At a fork branch R to Grange and Castle Crag (the farm vehicle track on the far right leads to High Doat if you decide to make the diversion) up the pasture to a gate in a wall. Turn R along the wallside. The path rises but the climb is soon over and a splendid scene over the Jaws of Borrowdale unfolds. A*n oblong boulder serves as a seat and looking over your shoulder reveals the mountainscape of Glaramara, Grains Gill and Great End* (*Walks 6 and 5*).

Pass a ladder stile where the way from High Doat rejoins. Cross the gated bridge over Scaleclose Gill and continue along our scenic balcony. Go over a footbridge which spans a stony gill below High Scawdel and along to a gate in a cross wall. Now we can look beyond the village of Rosthwaite into Stonethwaite with the sharp profile of Eagle Crag high on its southern flanks. Continue descending gently and cross another little gill and an old track from Rosthwaite to the Rigg Head quarries. Reach a gate and a pair of footbridges

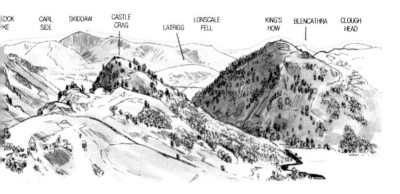

over Tongue Gill then walk a few yards past a quartz-streaked rock. From here look up the gill to the extensive heaps of quarry rid above.

Pass a small stream to a cairn at the junction with the quarry road from Grange. Continue your direction on the rough road past sheep folds to where the path begins to descend and the valley sides embrace a spectacle of Derwentwater and Skiddaw.

TO CASTLE CRAG: Branch R on a narrow shortcut path to a step between a wall and the crag. *Look down onto the old quarry road; from here you can see its set stones still neatly intact.* Continue to a stile in a ridgetop fence. Do not go over but keep to the fenceside until reaching and crossing another stile plus a ladder stile over a wall. * Note this spot.

Branch R by built up stone rid. (The upper ladder stile on the right is a short return.) Carry on up the well made zig-zag path taking care not to disturb the piles of stones on the sides. On approaching the summit, which is bounded by quarry faces, **supervise children closely** as the gentle nature of the trees and soft flower-decked turf belie the situation. After examining the memorial relax awhile and enjoy the view that has inspired writers through the centuries. Return to the ladder stile by the wall.*

Turn R and keep along the fence to a stile. Climb over carefully and descend the ladder and steep maintained path, not missing the memorial seat to the left of a cairn. *A plaque tells how Lady Agnes Hamer gave Castle Crag to the nation in memory of her husband.* Go down to the quarry road and turn R. Massive clapper stones bridge the stream but the road deteriorates as you

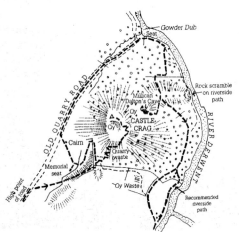

enter Dalt Wood at a gate. Keep ahead ignoring a branch left and cross the lively stream by the ford or raised sleeper. It is merely moments to the River Derwent at Gowder Dub; a popular gravel beach on the bend of the river. It is ideal for anyone young in heart to paddle, picnic or just turn R through the gate/stile onto the Rosthwaite footpath, find a seat and sit watching the red squirrels which abound in the trees.

Keep on the path to Rosthwaite. A little wooden sign indicates the way as the path swings away from the river. Cross a little stone causeway and make your way uphill, ignoring the first gap with an inviting path in the sidewall, turn L through the next gap and rise over a small spur. At the top meet a cross path.

** Note this point.   Turn R for Millican Dalton's Cave
                            Turn L to continue

TO THE CAVE: Turn R and go up the curving path, sometimes trickling with water, to the quarry holes. *The first is just a quarry. The second was Millican Dalton's 'living room' and his water source, drips from the roof, supplies even in the longest drought. The upper cave, his 'bedroom', has a message of wisdom carved for all to read. (It is not on the roof.) Millican Dalton was an eccentric lover of the outdoors who during the 1930 and 40s spent his summers in Borrowdale, living in the cave, and winter in a makeshift hut in Epping Forest. He loved climbing, scrambling, pottering about on the river and he guided parties of walkers amongst the hills. From the dressing floor in front of the caves is the best view of the Bowderstone Pinnacle peeping from the woods across the valley.* Return to **.

TO CONTINUE: Turn L (if you have been to the cave - straight on) and drop down to a cairn then, taking care over a glaciated slab, to a gap in a wall. Pass a quarry on the right and through the glades of High Hows Wood on a multi-cairned path. At a T-junction the paths part and join later.

To the RIGHT walk on to a gate at the woodland edge. Go through and continue until meeting the riverside.

Millican Dalton's Cave

To the LEFT (more adventurous) make a sporty attack by jumping over a wet patch and climbing a stile in a tangle of tree roots beside the river. Cross a little ditch occupied by wild mint and the lilac flowers of the marsh woundwort. Follow the river bank dropping over a wall end with ditch to the junction of the river and Stonethwaite Beck. Follow the bank until you meet the other path again.

Go ahead to a gate and you will see the New Bridge over the beck. (The path crossing the bridge leads to Rosthwaite. We do not take it but it is worth crossing over to inspect the tasteful repair.)

Continue along the beckside across little footbridges on a path now narrow, raised on the levee and hemmed by a fence and the waterside trees. Across the field on the right rises Johnny Wood. A gate leads to a ford and tempting stepping-stones (leading to Rosthwaite). Go straight on a permissive path between the wall and the stream to a kissing gate at Longthwaite. Keep ahead in front of the cottages to a bridge by the entrance gate to the YHA. Turn R into the grounds and walk in front of the hostel to follow the track into Johnny Wood. *Watch out for the flash of a dipper hunting in the beck, easily identified by its white rump, and for the gash in a ridge of glacial debris cut by the water. This is a moraine where the retreating glacier snout stayed a while.* On reaching a rock bar do not be lured too high but keep on a well-worn shelf to reach the continuation of the path at a fenceside and kissing gate. Follow the wallside on a path overhung by ancient oaks and go through a gate into a glade, then on into the woodland again to another gate above the wooden-clad holiday centre building of Glaramara. Follow the wallside to a gate above the car park then turn L and down to the start.

Castle Crag

This remnant of a volcanic plug was crowned by an Iron Age fort, much of which has since been quarried away, although some of the rubble ramparts are still visible. It is a scheduled site and must be treated with respect. It was one of Thomas West's recommended viewpoint stations in his *Guide to the Lakes* of 1778. The tiny valley where we walk on the west of the crag was formed by a stream running along the edge of glacier which once filled the valley. Castle Crag is probably 'The fortress' which gives Borrowdale its name - Borudale, Norse for 'the valley of the fortress'.

The Old Toll Road from Seathwaite to Honister

This was the original private quarry road and tolls were payable by the public. "Motor cars 2/6, Motor cycles 4d., Bicycles 2d." The new road, built in 1934 on an entirely different line, left the old road superfluous; now a pleasant route for walkers.

WALK 4: Borrowdale Wad and Stone

Lonely Launchy Tarn is defended by wet moorland

SUMMARY: Anyone interested in Lakeland's industrial heritage will enjoy this walk steeped in history. Some of the paths were working pony trails, or used by miners and quarrymen to and from their employment. It is difficult to imagine that 200 years ago the Wad mines needed to be heavily guarded against intruders. Our walk visits no summits but links the stone-set path up Sourmilk Gill with Seathwaite wad mines, Honister and Rigg Head quarries, returning along the valley. The plateau of High Scawdel with its lonely tarns can be wet underfoot, although on our visit, at the end of the 1995 drought, we managed dry shod; at Seathwaite, reputedly the wettest place in England, the river bed was a dry ribbon of stones.

		Short Return
Distance:	6¹/₂ miles (10¹/₂km)	5¹/₄ miles (8¹/₄km)
Grade:	Strenuous	Strenuous
Height gain:	1968ft (600m)	1066ft (325m)
Terrain:	Medium fell. Some rough, wet pathless walking.	
Summits:	Seatoller Common - 1476ft (450m)	Seatoller Common
	Shoulder of Dale Head - 1902ft (580m)	
Map:	OL4, HSW-WL	

HOW TO GET THERE AND PARKING:
Verge side parking at Seathwaite, at the end of Borrowdale road. Toilets, telephone, refreshments. The mine spoil heaps of the ore known as wad, graphite

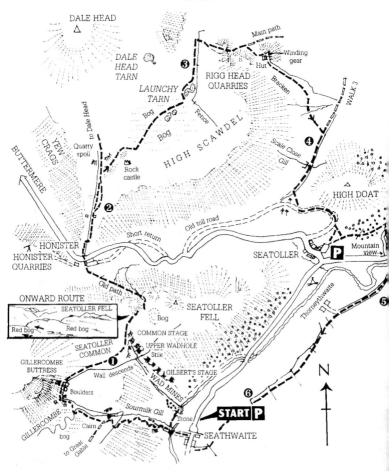

or plumbago perch on the western slopes above and an overall view is seen from the road.

WARNING: Old mine and quarry workings are dangerous and unstable. Do not enter passages or disturb spoil heaps.

The first shallow workings were high on the moor and the Grand Pipe of ore was successively worked by adits driven into the fellside, the latest and most productive workings being the lowest.

THE WALK: From just beyond the road gate turn R under the barn arch towards Sourmilk Gill and the campsite. Cross the River Derwent bridge which was reinforced and raised after the floods of 1966. Ahead is the reset path up Sourmilk Gill*. First cross R over the gill footbridge for in this pasture our intriguing walk into history begins. Go a few yards to the remains of the old mill and blacksmith's shop; a last resort effort to manufacture blacking for fire grates, paint etc. In the plantation above is the lowest and most recently worked level, Robson's Stage an unsuccessful drive to reach the Great Pipe 270ft below the next level. Cross R over the ditch, the remains of a leat bringing water from Sourmilk Gill to drive the overshot water-wheel which powered the mill crusher. Go along the foot of the plantation. *Just before the wall let into the turf is a reproduction marker stone of John Banks 1752 mine owner.*

The National Trust do not encourage walkers to use the old path through the mines as this is a historically sensitive area, so return to the path up Sourmilk Gill*.

Mount the stone path and the ladder stile. The beautiful falls and cascades of Sourmilk Gill need no added description but the fascinating stones underfoot are a geological experience in themselves. Pass Seathwaite Slabs (left), rocks used by climbers, and continue up to a bend. From this viewpoint over the cascade look over the top of the plantation to the flat topped spoil heap and ruined building of Gilbert's Level 1798. *The ruin was a guardhouse of two storeys enclosing the mine entrance and iron rail way which emerged at the front door. On the ground floor was a peat store and smithy and above were living rooms, an office, a wad room and a search room where the mine superintendent searched the miners at the end of each shift and inspected every tub of ore, for the wage of 10/6d*

The Wad mines from Sourmilk Gill

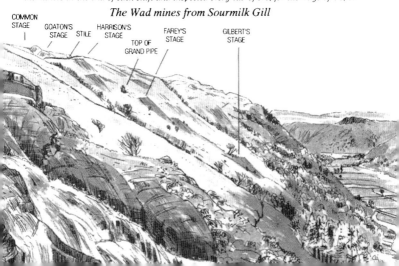

per week. The little gill outside is still named Privy Gill but its privy is long gone. The next level above is Farey's Stage, the main drawing level and the top of the Grand Pipe.

Continue up the path, taking care at the scrambly parts if wet, and as the path bends away left take another look over to the workings where a boundary wall, purposely built high to deter intruders, now with ladder stile, separates the open moor. Over the wall is Goaton's Stage and the Upper Wad Hole, a great quarry-like depression which we will see later.

Go along the wall until a gate gives access onto the moor. Pass the top waterfall and ignoring a path right, keep ahead to face a splendid view of Gillercombe. At the end of the stone path continue to a cairn. (The path turns left for Green Gable.) Go ahead by the stream and cross (where an island splits the flow 25yds left from the wall) then, jump tributary streams, follow the intake wall as it approaches then turns right under the base of the crag. *There are stone patterns and moraines (over the wall) left by ice, together with boulders.* Cross a ladder stile and in sporty manner pass huge boulders after which the way becomes easier and the views extensive over Seathwaite to Combe Head, Glaramara, Base Brown, Green Gable with the top of Great Gable just showing.

Pass between the wall and a rock then, descending only slightly on a thin trod leave the wall which dips away out of sight. Come onto a spur with jagged rocks overlooking the Mines gill and where the boundary wall with stile and the Upper Wad Hole can be seen below. Go up diagonally L along the edge of the steep slope aiming for the flat-topped spoil of the upper workings. **Do not be tempted to enter** even though there are signs of recent digging, but bid farewell to the wad mines and use your ingenuity to head north for the lowest point before the moor dips into the Honister valley, descending slightly to go between two peaty red bogs. The little cairned knoll to the right is Seatoller Fell. The way may appear pathless but it was a route used by miners and quarrymen between the mines and Honister.

Pass between the red bogs on a sheep trod then circle L by pools and Honister Pass is seen below. Join an old green path which makes a descending traverse left and keep a sharp eye to trace its progression down to the pass. (As you go look across the valley to our next objective - the slops towards Dale Head and the rock castle appearing on its right-hand skyline.)

Just before arriving at the pass there is an impressive view of the quarries on Fleetwith Pike, not closed but just ticking over. Cross the stream, go through a gap near the parking area corner and up the steps opposite (footpath sign), and through a gate onto the road.

SHORT RETURN: The Old Toll Road can be followed east down the valley to Seathwaite. It starts at the lower end of the car park and makes a pleasant easy return.

Gillercombe

TO CONTINUE: Cross the road and go straight up the hill with the fence on your right. *The vast face of the Buttermere and Westmorland Green Slate Quarry is a puzzling series of inclines and levels all used for transporting the stone, often by man-pulled sled, to the road from the great cavernous quarries within the mountain.* Reach a stile in the fence and before crossing amble over to the left to enjoy the impressive sweep of Gatesgarthdale to Buttermere. Carry on up the hill, now with the fence on the left. Pass Foxfold (two sheep folds) and two large cairns where the steepness eases and the height gained has earned a southern view. As soon as the Yew Crag Quarry rid heaps are seen above left, turn diagonally R (tiny cairn) towards a pointed rock on a dip in the skyline. There is the hint of a path. Just before the rock turn R (the rock castle seen previously is below right) and Launchy Tarn can be seen glinting ahead. Go on a trod towards the tarn ignoring trods branching left, and walking along the line of an old fence indicated by staggering iron poles at intervals.

Keep by the old fence across the moor. *The ground may be wet but it is a place of special charm where grass, reed and rush mingle their delicate hues and pools borrow their colour and throw it in reflection at the sky.* Pass to the L of the tarns, a hummock and, still guided by the old fence look north to where the slopes of Dale Head fall abruptly into the Newlands valley revealing distant Skiddaw. To the south the ridge of Seatoller Fell is seen in its true perspective against the high bulk of Glaramara.

Turn L at the new fence corner (ignoring the stile) and pass between Launchy Tarn and its offspring, a bit wet here, and along the path parallel to the fence and down to the pass, cairn. (Ahead is the old sheepfold of Wilson's Bield.) Turn R over the stile and take the lower path fork to descend gently to Rigghead Top Quarry with its black yawning chasm. Wend down the blue slate path past old blue ruins and black quarry holes from which the stone was mined. *The desolation is a perfect setting for the colonising fern - alpine lady's mantle making the borders of the re-made path an exhibition. To the left is a gigantic heap of rid, waste from the stone removed from High Scawdel, by cart and later lorry.* At the next level look behind at the arched tunnel leading into High Scawdel fell and used by the path. Go down steps past the foot of the great rid. Just below the corner of a ruin leave the pitched path and fork R to other stone buildings where the top winding gear of an aerial ropeway, used to lower the slates, is still in place. Go between the quarry hole and the house and ahead find a path down to the wall. (Ignore the stile below to the left.) Keep on the old quarryman's path above the wall towards Seatoller. Cross a gill and, across bracken slopes, an old wall. Turn L and descend to join a better path by the intake wall. Turn R and follow this path crossing a gated footbridge and over a low pass to the Honister valley. Below is Johnny Wood and Rosthwaite, home of the quarrymen. Go through the left-hand gate in the wall corner and down the cairned field path to the old road-track.

SHORT RETURN FROM HONISTER JOINS HERE: The old

Old winding gear

road is rough, but after the second gate becomes more amenable and Seatoller (toilets, refreshments, tourist information) is seen below.

VIA SEATOLLER: Carry on down the old road through two gates and turn L. The tourist information is on the left and the Country House restaurant on the right. Keep ahead to the car park (and toilets). To join the route again go through the gate at the rear of the parking area. (For a shorter return turn R just beyond the parking along the road to Seathwaite 1 ¹/₂ miles to the start.)

VIA MOUNTAIN VIEW AND THORNEYTHWAITE: Go round the bend and before four stately pines turn L down the steep grass slope. Just before crossing a stream cut down R to gain the rising path below and turn R towards the gate at the rear of the car park. (The Seatoller diversion joins here.) Turn L along the wall, cross over the ford, and through a kissing gate in the wall behind Glaramara House. Continue direction through the wood on the other side of the wall, pass two cross wall ends (ignoring a kissing gate in the wall above). Turn R down to Folly Bridge over the River Derwent and through the field and gates ahead to the road at Mountain View Cottages. Cross the road and along the lane to Thorneythwaite Farm (public footpath to Seathwaite). On reaching the home field before the farm turn L into a fenced footpath to Seathwaite. Go over a stile and along the wallside to join a vehicle track coming from the farm and continue ahead to a gate. *The view is across the flat glaciated valley to Sourmilk Gill spilling from its hanging valley of Gillercombe and our earlier ascent route.* Pass stand of pines and, ignoring a path branching down right, keep ahead to a kissing gate and continue above the intake wall. Go through a gate at a sheepfold, three more gates and Seathwaite is in sight. Pass through two more gates with cairns of gathered field-stones along the way and over the bridge into the hamlet. Turn R to the start (toilets, cafe, trout farm).

The Borrowdale Wad Graphite Mines

The earliest reference to the mines is found in the records of Furness Abbey in 1540 although earlier records of 1412 are thought to be inscribed in wad from the mines. It is possible that shepherds found surface expanses of wad and used it to mark their sheep. Another tale is that an ash tree was uprooted in a storm to reveal the wad.

The Seathwaite wad at its best was the purest in the world, which resulted in a long and colourful history which is well documented in Ian Tyler's *Seathwaite Wad*. The miners were searched after every shift, the main stages were guarded by substantial guard houses where raiders often needed to be repelled. There was a considerable local smuggling business. German miners were the first to exploit the wad in Elizabethan times, then in 1638 began a long period of ownership by the Bankes family. In 1891 the company was wound up. The Keswick pencil industry was founded on Borrowdale graphite and flourishes today. Its use was widespread, from moulds for casting metals (such as cannon-balls!), to a lubricant or grate blacking, a preservative and to quote Postlethwaite 'a present remedy for cholick'.

Honister Slate Quarries
The slate originated as horizontal beds of water deposited volcanic ash about 400 million years ago. Earth movements later tilted and converted these beds into easily cleaved slates or slate metal. The tilt of the two beds can be seen easily on the face of Honister Crag. Quarrymen were known to be active hereabouts in 1643. Honister Quarries flourished from 1728 to 1986. Fleetwith Pike has an impressive craggy face where you can easily pick out the inclines which once carried light tramways. The inside of the mountain is like a warren, with huge caverns left by the slate miners. There are tales of heroic skill and strength when loads of slate were run on wooden sleds down the screes to the Honister road. In the 1890s the Buttermere and Westmorland Green Slate Co employed 100 men here.

The history of the quarries is fascinating and is told by Ian Tyler in his book *Honister Slate, The History of a Lakeland Slate Mine*. The quarries are now a popular tourist venue, where you can take a guided trip into their interior.

Rigg Head Quarries
The veins of slate worked here for 150 years are the same as at Honister, yielding quantities of top grade slate. Many of the dark entrances to the closeheads can still be seen. It is dangerous to enter these as roof collapses are not unknown! Before quarrying, copper was mined around 1700.

WALK 5: Seathwaite Fell & Sprinkling Tarn

Stockley Bridge

SUMMARY: Grains Gill and Styhead linked by a visit to Sprinkling Tarn in its dramatic mountain setting is a justly popular walk, much of it along pitched stone tracks which provide easy walking, although the height gain does involve some effort.

We recommend a short detour to the summit of Seathwaite Fell; the hummocky plateau which separates the two valleys. On this lonely little mountain you will visit some delectable tarns and gain a magnificent view of its higher neighbours.

Distance:	6½ miles (10½km)
Grade:	Strenuous
Height gain:	1660ft (507m)
Terrain:	Medium fell and valley. Wet in parts. Some rough walking.
Summit:	Seathwaite Fell 2040ft (622m)
Map:	OL4, HSW-WL

The descent can be varied to pass Taylor Gill Force along an exposed path across the base of steep crags. This does require a head for heights but can be bypassed if necessary.

Boots are advised to cope with rough stretches and wet patches.

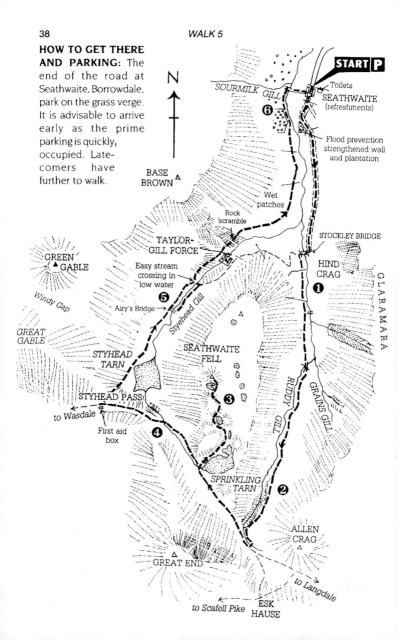

HOW TO GET THERE AND PARKING: The end of the road at Seathwaite, Borrowdale, park on the grass verge. It is advisable to arrive early as the prime parking is quickly, occupied. Late-comers have further to walk.

N

START **P**

SOURMILK GILL

Toilets

SEATHWAITE (refreshments)

6

Flood prevention strengthened wall and plantation

BASE BROWN ⌃

Wet patches

Rock scramble

STOCKLEY BRIDGE

TAYLOR-GILL FORCE

HIND CRAG

1

GREEN ⌃ GABLE

Easy stream crossing in low water

5

Airy's Bridge →

GLARAMARA

Windy Gap

Styhead Gill

GREAT GABLE

STYHEAD TARN

SEATHWAITE FELL

RUDDY GILL

GRAINS GILL

STYHEAD PASS

3

to Wasdale ←

First aid box

4

SPRINKLING TARN

2

ALLEN CRAG ⌃

GREAT END ⌃

to Langdale

to Scafell Pike ←

ESK HAUSE

THE WALK: Note the old plumbago mine spoil on the hillside, the site of extensive underground workings (Walk 4), then walk up the road to the hamlet of Seathwaite where there are toilets, a telephone box, refreshments at the farm and the opportunity to buy fresh trout on your return. Pass through the hamlet and, ignoring the track over the bridge on the left, go straight on up the valley through a gate by a plantation. *The trees were planted to stabilize the embankments made necessary by the floods of 1966 which nearly destroyed the hamlet.* As you move on look back to appreciate the scale of the near disaster. The path is straightforward, past knolls of glacial drift, so admire the glaciated U-shaped valley with the slopes of Hind Crag to the left (east). On the right is Base Brown with the graceful waterfall of Taylorgill Force where Styhead Gill and our return route plunges into the valley.

Stockley Bridge is an old packhorse bridge on the monks' route to Grange. The bridge was almost destroyed by the floods of 1966 but has been tastefully rebuilt. Its arch spans an attractive, rocky narrowing of the stream, and pools enhance the delicate hue of the Lakeland rock.

Cross the bridge, go through the gate and turn L to proceed up the V-shaped valley of Grains Gill. *Due to the high rainfall (176" per year at Sprinkling Tarn), the path is subject to erosion, but it has been repaired with pitched stones and although the going becomes more strenuous it remains easy underfoot.* Pass a gap in a wall end and on through a gate in a cross wall. *Hardy trees of birch and holly line the stream and stand in airy places where mowing sheep cannot eat the seedlings.* Height is gained easily and as you pass a gap in a low cross wall a glance back shows that you are already above the tree-line. The path spreads round a few flat-topped boulders which are very convenient for sitting and viewing the length of Borrowdale to Skiddaw with Dale Head on the horizon to its west. On again to where a rock slab leads onto a footbridge over Ruddy Gill. The path now steepens but is enhanced by the nearby cascades of Ruddy Gill. *Ever more dominating is the face of Great End; black and grim in summer but transformed when the buttresses are encrusted with winter ice or the gullies sketched in spring by lingering snow.* The path continues up the narrowing defile but suddenly the angle eases and the cairn indicating our path as a descent route is passed. Cross the stream and go on to meet another cairned path. (The path left leads to Angle Tarn, Rossett Gill and Langdale.)

Turn R along the red-coloured cairned path passing a small tarn to a gap where Sprinkling Tarn appears with its wonderful backdrop of Great Gable and Green Gable. Make your way down to the outlet of Sprinkling Tarn. **Note this spot** as we return here to make our descent.

SEATHWAITE FELL: Turn R along the tarnside path to the end of the tarn. The path has diminished but hold the same direction past a low rock buttress (right), a perched boulder (left) and then bear L for 20yds through a gap with

The rocky summit of Seathwaite Fell with Great Gable behind

a large boulder leaning against the bedrock which dams a small pool behind. In 50yds bear L again through a gap with scree to a tarn hidden in a hollow. Go round the left-hand side of the 'Hidden Tarn', known as Sprinkling Crag Tarn, cross the outlet stream and go up to the gap ahead. Climb up the slope to the L and gain the parallel ridge which is a grassy area strewn with ice-carried stone debris. Go along the ridge and cross a little depression with a Y-shaped tarn then mount the summit to the cairn 2040ft where the panorama is truly magnificent. Return, somewhat reluctantly (S), to the outlet of Sprinkling Tarn.

Set off R (NW) down the main cairned path facing the mountains of Great Gable (2949ft) and Green Gable (2527ft). Styhead Tarn lies in the valley from which the scree of Aaron's Slack rises to Windy Gap. Ignore the path branching left at the cairn where the left-hand rock wall ends. It is the start of the Corridor Route to Scafell Pike. Continue to the first aid box on Styhead Pass (the path left leads down to Wasdale). Turn R and march off down the valley to where Airy's Bridge spans Styhead Gill. From the bridge is a wonderful retrospective view of L to R Great End, Broad Crag, Scafell Pike and the lower peak of Lingmell.

CHOICE OF RETURN ROUTE:

a) Cross the bridge, continue down the main path to Stockley Bridge and return by the outward route. This is easy and straightforward.

b) Return via the old path beside Taylorgill Force. This route demands a steady foot and a head for heights but is scenically very rewarding. **Not for children**.

Keep along the left-hand side of the stream. The path is narrow and rough in places but the crowds have been left behind and other rewards will come. Just before the gill begins to steepen there are a few places to cross the stream and gain the main path if you change your mind. Keep on towards the plantation. The path becomes narrower and rough as it crosses an area

of red rock but is sound underfoot. Just before the first silver birch trees the path is a bit eroded. Continue with care then proceed along the fenceside. Ignore the stile leading into the wood. Carry on down the path to the point where the wall/fence swings away right and down to the waterfall.

The next part of the path requires a bit of easy rock scrambling. (If you are not the adventurous type bypass the exposed section by branching R down the scree, guided by the deer fence, where you can enjoy the beautiful waterfall of Taylorgill Force. Stride over the cross fence and join the main path below the scramble.)

The exposed path - keep ahead across the scree slope on the slightly rising narrow traverse path. At a rock step select a good handhold before you move. Keep going and the traverse gradually changes to a descent. Choose the left-hand path close to the rock wall where there are rock steps and on reaching the holly bushes stay under the arched branches where the rock has been worn smooth by many 'sit and shuffle' style scramblers as they descend to a level path with a perched wall complete with gate. Before you go through sit by the airy pathway and take to memory the silky falls of Taylorgill. Go down the path where the bypass path soon joins.

Taylorgill Force

Continue along the boulder fields of Base Brown where the path is boggy and intermittent. Pass a cairn on a boulder, descend a slight rocky step and go through a gap in a cross wall. Carry on to the top side of a plantation where you will find a ladder stile over a wall. Proceed to the lower corner of the next plantation where, across the water, the new flood defences turn the force of the stream. Continue to a gate giving access to the Gillercombe path descending by Sourmilk Gill. Turn R over the bridge, along the walled track and under the farm buildings into Seathwaite. Turn L to the parking and toilets, R to the tea room.

The Seathwaite Flood

Borrowdale is renowned for its prodigious rainfall. Seathwaite is the wettest inhabited place in England with 131" of rain per year. Keswick has a mere 57". Floods were recorded in 1898, but were not as damaging as those of August 1966 when two floods within a week caused extensive damage and almost swept the hamlet away. Neighbouring Seatoller was also awash when the river tore down the road. The River Derwent and Stonethwaite Beck have both been dredged and deepened whilst strong walls and gabions attempt to contain any flooding today.

WALK 6:   Combe Gill Horseshoe

Combe Ghyll

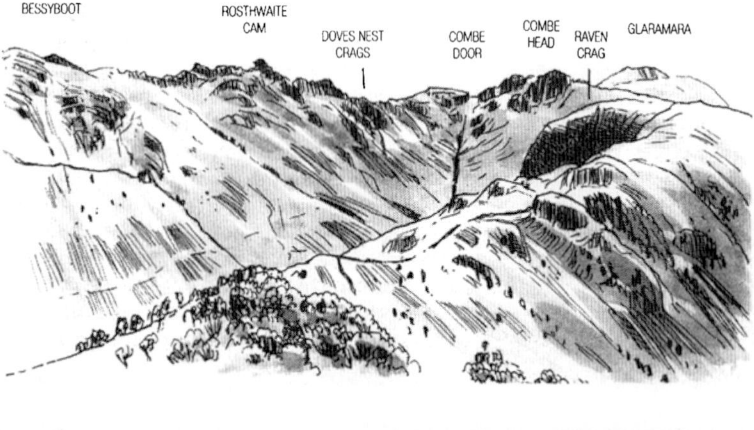

BESSYBOOT   ROSTHWAITE CAM   DOVES NEST CRAGS   COMBE DOOR   COMBE HEAD   RAVEN CRAG   GLARAMARA

SUMMARY: Lakeland horseshoe ridge walks are generally long and demanding. This is a miniature horseshoe but no less enjoyable, with a definite mountain air. The ridge of Rosthwaite Fell is a complex jumble of peaklets, wet hollows and tiny tarns; a wonderful place on a good

Distance:	5 miles (8km)
Grade:	Strenuous
Height gain:	2132ft (650m)
Terrain:	Medium fell. Rough walking on tiny paths, a broad worn path is joined for the return.
Summits:	Rosthwaite Cam - 2007ft (612m) Combe Head - 2394ft (730m)
Map:	OL4, HSW-CL

day. Views are ever-changing on the intricate path. Once embarked on this ridge walk there is no easy descent for there are steep crags on both sides. **DO NOT ATTEMPT THIS IN MIST.**

Combe Head with its aerial view onto the glacial mounds of Combe Gill makes a worthy culmination before a freewheel descent on the unmistakable worn path of the horseshoe's western arm.

HOW TO GET THERE AND PARKING: From Keswick take the B5289 up Borrowdale. Pass Rosthwaite and at Mountain View cottages turn left to Thorneythwaite. Park in 500yds on the extensive verge on the right. (Information centre, refreshments and toilets at Seatoller.)

THE WALK: Return down the lane to the road at Mountain View (ignoring two stiles on the right) and turn R. *The cottages were built as lodgings for miners at Honister Quarries and the windows stare into Combe Gill and our horseshoe route encircling it.* In 100yds turn R, public footpath sign, on the track through a field to a stone-arched bridge over the gill. (*The track turns right upstream to the old corn mill, mentioned in a will of 1727, now private and with no right of way.*) Go through the waymarked gate. Turn R a few yards then L up the fellside (confusing waymarks). Make your way directly up the strip of grass keeping well left of a broken wall. *The attractive mill building hides a water-wheel, still in place, and grindstones set in decorative paving.* Reach a signpost at the prominent right of way path. Turn R on the easy way where views abound. There is a complete vista west of Honister Pass from Seatoller at its foot to the quarried face of Fleetwith Pike at its head, and north over the ancient deciduous woodland of Johnny Wood to the Brund Fell and King's How Ridge (Walk 9).

The path mounts gradually and the waterfall in the deep gill can be heard and then seen. Go through a broken wall to a hawthorn, then keep L at an indistinct fork to pass the remains of an old sheepfold. Carry on to a gate in the intake wall and spin R immediately to another gate in the fence. Look up the line of the intake wall from which springs Intake Ridge, a popular scramble.

The path is now faint but take a rising traverse away from the gill towards a three-toothed rock on the near skyline. Pass to the right of the rock and discover the groove of an old path from a sheepfold below. Turn L up the very steep groove. It is tough but not rough and there are continually changing views to stop and admire. Pass a pointed boulder, go up a spur then the angle eases and the groove flattens but its continuation can be seen ahead. Pass a three-stones block and at the next ease of gradient a cairn. Stay with the path as it bends R then attacks the slope directly again to another R bend, cairn, to a shelf. To the side plunges deep Rottenstone Gill. Continue ahead with a small crag to the right and still the path goes up. At a second cairn bend R then leave the path for a break on a little bluff to identify the mountain panorama and let the aesthetic pleasure seep from the mind into the leg muscles for the easy

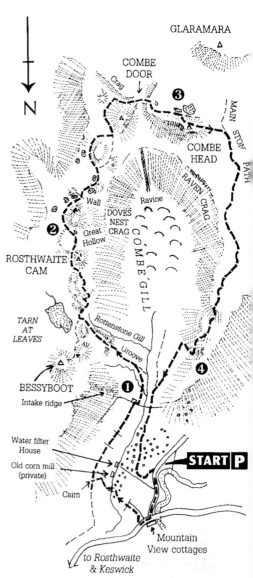

stroll to the pass at the head of the gill.

Before turning R on the ridge path go over the watershed where lies the pretty reed-fringed Tarn at Leaves in its sun-trap hollow under the slopes of Bessyboot's pyramid. Our onward way is to the sombre north-facing Rosthwaite Cam. Follow the path to a fork below a knoll. Keep R up a winding rock-stepped path towards the left of the summit block with excellent views east of Clough Head, the Dodds and Helvellyn. The path leads between boulders to a gap. (A narrow path right scrambles onto the fine summit block.)

Descend towards Great Hollow and on approaching keep L above a rock slope. Pass a captive pool and carefully follow the devious path with rock-step puzzles to a fine view over a string of tarns to Langstrath. Descend with the next little summit off to the right. Go over a stone wall and down, with a quick cameo of the Langdale Pikes, to pass a long pool (R) and a boulder complete with pool and sunbathing ledge (L). Fork R, just beyond climb a short rise and progress, allowing the path to take charge twisting, turning and revealing a new view with every bend.

Go round the back of a knoll and at cross paths turn L rising over the next shoulder to be faced by a wall of rock with horizontal strata. Continue towards it then veer R through a gap to a flat area with pools. This is Combe Door, the head of the Combe Gill Valley with Combe Head in front. Cross the floor to a junction of paths where we go straight on. (To the right the cairn indicates the treacherous way down the gill. **Not recommended**. The path

Rosthwaite Cam, across the Great Hollow

left is to Glaramara.)

Mount the cairned zig-zag path towards Combe Head. Pass a rock tooth and the path splits. (The left onward path passes by tarns to meet the main descent path.) The R fork makes a short easy upward traverse to the nearby summit. Do go for the summit; the reward is a magnificent outlook over the heart of Lakeland.

Carry on over the summit and down the slope bearing south to join the tarns path. Turn R to join the main path.

Turn R along the cairned highway which requires no description until reaching a red rockstep which is bristling with holds. The path then bends right and makes a steep well-cairned descent to the valley. Go through the gate in the intake wall and continue through light woodland along a wallside. The path bends L away from the wall to a stile at the lane. Turn L for 100yds to the parking.

Glacially formed scenery

The effect of glaciers on the scene is admirably demonstrated on this walk. The valley has been scooped and deepened by ice, which in retreat has deposited numerous mounds of moraines. When the ice depth was greater it covered the bounding ridges where it planed the present plateau with its characteristic knolls and hollows, many occupied by lovely pools. Boulders carried by the ice were deposited haphazardly when it melted. You can see them everywhere - balanced precariously or strewn over ice-smoothed slabs.

WALK 7:   Langstrath Valley Walk

SUMMARY: This easy walk, up one side of the valley and down the other, is very popular, yet the higher reaches of Langstrath retain a sense of mountain wilderness in its stony strath backed by steep-sided fells. Interesting features of the walk are the dubs - deep, black pools trapped by vertical rock walls. Many shallower pools make excellent cooling-off spots in hot weather.

Distance:	6 miles (9½km)
Grade:	Easy
Height gain:	460ft (140m)
Terrain:	Easy. Good paths but stony in parts.
Map:	OL4, HSW-CL

HOW TO GET THERE AND PARKING:
Drive up Borrowdale, past Rosthwaite turn L to Stonethwaite. Just before the hamlet there is a good parking space on the right.

Eagle Crag dominates the old circular sheepfold, constructed with water worn stones

THE WALK: Start at the telephone box in Stonethwaite centre and take the path signed Greenup Edge and Grasmere. Go along the walled path to a bridge over Stonethwaite Beck. *Before going over look in the wall for debris indicating the flood height of the strem, normally flowing gently with wagtails picking amongst the stones and families of mallard paddling in the pools, and notice the wise siting of the farmsteads and the village of Rosthwaite perched about The How.*

Cross the bridge, go through the gate and turn R on the public bridleway, now part of the Cumbria Way, and through another gate to walk along the intake wall with the woods of White Crag above. Pass an old sheepfold and along to another gate where we ignore the path to Dock Tarn and keep ahead on the walled path. *You cannot fail to notice the campsite across the beck and be tempted to pitch your own tent there one day. No serried rows with night-lights but choose your own spot and leave the valley as you found it when you go.* As we progress a junction of two valleys, with Eagle Crag rising between them, comes into sight. Straight ahead is the V-shaped Greenup Gill with an old, but still popular, pony path leading to the pass over Greenup Edge and across the moor to Far Easedale and Grasmere. The valley turning right is Langstrath.

The path becomes better underfoot where the wall ends. Cross a bridge over a side stream, through a gate in a cross wall then pass a ruin with a double sheepfold; the upper one built round the roots of a great yew tree. Continue under an old ash to a gate in a cross wall with its top hinge supported by a jutting stone. On the right the beck now passes through Galleny Force where the water is strangled by a band of hard rock. Cross a side stream on set flood-stones and hanging fence. Stop here and look across the beck. *The flat area is Smithymire Island thought to be the site of the Furness Abbey smelter*

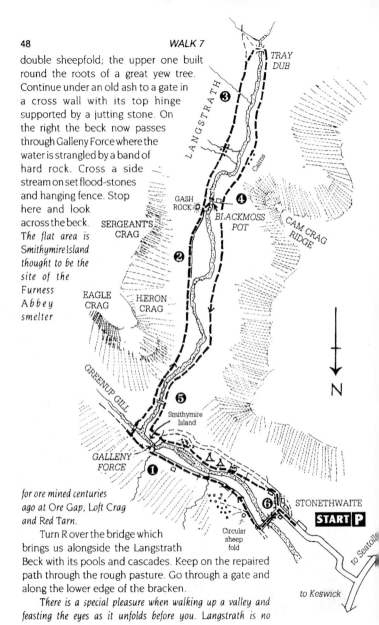

for ore mined centuries ago at Ore Gap, Loft Crag and Red Tarn.

Turn R over the bridge which brings us alongside the Langstrath Beck with its pools and cascades. Keep on the repaired path through the rough pasture. Go through a gate and along the lower edge of the bracken.

There is a special pleasure when walking up a valley and feasting the eyes as it unfolds before you. Langstrath is no exception with shapely Bowfell at its head; the slabs of the left-hand ridge being of volcanic ash uplifted to the mountaintop. The path now runs beside a wall. (To the right is a footbridge leading to the return path if needed.) *On the bank to the left of the bridge orchids hide from the sheep in the damp grass. Please avoid treading on them as they take up to 14 years' growth before they produce seeds.* Go through a gate by a larch tree and on up the valley. The path soon goes between a rock wall and section of old wall. From here look ahead and up to the left. This is Sergeant's Crag, its face split by a deep cleft. *This was the type of rock climb which challenged the Victorian climbers and was first ascended in 1893 by O.G. Jones and J.W. Robinson. Now it is a challenge for modern ice climbers when winter conditions allow.* The path is part of the Cumbria Way which runs from Ulverston to Carlisle. Pass to the R of a large boulder, Blea Rock, and when reaching the fence end you will see a ladder stile over the next wall. Do not cross yet but turn R to the beck for a view into Blackmoss Pot. Cross the stile to the open fell (it is possible to cross the beck here in low water). As progress is made up the valley Esk Pike comes into view to the right of Bowfell. The pass between them is Ore Gap previously mentioned. What a trudge to work and back on a stormy day. Pass a ruin and cairns built of stones cleared from the path. On the left-hand fellside the old pony track winds its way up Stake Beck to the Stake Pass and over to Langdale. Cross a major stream by two ash trees which should get a

medal for survival and fork R to the main stream heading for the upper group of trees to the footbridge above the gorge at Tray Dub.

Turn R and begin the return down the valley. The path is unmistakable with more stone piles under Cam Crag, its prominent ridge being a popular scramble. Looking down the valley the six knobbles around Dock Tarn span the gap. Go over a stile in the intake wall

Blackmoss Pot

and pass by cross walls and ruins. On the right is the footbridge used by the short return. Pass a fenced area of saplings, where, under its protection purple orchids grow in profusion. Go through a gate where the noisy beck runs through blue rock and pass by a line of larches. Just round the bend of the path is Smithymire Island (the flat bit). At the next wall corner fork down R to a stile by Galleny Force and along the path which leads through pleasant waterside scenery. Go over a ladder stile and through the campsite keeping to the beckside path. Keep ahead over a ladder stile and through a field to the hamlet at the Langstrath Country Inn (open all year for refreshments) and the start just beyond.

Blackmoss Pot gorge was formed by the cutting action of the stream as it flowed from a lake, now seen as an extensive alluvial flat.

Stonethwaite

Thick stone walls were a way of clearing the valley pastures. Often the stones are rounded, washed down by the river. Other surplus stones were gathered into mounds, called 'clearance cairns'.

WALK 8:   Dock Tarn and Great Crag

Dock Tarn

Distance:	4½ miles (7¼km)
Grade:	Moderate
Height gain:	1148ft (350m)
Terrain:	Medium fell on good paths
Summit:	Great Crag - 1462ft (446m)
Map:	OL4, HSW-CL

SUMMARY: A classic, very popular circuit which visits Dock Tarn, an attractive little indented pool set in a wonderful landscape of rock knolls rising from colourful boggy basins. A surround of heather adds colour in season.

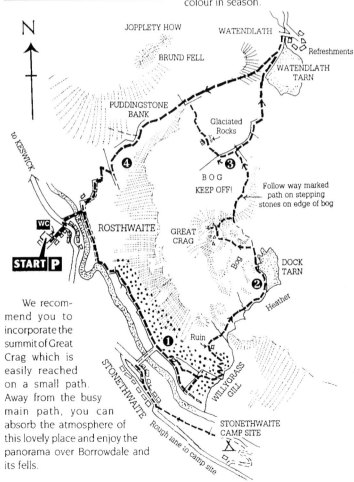

N

JOPPLETY HOW

WATENDLATH

Refreshments

BRUND FELL

WATENDLATH TARN

to KESWICK

PUDDINGSTONE BANK

Glaciated Rocks

4

3

B O G KEEP OFF!

Follow way marked path on stepping stones on edge of bog

WC

ROSTHWAITE

GREAT CRAG

Bog

DOCK TARN

START P

2

Heather

We recommend you to incorporate the summit of Great Crag which is easily reached on a small path. Away from the busy main path, you can absorb the atmosphere of this lovely place and enjoy the panorama over Borrowdale and its fells.

1

Ruin

STONETHWAITE

WILLYGRASS GILL

Rough lane to camp site

STONETHWAITE CAMP SITE

Much of the walk is on well managed paths; the steep climb through the oak woods above Stonethwaite is on a pitched stone zig-zag track, and later, stepping-stones alleviate much of the worst bogs. Only the descent to Rosthwaite is a trifle stony.

HOW TO GET THERE AND PARKING: From Keswick take the B5289 Borrowdale road to Rosthwaite. Car park, toilets, shop and hotel refreshments.

THE WALK: Turn L along the car park lane to the road. Go L for a few yards then R on the lane signed public bridleway to Stonethwaite and Watendlath. The open pastures left allow a view of Castle Crag and King's How as they close together to form the Jaws of Borrowdale allowing path, road and River Derwent to squeeze through. Cross the Stonethwaite Beck bridge and turn R on the public byway to Stonethwaite.

The path, the old pony track from Rosthwaite to Grasmere via Greenup Gill, has walls low enough to allow an outlook. Go through a gate swung on stones with old iron mountings. *Now have a look over the head-high wall to see the village, raised from the floodplain and sheltered by knolls backed by the fells to the west which yielded building stone, slate, lead and wad from which residents drew their livelihood.*

The scene changes and the path bends into Stonethwaite valley with the dark outline of Eagle Crag ahead. Go through a gate by a group of hollies, their winter colours contrasting with the oak wood above. *Note the pollarded ash trees in the fields, used for fuel, charcoal and poles.* Pass the lane which leads over the Stonethwaite Beck bridge to Stonethwaite (refreshments, telephone) and ahead through the gate on the public bridleway to Grasmere. The path is stony, but not for long. Do a short-cut fork L up the grass by a circular sheepfold and passing above it, go up the leftward rising diagonal path across turf with large boulders. The path runs beside a little rill then through short bracken to an awkward stile in a crosswall. Go over and turn L up the main path into the once coppiced oak wood. Cairns indicate the way to a wooden stile in a converging wall. Go over then linger to look at the tumbling

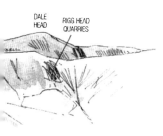

waters of Willygrass Gill, its music held by the oak canopy. The hillside is steep but the pitched path eases the labour until you reach the edge of the wood and a surprise viewpoint. Eagle Crag splits the Stonethwaite valley, to its left the pony path mounts Greenup Gill to Easedale and Grasmere, to its right the Langstrath pony path over the Stake pass to Langdale is now used by the Cumbria Way.

Pass a roofless ruin (wind shelter) with an easing of gradient, carry on along the cairned path through heather. On the right the cascades of the gill sing again. Pass a bend by a wall end, cross a stream and from the broad path look across to Greenup Gill where morning light highlights the glacial moraines left in the valley as ice retreated. Go over a stile in a crosswall and along by the gill to its outlet from Dock Tarn.

The tarn is a very popular destination and its initial sighting invites all to sit by its side and share its tranquillity.

Walk along the left-hand side and when the tarn is about 50yds behind turn L (just before stepping-stones). Go along a shallow depression, pass a pool and a bog then bend R to gain an upper depression. The narrow path mounts on its left-hand side then levels and comes face to face with the rocky side of Great Crag. (To the left is the smaller cone of the south summit.) Fork half R up the path to a flat summit ridge with pools, an array of cairns and a fine panorama from the topmost cairn. Continue direction (the path divides - left loop down a short rock scramble - right loop is easy) to a dip then up to the north summit. Watendlath is a perfect foreground for the view north to Skiddaw but for the best of Borrowdale move to the small cairn west.

Return to the dip and turn L on a descending path which bends to the left then divides. Either branch will lead to the main path from the tarn. At the main path turn L down the set stones to a kissing gate in a cross wall. Read the request notice then cross the stream and follow the path marked by green-topped guide poles around the edge

ENLARGEMENT OF GREAT CRAG

of the bog, an amusing exercise in using step-stones. At the signpost choose
your onward route.

TO WATENDLATH: Turn R and follow the path passing a plantation then
along the edge of the tarn to join the main path from Puddingstone Bank.
Turn R and cross the packhorse bridge to the picturesque hamlet of
Watendlath (refreshments). Return to the packhorse bridge and keep ahead
to the gate by the tarn outlet where the resident ducks expect an offering.
Fork R up the steep pony path and on gaining some height stop for the classic
view of Watendlath backed on the east by the slopes of High Tove with High
Seat to its north. *An extensive bog-ridden moorland ridge separates Watendlath and
Thirlmere sporting few paths (it is possible to see the line of cairns on the old pony track
over to Harrop Tarn and Thirlmere).*

The path continues to climb and when an attractive planting of mixed
trees falls behind there is a panorama of the central Lakeland mountains to
enjoy until meeting the short route at the highest point Puddingstone Bank.

TO PUDDINGSTONE BANK: Continue the green pole route through the
myrtle. Rub a leaf (without picking it) and smell its delightful fragrance. Go
through a kissing gate and along to some ice-smoothed rock. *From here Great
Crag looks darkly impressive and from Watendlath the pony path can be traced up the
valley where it runs along the intake wall and over the moor to Blea Tarn, Harrop Tarn
and Thirlmere with High Seat prominent to the north-east.* Go through a kissing gate
in a wall and over planks to the main path at Puddingstone Bank where the
route from Watendlath is joined. Turn L. Pass a group of pines at Birkett Leap,
then ignore the kissing gate on the right to Keswick and the Bowder Stone,
cross a clapper bridge to go through another kissing gate. Kind hands have
repaired the well worn path as it descends to a gate in the right-hand wall.
Go through and down zig-zags to walk between a fence and a wall. Go along
a raised causeway to cross a stream then proceed on a sheltered path to join
our outward route. Turn R over the Stonethwaite Beck bridge and into the
village (shop and hotel). Cross the main road to the lane and parking.

WALK 9: Brund Fell and King's How

SUMMARY: A popular walk which packs a lot of interest in a short distance
and certainly feels longer than it is! Beautiful woodland, river and rock
scenery, rough steep fell and a variety of little summits make a fine
combination.

The Bowder Stone

HOW TO GET THERE AND PARKING: From Keswick take the B5289 Borrowdale road. Park at the Bowderstone car park, on the left, ½ mile past the turn to Grange.

THE WALK: From the car park drive turn L on a path signed to the Bowder Stone. Blue stone steps lead down to the road. *The great quarry cave, often used for shelter and enjoyment of rock scenery and known as Quayfoot Quarry collapsed in the 1970s after earth tremors shook the area. There are views across the valley to Goat Crag and down the valley to Skiddaw.* Go through a gate and along the path (in 1842 the only road up the valley) with Woden's Face, a small crag, on the left. The Bowder Stone has a substantial staircase leading to the top. *This was popular with the early tourists and a must, along with Lodore Falls, if Borrowdale was to be done thoroughly. Tourists were encouraged to shake hands under the Bowder Stone through a small hole, chipped out specially for the purpose.*

Distance:	3¾ miles 6km
Grade:	Moderate
Height gain:	1302ft (397m)
Terrain:	Low fell. Good paths, steep and stony in places.
Summits:	Brund Fell - 1376ft (420m) King's How - 1285ft (392m)
Map:	OL4, HSW-CL

Pass Bowder Stone Cottage, the old tourist guide's house, and continue along the path, now rougher, to the road. Cross the road and turn L. It is better to walk along the bank of the River Derwent than round the blind bends of the road especially as the clear water shows to perfection the colours of the river bed rock, fish darting and pools formed by the swirling current. Cross a small sidestream then you are forced to go up L to regain the road. Carry on along the roadside footway and just round a bend look for a parking area on the left. Cross the road to it and go through the gate signed public bridleway, then ahead steeply through the mixed woodland alongside a wall. The ascent of Brund Fell has begun. Pass a wall end and a stream then the gradient eases for a while but steepens once again. *Away from the sound of the road and river the songs of many birds cheer*

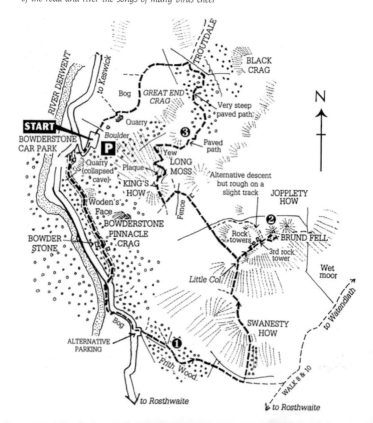

CAFELL   LINGMELL   GREAT GABLE   HIGH SCAWDEL   DALE HEAD   CASTLE CRAG   RIGG HEAD QUARRIES

Looking out over Rosthwaite from the way up Brund Fell

the climb. Respite comes on reaching a gate in a cross wall. Go through and bend L over a rise graced with a beautiful birch tree. Walk on and look out for a gated ladder stile in the wall above left. Before going over look at Rosthwaite village below sited at the hub of valleys. Stonethwaite to the left, Seathwaite to the right with Combe Gill leading to Glaramara in between and a circle of mountains behind.

Go over the ladder stile and up the side of the wood, cairns. *Watch out for buzzards wheeling around the hillside in search of prey.* On breasting the crest by a forlorn hawthorn Brund Fell can be seen ahead. The path levels then rises up a grassy rake (ignore a trod traversing left). Continue with a steep pull up to a gap. The view over Borrowdale is terrific and will halt the keenest summit bagger. Make a determined effort up the next slope and arrive at the ridge. King's How is across to the left. Observe the lie of the intervening land and the path along it to King's How for we will use this way. Note a path joining it from the north side of Brund Fell as this is an alternative choice.

Fork R and slightly uphill (cairn - return to here). Go along a path through heather towards a rock tower up a rocky step with the tower to your left. Pass a second tower to the third rock tower and branch R. Go ahead skirting a small bog for 50yds and clamber onto Brund Fell summit. The view to the east over High Tove shows the undulating summits of the Helvellyn range.

TO KING'S HOW: Return to the third rock tower then either **a)** Return to the ridge and the cairn. Turn R on the path previously observed descending into a bowl.

or **b)** Turn R down a trough and negotiate a steepish slope towards a wall. Traverse L under the crag to gain the wallside. Turn L on a path improving as other ways join from the left. Take care not to snag your hair or clothes on the barbed wire aggressively protruding from the wall. Meet the path from the

CASTLE CRAG · SKIDDAW · KING'S HOW · BRUND FELL

King's How and Brund Fell from the start of Walk 6

cairn, turn R.

Go along to a ladder stile on the left. Go over and on the broad grassy path towards King's How. Pass a cairn and a sheepfold then proceed to a stile in a fence. Go over and fork L up the zig-zag path, one of many, and up to the rather weary little cairn for such a popular summit, with tranquil scenes over Derwentwater and the wooded Castle Crag standing in the Jaws of Borrowdale.

Leave the summit, eponymous to Edward VII, on the north (towards Derwentwater) and look for the memorial plaque placed by his sister Louise who gave Grange Fell in his memory. Continue down and at a cairn turn L on a broad path which winds about and clambers down a rock staircase between silver birches. Keep R through the birch grove and down set-stones to cross the stream issuing from Long Moss. Go round the edge of the moss and down the repaired path by the fence. Bend L away from the fence and stile and descend a long staircase through the woods. Above and to the right towers Black Crag. On approaching a wall turn L then drop down to cross a stream and go up the other side. Ignore a ladder stile on the right and bend L to go through a gate in a wall. (Above left is Great End Crag, scene of a fire in the 1940s.) On reaching an open bowl fork L keeping above the spring line. Keep L towards an old quarry cave and dressing floor. Go across the floor and along to a big square boulder. Keep ahead across the stream and over the stile into the rear of the car park.

Borrowdale Slate

Two beds of fine, cleaved slate called 'slate metal' lie at the base of the volcanic rock. The main quarries were at Rigg Head (opened in 1832) and Quayfoot, with several smaller Borrowdale ones around Castle Crag and the Bowder Stone. The fine volcanic ash which formed the slate contains showers of coarser material (breccia) and embedded fragments of older rock, which together forms an attractive pattern. Quayfoot Quarry yielded heavy slates and good building stone. It was also called Rainspot Quarry after its characteristically dappled slates.

WALK 10: Through the Jaws of Borrowdale to Watendlath

Watendlath

SUMMARY: The woodland walk by Lodore Falls followed by the upland valley to Watendlath is justly popular. We suggest incorporating this with a stroll down the valley from Rosthwaite to Derwentwater. The whole walk is a wonderful combination of the best of Borrowdale scenery - riverside, woodland, fells and rocks, with a chance to obtain refreshment at Watendlath before the final fell crossing to Rosthwaite.

Note: On your drive up Borrowdale it is important to glance at the marshes which border the head of the lake for our path crosses these on raised walkways. At times of flood these are under water and the route is impracticable.

HOW TO GET THERE AND PARKING: Car park, Rosthwaite (toilets).

Distance:	7½ miles (12km)
Grade:	Moderate
Height gain:	852ft (260m)
Terrain:	Valley, woodland and low fell, along good paths.
High point:	1066ft (325m) above Watendlath
Map:	OL4, HSW-CL

THE WALK: At the car park entrance turn R past the village hall, where parking is also allowed, to the interesting buildings of Yew Tree Farm (sign, footpath to Grange). Notice how boulders and stones are used in alternate rows.

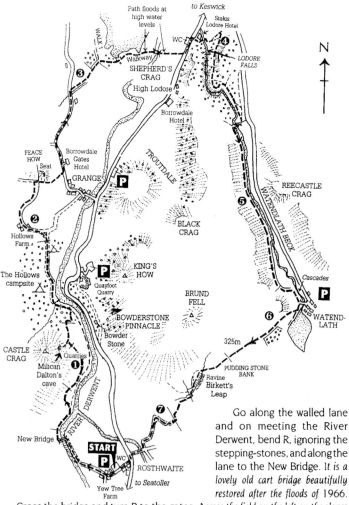

N

Go along the walled lane and on meeting the River Derwent, bend R, ignoring the stepping-stones, and along the lane to the New Bridge. *It is a lovely old cart bridge beautifully restored after the floods of 1966.*

Cross the bridge and turn R to the gates. *Across the field on the left on the slopes of High Doat is Johnny Wood, an ancient woodland of oak, ash and beech.* Go over a stile by the right-hand gate and along the riverside path.

At a fork keep L (the right-hand path at the water's edge involves a tricky scramble.) The path is really an old quarry track. On reaching an old wall the path begins to rise and is cairned. O*n the left is a quarry in the slates of the* *Borrowdale Volcanics, its rid being reclaimed by delicate larches and the pink flowers* *of herb robert.* Go through a gap in a wall and up an ice-scratched slab ignoring a small path to the right, and up to a T-junction. Turn R (Millican Dalton's cave, an old quarry, is up the path to the left - see Walk 3), pass through a rock cutting and down to a gap in a cross wall. Turn R and if you look up from the gaudy-coloured path you may be able to distinguish the Bowderstone Pinnacle rising from the trees on the opposite side of the valley. Cross a little causeway to a riverside glade. Here the river, road and path squeeze through the wooded Jaws of Borrowdale. As you approach a gate divert up R for a while where there is a seat, sited to give a view of the river as it turns a corner forming the wide pool of Gowder Dub. Go through the gate, ahead over a footbridge and follow the track skirting the Hollows campsite. At the edge of the wood branch L at a triangular junction keeping L onto the surfaced lane to Hollows Farm. Go straight through the paved yard and out of the far gate to a bridge and gate beyond. *The underlying rock is now the smoother Skiddaw Slates and as the* *valley opens out King's How can be seen over the river and the roofs of Grange peep* *through the treetops.*

Near the top of the rise pass a standing stone on the left of the path then turn R on a minor path ignoring a "private" gate (leading into the grounds of High Close) and go through the next gate. *This is Peace How, a* *little knoll donated to the National Trust by Canon Rawnsley, one of the founders of the* *National Trust.* Leave the path for a while and make your way up diagonally L over to the stone seat on the summit. The tranquil scene is truly beautiful. Find the path once more which winds round the knoll and down to the road. (Grange village is 500yds down the road on the right, toilets).

Turn L along the road, pass the Borrowdale Gates Country House Hotel and High Close. Pass a modern barn on the right then turn R on a public footpath to Lodore. Go along the path crossing the low-lying pasture (ignore a field path to the left) and over two plank bridges to a kissing gate. Continue to a wall corner and where the wall turns fork R over the heathland to a wooden walkway crossing the valley floor, where Derwentwater glints silver through the bushes. Keep R on the lakeshore and through a damp oak wood which sprouts fungi of odd shapes and hues, purple puff-balls etc.

The walkway continues, narrow with passing places, carrying the path over the flood-prone lake fringe. Cross the river bridge and walk on towards the road. A*head is Shepherds Crag, a very popular climbing venue which has launched* *many adventurers into the sport.* At the road turn L for 100yds (public toilets), cross and turn R under a copper beech tree to the 'Entrance to Waterfalls'. Turn L behind the Lodore Hotel. There may be a very small fee for entry to these private grounds. Many paths wander about so keep moving uphill through the woods. *The views into the boulder-choked bed of Lodore Falls are*

*disappointing except after heavy rain, but there are many ferns, grasses and mosses to
see along the path.* Make a zig-zag L away from the falls and back R along the
base of a crag to a wall. Keep along the valley which widens still in woodland
and ignoring paths to the left do not leave the stream. There is a fence up to
the left and the ground gradually becomes less stony and flatter. Keep the
roar of the water on your right as the path narrows and becomes gloomy,
soggy and, for the first time since the hotel, it runs close to the beck. Another
path joins in but continue ahead to a ladder stile over a wall. Turn R and cross
the beck by a footbridge (sign plaque). Turn L to Watendlath on a permissive
path, and walk with sheer pleasure a beautiful streamside mile up the valley
unconscious of the narrow road and any traffic it contains. Soon Watendlath
comes into sight. The path leaves the beck up steps and runs above the level
of the wall. The path begins to descend by the wallside. Branch R towards the
beck and look on the right bank of the path for the delicate white and purple
flowers of the Grass of Parnassus. Cross the ditch and at last there is a
waterfall to enjoy and the picturesque hamlet of Watendlath (refreshments).
Do not cross the packhorse bridge but keep ahead to the gate by the tarn
outlet where the resident ducks expect an offering. Fork R up the steep pony
path and on gaining some height stop for the classic view of Watendlath
backed on the east by the slopes of High Tove with High Seat to its north and
Middle Crag to its south. *This is an extensive bog-ridden moorland ridge between
Watendlath and Thirlmere sporting few paths (it is possible to see the line of cairns on the
old pony track over to Harrop Tarn and Armboth in Thirlmere) yet with a unique
atmosphere well worth sampling (see Walk 34).*

The path continues to climb and when an attractive planting of mixed
trees falls behind there is a panorama of the central Lakeland mountains to
enjoy. Cross a stream by a fir wood and branch L on a rocky path; a short
distance and Rosthwaite can be seen below. The rough path demands your
attention but, after passing a group of pines at the ravine of Birkett's Leap,
conditions improve underfoot. Ignore the kissing gate on the right to
Keswick and the Bowder Stone, cross a clapper bridge to another kissing gate
and go through. Kind hands have repaired the well-worn path as it descends
to a gate in the right-hand wall. Go through and down zig-zags to walk
between a fence and a wall. Go along a raised causeway to cross a stream
then proceed along a sheltered path which leads to a lane. Turn R over the
Stonethwaite Beck bridge and into the village (shop and hotel). Cross the
main road to the lane and parking.

Sir Hugh Walpole (1884-1941) was a historical novelist who set many of his
stories in Borrowdale. Watendlath was the setting for Judith Paris' home. Few
of today's tourists will have read his works which were very popular in the
1930s.

WALK 11: Walla Crag and Derwentwater Shore

CLOUGH HEAD   WALLA CRAG   GREAT DODD   CAT GILL   FALCON CRAG   BLEABERRY FELL

The Walla Crag walk viewed across Derwentwater

SUMMARY: One of the classic walks of Borrowdale, it combines the splendid vantage points of Walla Crag and Castlehead with the lakeshore delights of Derwentwater. Woods, crags and water blend into an unforgettable vista through the Jaws of Borrowdale to the higher fells behind. Paths are excellent. The laid path up Cat Gill makes an alternative start or can be used for a shorter walk in attractive surroundings.

HOW TO GET THERE AND PARKING: Take the Borrowdale road from Keswick and in 1 mile park on the left at Great Wood car park.

THE WALK: Set off on the footpath signed to Ashness Bridge. After climbing the initial slope turn R along a plantation of larches, a younger patch on the gentle swathe of mature deciduous woodland. At the next fork go straight on towards Ashness Bridge. In summer views will be restricted by foliage but soon the sound of running water heralds the approach to Cat Gill. THE SHORT ROUTE TO WALLA CRAG VIA CAT GILL turns L here.

Distance:	6¼ miles (10km) - full round
	5 miles (8km) by Cat Gill
Grade:	Moderate
Height gain:	1016ft (310m)
Terrain:	Low fell, woods and lakeshore
	Good paths.
Summit:	Walla Crag - 1243ft (379m)
Map:	OL4, HSW-CL

Cross the bridge over Cat Gill, once the home of wild cats, and keep on the path which descends a little by a wall then begins to traverse the fellside. *From here splendid views up Borrowdale sweep to the south-west whilst close above the*

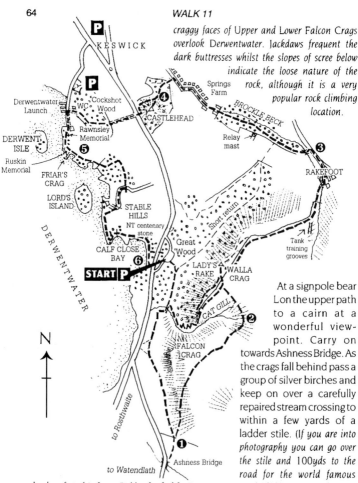

craggy faces of Upper and Lower Falcon Crags overlook Derwentwater. Jackdaws frequent the dark buttresses whilst the slopes of scree below indicate the loose nature of the rock, although it is a very popular rock climbing location.

KESWICK

Springs Farm

Derwentwater Launch

Cockshot Wood

WC

CASTLEHEAD

BROCKLE BECK

DERWENT ISLE

Rawnsley Memorial

Relay mast

Ruskin Memorial

RAKEFOOT

FRIAR'S CRAG

LORD'S ISLAND

STABLE HILLS

Short return

NT centenary stone

Great Wood

Tank training grooves

CALF CLOSE BAY

LADY'S RAKE

WALLA CRAG

START P

CAT GILL

At a signpole bear L on the upper path to a cairn at a wonderful view-point. Carry on towards Ashness Bridge. As the crags fall behind pass a group of silver birches and keep on over a carefully repaired stream crossing to within a few yards of a ladder stile. (*If you are into photography you can go over the stile and 100yds to the road for the world famous calendar shot of Ashness Bridge backed by Derwentwater and Skiddaw.*) Turn sharp L up the fell path which climbs and steepens at a rocky bar. As height is gained the bracken becomes stunted and the sliver of silver to the north lengthens into Bassenthwaite Lake. Pass a large ash tree which grows awkwardly from a rock and gain a shelf where the path bends left. *Keep your eyes open for a falcon hovering, the peregrine is still around its named crag.* The angle eases and gradually our direction turns northward with the crags hidden below to the left. *Away westward the horizon is a jumble of mountain peaks which the profile may help you*

FALCON CRAG

to Rosthwaite

Ashness Bridge

to Watendlath

DERWENTWATER

N

Above:
The path around
Derwentwater has
duckboards over the
boggy bits (Walk 1)

Left:
From the Cat Bells
path (Walk 2) there is
a fine view over
Derwentwater to
Blencathra

Left:
The woods in
Borrowdale are a joy
to walk. The start of
the path to the
Bowderstone (Walk 9)

Below:
The path from
Rosthwaite to
Stonethwaite comes
close to the river
(Walk 8)

unravel. Can you spot the 'Bishop of Barf'? It is a pinnacle of rock on the western fellside above Bassenthwaite Lake. The 'Bishop' is painted white by the Keswick Mountain Rescue team. A formidable task in view of the lichen-friendly climate (see Walk 17 p91). The path gradually bends away from the crags and at an ice-borne boulder we can see Keswick, Walla Crag and the summit peaks of Blencathra peeping over the moor.

Do not allow the demanding scenery to lure your attention from the path. Suddenly the ground to the left falls away in the precipitous erosion of upper Cat Gill. During the circuit of the cirque glance right to the summit cairn of Bleaberry Fell (Walk 28). The path is now fringed with purple heather and there are two peaty streams to cross before gaining a broad, green cairned path leading to another cairn near a wall and route junction.

SHORT RETURN VIA CAT GILL: At the cairn turn L and begin the descent on a green velvet path. Keep by the wall on the path which steepens dramatically as it nears the gill. (The stile in the wall right is an ascent path to the summit of Walla Crag.) Pick your way down with the wall at your right hand and find a handrail leading onto a newly repaired section of the path, an excellent piece of work gratefully accepted by all who use it. A kissing gate stops animals entering the ravine. Pass another kissing gate then keep down beside the wall ignoring the path which crosses the gill. Reach the gate near the bridge crossed on the outward route. Keep R and soon make the left turn down to the car park.

THE SHORT ROUTE TO WALLA CRAG VIA CAT GILL: Keep L up the pitched stone path to a kissing gate. The path has been recently repaired and stones and steps makes light work of the steep slope. A fine array of mosses and lichens decorate the rocks but the deep cleft of the gill and the bouldery nature of its bed makes waterfall watching almost impossible. Go through the next kissing gate and mount a series of zig-zags. Note the remains of felled trees where beetles and weather have eaten away the heartwood leaving a wooden pipe. When the path straightens beside the wall look for a stile on the left, climb over and walk on the opposite side. A strip of woodland robs the path of views as it passes along the top of White Crag. A great toppled birch indicates the head of Lady's Rake. Ten metres ahead is a stile where we join the route from Falcon Crag.

TO CONTINUE THE ROUTE TO WALLA CRAG: Keep ahead up the moor to a stile in the wall. Go over the stile and join the ascent route from Cat Gill. Turn R and climb gently up the broad path with a spreading outlook to the summit cairn of Walla Crag. There is not only an all round view but a smooth rock platform from which to enjoy it.

Leave the summit and - a) Rejoin the wall. Cross it by a stile and turn L to the broad green sheltered path.

or b) Use the popular path on the edge of the crag which passes rocky buttresses and the top of a narrow gully. At a fence with kissing gate join the sheltered path at a cairn.

Continue down the path (ignore a gate in the wall to the left). *Below are the white houses of Keswick, neat and Lego-like at the foot of Skiddaw.* The path narrows and drops into the Brockle Beck valley. Go over a stile and, passing a set of old slot gate stones, cross a footbridge over Brockle Beck and turn L along the lane at Rake End Farm. In 100yds turn sharp L to find a kissing gate signed public footpath to Keswick and Great Wood. Cross the field and the bridge then go along the beckside path. The beck soon cuts into a deepening valley and from the path Walla Crag looks impressive in profile. At a kissing gate turn L for short return to Great Wood.

To continue keep straight on the public footpath to Keswick. Pass Castlerigg Relay Station and follow the main path (ignore a right bend to a bridge over the beck) through the once-coppiced Springs Wood to a kissing gate. Pass barns and go ahead to the surfaced lane at Springs Farm. Once over the bridge go along the quiet lane on the edge of Keswick for 400yds with our next objective, the wooded knoll of Castlehead, to the left. Opposite Wood Close, with a prominent white wall, discover a narrow path L to Castlehead and Lake Road. Go along it to a kissing gate and enter the fine oak wood. Mount the steps then fork R on a rising path which steepens to arrive at a fence corner. Fork L to the summit viewpoint which displays a wonderful picture of Derwentwater framed by interlocking mountain peaks and valleys. They are identified by a direction indicator.

Return to the fence corner and, turning left onto the previous line of travel, make your way down through beech and oak until above the road. Turn L and do not miss the memorial stone to Sir John Scurrah Randles (set off to the left) who donated this beautiful area for all to enjoy. In 50yds cross the busy road to a narrow gravel path opposite, which leads between fields to Cockshot Wood. Enter the wood and go straight ahead over a rise to the

From Castlehead. The dolerite plug makes a fine vantage point

lakeshore road (toilets on right - summer only) and boat landings. On the right are tea room and toilets open all year. *This is just the place for children to feed the mallards and there are many seats for relaxation along the lake shore.* Turn L then at the next junction go straight on towards Friar's Crag. Pass a memorial plaque to Hardwick Drummond Rawnsley, one of the founders of the National Trust. Across the strait is Derwent Isle and a short distance on and to the left of the path stands another memorial stone to John Ruskin, artist, writer and critic. A few steps further, protruding into the lake, is the much photographed viewpoint of Friar's Crag. *If the water is low you will be able to see the plaques which record the lowest lake levels.*

From the crag turn R to circle the memorial and descend steps to a kissing gate at shore level. Continue round the bay then enter woodland by a kissing gate to a bridge over Brockle Beck. Progress through the very swampy woodland on a solid path to a road. Turn R on the access road towards Stable Hills Cottage. Go through a gate at a cattle-grid in the direction of Calf Close where the path branches L and we gain the shore again opposite Lord's Island. Walk on the gravel path above the shoreline to a gate in the shadow of some shapely yews. Pass through the grove, the branches alive with tits, then on the fringe of the shore note the National Trust centenary stone, tastefully carved, pass over footbridges and alongside winter floodlines to a fence corner and National Trust contribution box. Turn L to a slit stile and go straight across the road and into Great Wood. Keep ahead up the bank by an ancient beech to the car park.

The Islands of Derwentwater

The four main islands are drumlins. St Herbert's Isle was the hermitage of the said saint which later became a place of pilgrimage. Friar's Crag was where the pilgrims waited to make the crossing.

In the 1770s Joseph Pocklington built various follys on Derwent Isle and organized an annual regatta which involved a mock battle.

Derwent Isle was formerly the home of German miners who came in Elizabethan times. The locals mistrusted them, hence their island home. Later, some married local girls and became fully integrated into the community.

Castlehead and the Drumlins

The remnant of a volcanic plug, its dolerite rock is different to that elsewhere in the valley (apart from Friar's Crag). The other surrounding hillocks, including Cockshott Wood, are drumlins. These were formed by moving ice which moulded soft sediments left by the glacier into their typical drawn-out dome shape. The ice was moving north towards the Solway. Keswick is surrounded by drumlins, and the walk along the lakeshore runs around several. You may also notice an 'esker'. This is a gravelly ridge left at the base of a crevasse when the ice was stationary for a while.

Lady's Rake

After the Jacobite rising of 1715, it is reputed that the Countess of Derwentwater escaped with her jewels up this break in the crags. Presumably it was much less overgrown then than it is now.

Lower Falcon Crag

You may see rock climbers at this popular venue for it sports many steep and difficult routes.

WALK 12:   River Greta and the Keswick Railway Walk

Old railway bridge, River Greta

SUMMARY: Since the National Park renovated the old railway track between Keswick and Threlkeld it has become popular with both walkers and cyclists, and provides very easy walking with a touch of history.

Our walk threads a way through the woods of the Greta valley before gaining the old rail track and a quick, easy return to Keswick. If you finish early you could have a dip in the pool, visit the nearby Cumberland Pencil Museum, the more general Fitzpark Museum, or stroll round the attractive town centre. The Moot Hall houses a useful information centre.

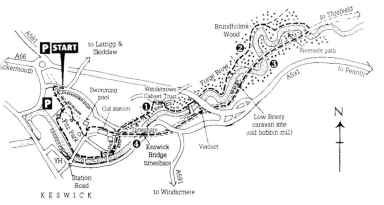

HOW TO GET THERE AND PARKING: From the roundabout at the junction of the A66 and A591 north of Keswick, turn towards Keswick and left in 100yds* to roadside parking just past the stump of an old bridge.

* or continue 200yds towards Keswick to Crosthwaite Road car park on the left.

THE WALK: Opposite the stump of the old railway bridge go L through a gate into the park on a surfaced path past the BMX track. Follow it R to the riverside, (where a path joins from the Crosthwaite Road parking) and turn L along it. Pass by a footbridge to the road and instead go under the road observing the ironwork and additional brickwork where it was widened.

Continue along the path where an æsthetic planting of trees and shrubs blend with formal lawns to enhance the streamside. On reaching a circular lawn bend L to discover a gate under horsechestnut trees leading onto the road. Cross over and turn R. An old railway bridge is almost hidden by the trees. Go under the bridge and immediately take the second R turn on a permissive path to Keswick Bridge.

Walk along a rhododendron aisle which borders the Keswick Bridge Timeshare, once the subject of some controversy in the area. Brief

Distance:	4¾ miles (7½km)
Grade:	Easy
Height gain:	230ft (70m)
Terrain:	Woodland and old rail track. Good paths.
Map:	OL4, HSW-NL

glimpses of Walla Crag appear on the right. Cross over an old sunken lane and as you walk the sound of the river, muttering in its deep ravine below, is overcome by the road of the traffic up left on the bypass. The aisle narrows to a single width path.

On reaching the drive of Bundholme Country House Hotel turn L to the entrance gate and R on the surfaced road. Note the sign on the left-hand verge 'Footpath to Brundholme Wood 300m'. Walk the 300m to the disabled Riding Centre of the Calvert Trust and at the car park turn R down steps to join a track. Turn L along the track and past houses descending to the bridge at the Old Smokehouse. For a view of the river it is worth going onto the bridge built by J.B. Hardisty in 1817. You will also get a view of the architecturally striking new bridge which carries the bypass. The Greta river bed contains many boulders brought into the valley by glaciers.

Hereabouts was located the Brigham Smelter, built in 1565, the largest in Europe. By 1567 six furnaces were busy here, fuelled by charcoal from the surrounding dales and processing ore mainly from the Newlands mines. Packhorse trails radiated in all directions, built to carry the charcoal. Destroyed by Cromwell in 1661, rebuilt and active until 1715.

Return to the path, go through a kissing gate and keep on the level path. The new bridge is impressive viewed from beneath as we pass its foundations springing from the ochre, russet and blue Skiddaw Slates. Pass through evergreens to the young birch plantation on Forge Brow. *Fly agaric fungus grows hereabouts. It is recognised by its vivid red cap with white spots, is highly poisonous and best left untouched.* Descend to river level where there is an old weir backed by the wall of the railway, a pleasant spot to sit and watch the water weaving its way around the boulders. The path continues gaining height again and when Briery caravan site on the opposite side of the river drops behind look for a three-way signposts. Fork L towards Latrigg. (Turn right to reach the railway for a shorter return.)

The path is narrow and runs through an oak wood. Ignore an uphill path and maintain direction to cross a plank bridge (ignore a footpath leading down right). Keep ahead as our path

Greta bridges - the old and the new

follows the curve of the meandering Greta where in autumn the views over the valley are fantastic. Cross a forestry track. Branch R down steps to the river. Keep along the riverside and where the main track bends L uphill, continue by the riverside to where the woodland ends at a stile. Cross the pasture to an exit stile and steps to the dismantled railtrack and seat.

Turn R over the river bridge and freewheel the 2 miles back to Keswick, the bridges forming the major interest on the way.

The walk along the railtrack is smooth underfoot and suitable for cyclists of all ages. An alternative path loops R staying close to the river bank but is short-lived. Cross the bridge then look down on the weir before moving on to a gated bridge. Pass the caravan site to the Low Brierly Bobbin Mill station.

Beyond is a screw bridge (notice the brickwork of the arch). The railtrack next serves as a high balcony which offers a wonderful view of the valley with Latrigg and the western tongues of Blencathra behind. Branch L up to a gate to go over the spur and under the bypass viaduct with its graceful sweeping arches unseen by its speeding occupants. Continue to a beautiful bridges built of blue Lakeland stone with red sandstone copings.

Ignore the steps leading down right and stay on the railtrack to reach disused Keswick station. The ironwork is still intact with oak-leaved capitols. Turn L behind the swimming pool (drinks machine in the foyer) then make your way across the cobbled garden and R to the park gate and road. Turn R down steps, pass under a mighty sycamore and walk on past the children's playground to join the outward route near the BMX track.

Low Briery Bobbin Mill

Closed 1961 after existing for six centuries. In the early 19th century it was a water-powered pencil mill.

Bobbins were exported as far as Uruguay, South Africa and Hong Kong. Produced 4 million bobbins per year. Used for silk, cotton, Irish linen and wire which was inserted into old £1 notes. Used coppiced ash, birch, sycamore, lime, alder and teak. Poles were harvested when 18-23 years old.

Keswick to Penrith Railway

Opened 1865, closed in 1972. The coming of the railway, built to carry coke to the iron works in west Cumberland, also heralded the beginning of Keswick's tourist trade. The bow girder bridges over the River Greta are a feature of the walk. The railway engineers had problmems with a bank of blue clay which they tunnelled ½ mile east of Keswick. In wet weather landslips occurred.

CHAPTER 2

Newlands and the North West

Newlands, named after marshes at the lower end of the valley were reclaimed, is always quieter than its neighbour Borrowdale. Access is by tortuous narrow lanes which need care to drive safely. The reward is free parking (at the time of writing).

The surrounding fells are of Skiddaw Slate, which promotes a more uniform landscape than the knobbly volcanic rock of central Lakeland, resulting in shapely conical peaks and steep-sided ridges with crumbling crags and shattered screes rising from a clothe of bracken. Slate is a misnomer, for there is sandstone intermingled with the shales.

Mining was an important activity hereabouts two centuries ago and the legacy is a network of smooth paths which are delightful to walk.

The north-western part of this area has been taken over by forestry, where walkers are welcome and tourism is an important part of the forest economy.

Newlands Church

WALK 13: Hindscarth via the Dale Head Miners' Path

Old mine building ruins below Dale Head with Eel Crags behind

SUMMARY: The northern side of Dale Head, the fine mountain which commands the head of Newlands, was explored in Elizabethan times for its copper deposits. Now you can walk the old miners' track which zig-zags high into the combe below the summit. At the Hindscarth Edge col the sudden view is breathtaking over to Honister with a ring of high fells beyond.

The return over Hindscarth on a popular but stony ridge path serves to emphasise the pleasant green paths of our ascent.

HOW TO GET THERE AND PARKING: From Braithwaite or Portinscale follow signs to Stair then Littletown. Parking at the bridge just before Newlands church.

THE WALK: Walk back up the road for 100yds and find a stile sharp R. Take the lower of two paths which slants gradually up the hillside to join the old mine track and continue up the valley along it. *You will already have noticed the beautiful U-shaped ice-worn valley. The bastions of Eel Crag, Gray Crag, Red Crag and*

Distance:	6¼ miles (10km)
Grade:	Strenuous
Height gain:	2264ft (690m)
Terrain:	High fell. A mix of grassy and rough paths.
Summit:	Hindscarth - 2384ft (727m)
Map:	OL4, HSW-WL

Miners Crag form the eastern wall, Dale Head dominates the valley head and the silvery slopes of Hindscarth form the west. As you walk easily up the valley our route can be seen in profile rising to the pass between Dale Head and Hindscarth then returning over its shorn summit and down

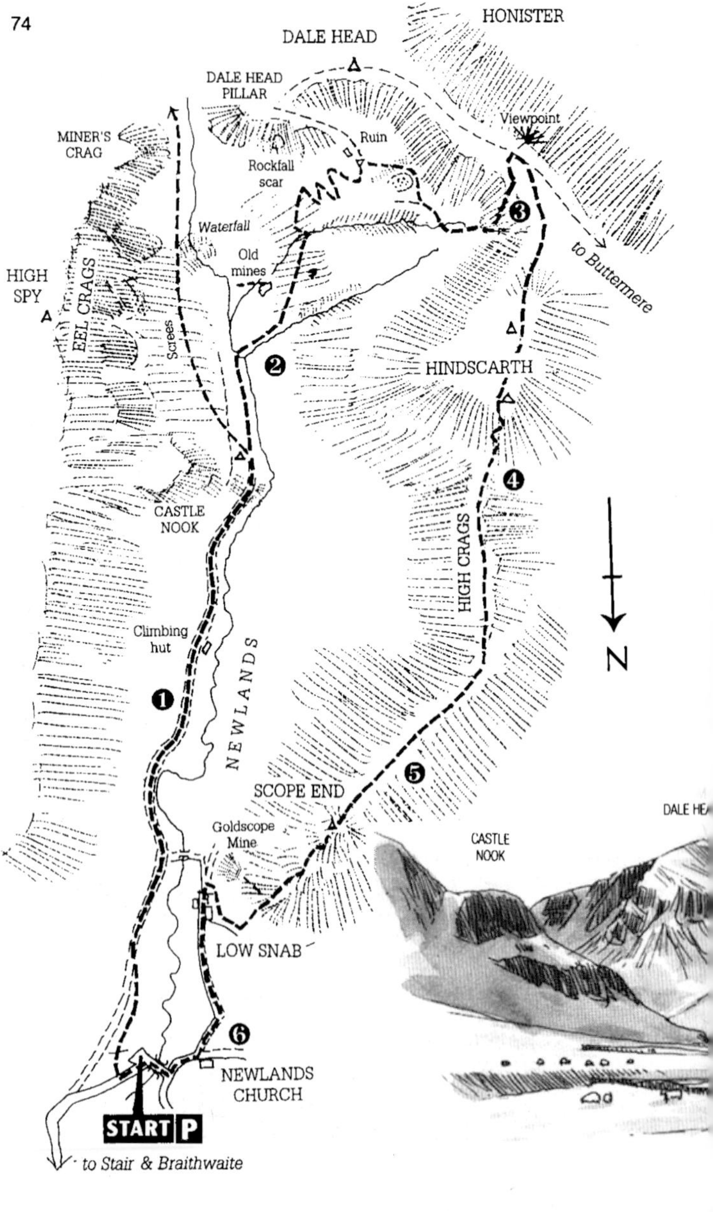

HONISTER

DALE HEAD

DALE HEAD
PILLAR

MINER'S
CRAG

Ruin

Viewpoint

Rockfall
scar

❸

Waterfall

to Buttermere

HIGH
SPY

Old
mines

EEL CRAGS

❷

Scapes

HINDSCARTH

❹

CASTLE
NOOK

HIGH CRAGS

Climbing
hut

❶

NEWLANDS

❺

SCOPE END

Goldscope
Mine

CASTLE
NOOK

LOW SNAB

❻

NEWLANDS
CHURCH

START P

DALE HE

to Stair & Braithwaite

N

the Scope End ridge. Pass the Carlisle Mountaineering Club hut and, just before going through a gap in the Castle Nook spoil heap, sit on a convenient flat stone and enjoy the view of pastoral Newlands and Skiddaw.

Carry on past the bluff of Castle Nook to a fork and cairn. Keep ahead on the track, now green underfoot and descending to the stream (the left fork rises to the pass at the valley head). Notice the continuation of our track, a green zig-zag on the opposite fellside. Keep along the stream to where a tributary, Near Tongue Gill, joins it from the right. Cross over - there are stones to leap onto - proceed 100yds up the gill and branch L up a diagonally rising rake which soon improves as the miners' path seen from below.

This seldom used path brings a sense of adventure as you scan the wild aspect above and the grim, grey sweep of the sombre combe broken only by the white plume of an elegant waterfall. Cross an area of spoil then look down the line of the vein to a sheepfold and the gaping chasms of the Elizabethan Longwork (1607). Continue to Far Tongue Gill and before turning into it look back north at the enhanced view of Skiddaw, then cross the gill.

The path begins to climb again. *Under the turf of the fell lies the junction of the Borrowdale volcanics, exposed in a recent rockfall on the face of Dale Head Pillar, and the Skiddaw Slates containing the mineral vein.* Keep on the path to reach a cairn where the gradient eases at an upper combe. A branch left goes past the ruined mine building, which still affords windshelter, and up a narrow path to Dale Head (753m) which is considerably further and higher than it looks and not on our itinerary. Ahead our onward route aims for the col between Dale Head and the silvery sloping slabs of Hindscarth. *The ground hereabouts is strewn with spoil containing fragments of ore, weathered to a brilliant turquoise.*

From the cairn there is no path so descend into a reedy hollow to avoid a scree slope. Traverse below the scree and uphill on an emerging trod where

MINE   HINDSCARTH

the sheep lead to the best crossing of a gill above its ravine. Bear left up the grassy tongue which is steep and calls for frequent halts to identify the peaks of Blencathra and the Helvellyn Range spread behind High Spy and the intervening valleys. At the col on Hindscarth Edge a marker stone notes the junction of paths. Our route takes the first on the right.

Do not set off yet. From here you must go ahead a few yards, carefully, to the edge of Yew Crags for the prize view of the day; Honister and Buttermere with a vast panorama of central Lakeland Mountains. Now you can return to the marker stone and set off for the summit of Hindscarth.

Go along the path stretching across the slope towards a large cairn, passing a small cairn at a path joining from the left. The large cairn is perched on the southern end of the summit plateau of Hindscarth. Carry on to the main summit 727m and the windshelter at the northern end of its flat top where the outlook is over, left to right, Grasmoor, Crag Hill and Grisedale Pike.

The ridge with the descent path now drops away ahead. Go down the path, a bit steep and stony at first, then cross a ridgetop moor and a little airy traverse on High Crags and on through the heather to a glimpse of Keswick and Derwentwater. Down on the western side is the almost forgotten little valley of Scope Beck (Walk 14). Take care down the Scope End path which winds about in a series of intricate rock steps to end at the wall/fence junction. Turn R and down the track passing Goldscope Mine on the right (see p78) to turn L into the farmyard. (Refreshments highly recommended with real walkers' pots of tea.) Follow the farm track to the road near Newlands Church, turn R and cross the bridge to the start.

WALK 14:   Scope Beck

SUMMARY: A short, easy walk into a seldom visited but rugged valley to visit the dam at its head. Smooth, grassed-over quarry paths are a delight to walk. You pass the Goldscope Mines, where German miners sought copper in Elizabethan times.

HOW TO GET THERE AND PARKING: Parking area just before the bridge near Newlands church.

Distance:	3¼ miles (5¼km)
Grade:	Easy
Height gain:	262ft (80m)
Terrain:	Gentle valley walking on green paths. Some wet patches.
High point:	The dam
Map:	OL4, HSW-WL

Scope Beck dam

THE WALK: Cross the bridge over the Newlands Beck and in 25yds turn L to Newlands church. Turn L on a track to Low Snab. As you walk look ahead and slightly R to see the valley of Scope Beck draining the combe between Hindscarth and Robinson. Cross a bridge and keep ahead through a gate on the permissive path to Low Snab Farm (refreshments) where you can sit with a pot of tea and contemplate the noise and bustle in this quiet valley when the mines were at their heyday.

Go through the farm gate onto the continuation of the track. Above on the right is the spoil and workings of the Goldscope Mine. Turn R up the grass onto an old green track. Our onward path keeps R to the fence but if you want to visit the mine go uphill on a path through the bracken to a junction with a traversing path and turn L along it to the level top of the mound of spoil. The entrance is an impressive cleft. **Old mines are dangerous and must not be explored,** *but just stand inside the entrance to feel the draught, a steady 42°in all seasons, and note on the right wall the cut-out support brackets.*

Return along the traversing path to the junction then keep ahead to the green path by the fence and turn L. A short climb leads round the shoulder of Scope End (ignore the ridge path branching left) then the green path rises gently to arrive at more spoil heaps. Pass a mine adit now in use by the sheep, delicate ferns and sorrel as a haven from the weather. Immediately past the adit turn L up the slope to gain the level of a quarry and turn R along the path leading from it. The path, once the line of a leat which carried water from the dam to the mines, now forms a balcony giving a fine view of the valley as progress is made past another adit. Robinson dominates the head of the valley its flanks running into Little Dale, the combe above the dam. Pass an

area of scree and a jutting rock where the path has been supported. A little further and the dramatic valley head comes into view, the dam being almost insignificant as the eye fixes on the contorted rock strata of the crag-strewn valley walls.

At a large boulder striped with quartz fork L on an upper trod as our path goes into a boggy patch and both that and the trod disappear. Aim for the waterfall to the left of the dam and as you get nearer another trod will help you to reach the pretty tarn held by the dodgy-looking dam.

Cross the twin outlet streams and tiptoe over the dam. Up the valley are the waterfalls of Scope Beck in an impressive ravine. Turn R and find a trod above a patch of rushes to join the path coming down the valley. Walk down the valley enjoying the view to Skiddaw and Blencathra. The path broadens on meeting the intake walls, becomes enclosed and leads to a gate and a stile. Go through and along the fenced path past Low High Snab to meet a surfaced lane. Keep straight on (ignore the road to High Snab and two public footpath signs) to Newlands church. At the road junction turn R and cross the bridge to the parking.

Goldscope Mine

One of Lakeland's earliest mines mentioned in the Close Rolls of Henry III, worked in 1561, by the first mining company formed in the north of England. A copper smelter was built at Keswick in 1565 to process the ore from Newlands. Goldscope produced both lead and copper pyrites, the latter being very rich in silver and also contained some gold.

Robinson in his *Natural History of Westmorland and Cumberland* of 1709 states that 'for securing of this rich vein, no cost of the best oak wood was

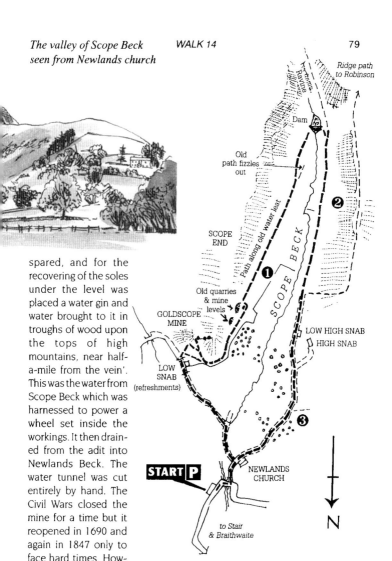

spared, and for the recovering of the soles under the level was placed a water gin and water brought to it in troughs of wood upon the tops of high mountains, near half-a-mile from the vein'. This was the water from Scope Beck which was harnessed to power a wheel set inside the workings. It then drained from the adit into Newlands Beck. The water tunnel was cut entirely by hand. The Civil Wars closed the mine for a time but it reopened in 1690 and again in 1847 only to face hard times. However a rich vein of lead was found, which made a remarkable profit, until the cost of pumping water out became too great and the mine closed in 1864.

WALK 15: Ard Crags and Keskadale Edge

*Ard Crags from
Rigg Beck*

SUMMARY: 'What's that striking little pyramid amongst the Newlands peaks?' is an oft asked question. It proves to be Ard Crags and although the illusion of a conical peak is a sham it does provide one of the best mini ridge walks in Lakeland with an atmosphere out of proportion to its height. On one side is the steep unbroken mountainside which stretches from beyond Crag Hill to Causey Pike; on the other, across Keskadale, lie Hindscarth and Robinson. Our walk completes a horseshoe ridge by returning to the road down Keskadale Edge. A field path and quiet lane avoids a busy road walk.

HOW TO GET THERE AND PARKING: 2³/₄ miles from Braithwaite on the Buttermere road, park in a small quarry just before Rigg Beck.

THE WALK: Start up the Rigg Beck valley dominated by Causey Pike which quickly fades into insignificance and is replaced by the shapely cones of Ard Crags. *As you progress up the valley patches of oak woodland, hardy relics of the ancient forest which once covered the Lakeland fells, can be*

Distance:	5 miles (8km)
Grade:	Moderate
Height gain:	1561ft (476m)
Terrain:	Medium fell. Good grassy paths
Summit:	Ard Crags - 1905ft (581m)
	Knott Rigg - 1823ft (556m)
Map:	OL4, HSW-WL

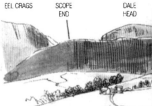

EEL CRAGS   SCOPE END   DALE HEAD

seen on the slopes of Scar Crags.

Turn L at the intake wall/fence corner, cross the beck and follow the wall up the fell. The path mounts steeply towards the ridge, where Hindscarth and Robinson make an impressive appearance and then the ridge path is joined. Turn R along the broad ridge where the southern panorama across Keskadale is excellent. (Note our onward route around the head of the V-shaped valley of Ill Gill to the left of Ard Crags.)

Go straight up the steepening ridge of Aikin Knott, the first cone of Ard Crags. The green path soon gives way to heather and rock. *From here look back to just inside the intake wall where the pattern of old cultivation terraces stand out clearly.*

The path steepens and winds about but is clearly defined and there is no difficulty. From the summit of Aikin Knott carry on up the east cone of Ard Crags where the view into Rigg Beck is dramatic, and yet another cone looms ahead. This is soon conquered and the summit ridge is gained.

Go along the fine ridge, wide enough for a comfortable path, narrow enough to allow views down into each side valley. To the right is a vast unbroken mountainside which stretches from Wandope, Crag Hill and Sail, past Scar Crags to Causey Pike. Pass the meagre cairn on the summit and continue, getting a thrill by looking down the dramatic gully on the left, and descend gently through heather slopes making a mental note to return in late August when all will be a blaze of colour. Go uphill again to the first knoll of Knott Rigg but carry on to a small cairn on its west end for the view of Buttermere's meadows and the spread of mountains beyond.

Turn sharp L dropping down the grass slope to fenced areas guarding nasty-looking bog holes on the end of the Keskadale Edge ridge. Our onward descending path is narrow but clear along the ridge ahead. (An old path traverses on the right 50ft below and parallel to the ridge.) Pass a cairn and down the winding ridge-path with tingling views into Ill Gill. *Another area of old forest clings to the slope of Ard Crags, its windward trees bowed under the weight of the gale.* At the steep end of the ridge look R to find a slanting grassy rake to make an easier way down to the fence path. Turn L and skirt Keskadale Farm to meet the road.

Southern outlook from the ridge below Aikin Knott

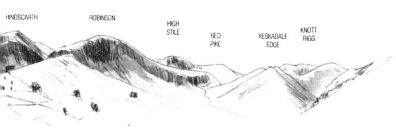

HINDSCARTH   ROBINSON   HIGH
                                 STILE   RED   KESKADALE   KNOTT
                                              PIKE   EDGE   RIGG

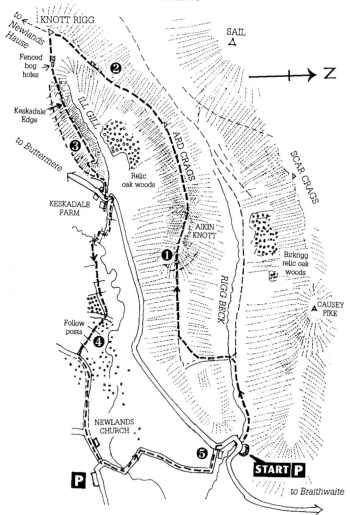

Turn L and cross Ill Gill bridge. The road can be followed to the start but this is not recommended as the road is narrow, and often busy.

Turn R, public footpath sign, beyond the bridge and down the gravel track. Go straight on at a gate following down the gill to cross it and turn L to a footbridge over Keskadale Beck. Turn L and cross the pasture, the scene a gentle, pastoral relaxation in contrast to the fells. Go up the rising track ahead and straight across the field, aiming for a prominent oak tree with Cat Bells behind, to a stile and footplank leading into a rush-grown field. Yellow-topped poles indicate the way along the right-hand fence with planks across the ditches. Leave the field at a stile/bridge across another pole marked field to a 5yd wall and stile bridge and go straight across two fields to approach the Newlands valley. Keep ahead (ignoring a gate right), to a narrow surfaced lane edged with oak and hazel. Turn L to Newlands church and its little adjoining school. From here admire the Newlands valley then carry on to a road junction. Turn L along and across Keskadale Beck to make the final climb out of the valley to the road at Rigg Beck. Turn R to the parking.

The Relict Woods
These old woods were coppiced, which accounts for their straggly appearance. The bark was used for tanning leather, whilst the timber was used to make oak swills and woven baskets.

WALK 16: Newlands - Outerside and Barrow Ridge

SUMMARY: A satisfying hill walk which visits some low summits with excellent views. Height is gained easily along the old mine track. The ensuing ridge walk is a delight culminating in a steady descent to Braithwaite. Parking here is difficult even for residents so we advise using the ample parking at Uzzicar, reached by a gentle streamside stroll from the village.

HOW TO GET THERE AND PARKING: From the Keswick bypass and A66 turn L to Braithwaite. Take the Newlands valley road, pass the screes of Barrow mine and park just beyond at Uzzicar (1½ miles from Braithwaite).

Distance:	6¼ miles (10km)
Grade:	Moderate
Height gain:	1830ft (558m)
Terrain:	Medium fell. Generally easy walking on good paths, which become a little rougher on the hill top.
Summits:	Outerside - 1863ft (568m)
	Stile End - 1466ft (447m)
	Barrow - 1492ft (455m)
Map:	OL4, HSW-WL

THE WALK: From the parking area cross the road to the footpath sign and turn L up the gently rising track, the old trackbed of a light tramway to

BLENCATHRA

the cobalt mines, and parallel with the road. The height gives an immediate view over the Newlands valley drained by Newlands Beck which will guide our return. *On reaching the deep valley of Stoneycroft Gill look down at the buildings of Stoneycroft, the site of a smelter which drew lead ore from as far as Greenside Mines, the other side of Helvellyn.* Across the valley stands the peak of Cat Bells and the ridge rising onward to Maiden Moor.

The track bends up the Stoneycroft valley between Causey Pike (left) and Barrow (right) gaining height easily up the deep V-shaped defile, cut most of the way into the bedrock. Pass a level area on the left and as the valley begins to widen out Outerside is seen ahead whilst Helvellyn fills the narrow horizon behind. Keep up the progress and the western side of the valley pulls away revealing the summit and ridge of Causey Pike with Sail across the valley head.

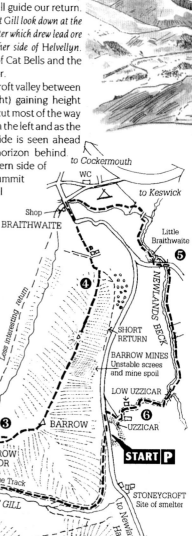

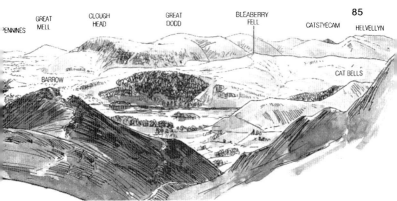

View over Barrow from Outerside

At a cairn ignore the many branching paths, halt a minute to look at the wonderful view of Derwentwater backed by Walla Crag and Clough Head. Carry on along the track, pass a cairn and a sheepfold then halt at the next cairn just beyond. Ahead the valley flattens into a wide pass before plunging into Coledale. This cairn is where we leave the track which makes its way to the pass and culminates in the area of red screes round the old mines. Take a short-cut by forking diagonally R, walking on the right of an old groove, on a trod which traverses the fellside. Pass a tiny ruined fold with stones and carry on to meet a better path coming from the pass. Turn R along it and climb up the ridge. The deep valley of Coledale is now north (left) with the Force Crag Mines at its head and bounded by the monstrous slopes of Grisedale Pike. Carry on to the summit of Outerside where the panorama is truly breathtaking.

Continue over the top and down the ridge and zig-zag path, making the steep descent reasonable, to the depression of Low Moss. There are paths everywhere so pass the pool, turn L round it, then bend R on the widening path (or take one of the many combinations) and go up to the summit of Stile End. There is an insignificant cairn but a rich view north over the Whinlatter Forest.

Set off along the second path right, at 90° to your approach (facing the Stoneycroft valley) and descend the steep path to the next gap, Barrow Door. (Turn L for a short return to Braithwaite.)

Keep ahead and it is an easy ascent up the shoulder of Barrow. Suddenly a magnificent aspect to the south opens out and the summit is a worthy culmination to the day's climb. Do not forget to look back at the grandeur of the mountains surrounding Coledale.

The enjoyment is by no means over. Carry on along the ridge with an

CAUSEY PIKE   SCAR CRAGS   SAIL   CRAG HILL   OUTERSIDE   SAND HILL   HOBCARTON PIKE   GRISEDALE PIKE

The ring of peaks around Coledale from Barrow

excellent view of Derwentwater all the way. Pass old workings at a little gap with two cairns, up the short rise and down the ridge again to a cross path about 500yds above the plantation. (Short return R to the Newlands road, turn R to the start.)

Keep ahead to a small three-way signpost, turn L to go through a gate under oak trees. Cross the pasture and straight on (signpost) the public bridleway through the yard at Braithwaite Lodge. Pass an old yew tree then go down the drive to the road.

Turn L into the village, pass a shop, cross the bridge and turn R (signed Keswick) then in 50yds locate the public footpath on the right opposite Old Farm Mews. (Toilets 100yds ahead just beyond the triangular traffic island. Pub refreshments in the village. Shop in the campsite.)

The footpath runs along Coledale Beck past houses and through the campsite. Go over an exit stile and on to a footbridge over the beck. Continue along the opposite bank with the wooded knoll of Swinside ahead. Pass the confluence of the Coledale and Newlands Becks and continue up the Newlands Beck to Little Braithwaite Farm. Go through the yard to the surfaced road. Turn L for 50yds, go over the bridge and turn immediately R through a kissing gate onto a streamside footpath. The path runs between the stream and the floodbank and flowering gorse makes an attractive setting to the views across the fields, reclaimed from former marshes. As you progress great scree-like scars triggered by former mining can be seen on the slopes of Barrow above. Turn R over an old stone bridge and along the hedged path to Low Uzzicar. Follow the track round at High Uzzicar and go through the farm gate. The parking is on the road directly above.

The Cobalt Mine

A promising vein high on the fell proved a financial disaster. At great expense a road, tramway and smelt mill were built with crushing mills and dressing floors. The good track up Stoneycroft Gill is a legacy of the work.

Barrow Lead Mines
These date from 1680. A huge water-wheel was located at Uzzicar. Lead was smelted from Elizabethan times at Stoneycroft, where a flue was built up the hillside. A disaster occurred when a shaft was being sunk in the stream, the dam burst and drowned the men below.

Braithwaite
Cumberland pencils were manufactured here from 1868 to 1898 until a fire demolished the factory. The village also had a woollen mill and housed miners. In its heyday population was more than double its present number.

Force Crag Mine
Until 1990 the mines road up the valley was busy for this was the last working mine in Lakeland, closed after a huge rock fall in 1990. Lead, silver and barytes were produced.

WALK 17: Barf, Lord's Seat and Whinlatter Forest

Barf

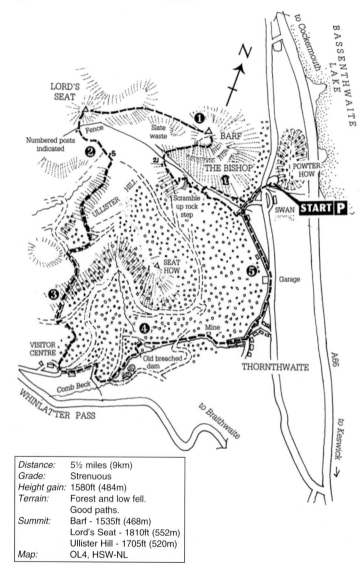

Distance:	5½ miles (9km)
Grade:	Strenuous
Height gain:	1580ft (484m)
Terrain:	Forest and low fell.
	Good paths.
Summit:	Barf - 1535ft (468m)
	Lord's Seat - 1810ft (552m)
	Ullister Hill - 1705ft (520m)
Map:	OL4, HSW-NL

SUMMARY: The white painted stone 'the Bishop of Barf' is a landmark seen from afar, which attracts curiosity. Its host Barf is a fine little rocky peak well worth the effort of its steep approach. Once on top it is an easy stroll to the higher Lord's Seat where the view over the Solway to Scotland expands. We skirt the western slopes of Ullister Hill on an easy path which descends, passing many viewpoints, to the Whinlatter Visitor Centre (café, toilets, shop, cycle shop and hire). Return via the valley of Comb Beck with a visit to the tranquil pools if time allows.

HOW TO GET THERE AND PARKING: From the A66 west of Keswick at the southern end of Bassenthwaite Lake turn L to Thornthwaite and in ¼ mile park at Powter How car park near Swan House.

THE WALK: Return to the road where an old VR post box is still in use in this quiet backwater away from the current of tourism around Keswick. Cross the road and turn R into a narrow lane. At a junction turn R and make a choice of route opposite signed public footpath to Lord's Seat and Barf.

a) Turn R uphill then R through a kissing gate. (The Danger sign is for the approach up the scree to the Bishop rock.) Pass by a miniature 'Bishop' stone indicating his path. Continue along the path and bear L to cross a ford over Beckstones Gill, go over the stile and R up the forest path.

b) Continue up the lane, cross a ford, then fork R over a stile. This reveals a narrow path in the forest. The path makes its way through at least six varieties of trees from which to view the inhospitable hillside of Barf and the striking white figure of the Bishop (looking rather like a frog from this angle) on his hillside perch, and rises up the left-hand side of the stream to be joined by path a).

Follow the path. The path runs by a fence and begins to climb gently at first, then much more steeply. Ignore a stile over the fence on the R and plod up enjoying rests with such views as the forest allows. *Gradually the crags of Barf look nearer and at a clearing its folded rocks of Skiddaw slates can be seen, uplifted, bent and contorted into unstable piles*. The path steepens passing post 21 up a series of bends. The trees become less dense and the path is interrupted by a multicoloured rock bar. Find the way which suits your inclination and continue up the path to a forest road. Turn R on the road, more like a wide path to a fence at the woodland's edge. Go over the stile and onto the open fell.

Cross the red stream and up the rising path which offers an ever expanding scene over the Derwent valley, Keswick and away to the ridge of the Dodds and Helvellyn beyond. At a path junction keep R to a little bluff which juts out airily into a view of Bassenthwaite Lake. Carry on over rocks which contain the tiny silver shrimp-like fossil graptolite, which lived over 500 million years ago, to the summit cairn of Barf. The view is east to the great bulk of Skiddaw (931m) from this angle rising from the lake in successive ridges to a noble summit.

From the Barf cairn take the path north-west which leads down a shallow valley then rises gently towards Lord's Seat. Views open over the Solway to Criffel on the northern horizon. Cross a track and carry on to the summit of Lord's Seat. *When you have enjoyed the estuary view west and looked south to identify the interleaved mountains of Grisedale Pike, Grasmoor and beyond, it is interesting to turn back east to the Derwent valley. Imagine during the ice age how a glacier which poured over The Dodds from Helvellyn, was blocked by the bulk of Blencathra and forced west to flow down the Greta Valley, removing the top of Latrigg before smoothing and shaping the Derwent valley we enjoy today.*

Turn L (south) to start the downhill journey heading for a stile in a fence. As you walk the well-made path the view is west over the forest to the Vale of Lorton where the River Cocker flows from Crummock Water past Cockermouth to the sea. At Pole 5 fork R. The path skirts pleasantly along the western slope of Ullister Hill to join the Whinlatter Forest Green Route at Pole 53. Continue ahead on the Green Route downhill. The mountain bike track joins the forest road from the left for a short way so be aware of riders until arriving at a clearing, Post 3, where the bikers shoot off into the trees. Keep L on the forest road passing a viewpoint over to Keswick and Derwent Water. At Post 2, viewpoint seat and information panel, follow the Green Route round the road corner and R into the forest on a steep path which zig-zags down to a clearing with log seats. A green, red, blue post indicates the path leading downhill. Look for a path L with a squirrel carving and in a few strides you will see the Visitor Centre ahead.

Turn L to pass below the cycle shop and L along the lower road, which becomes a forest road past a cottage. Keep on to the edge of a plantation where a path R (blue marker) drops into the valley of Comb Beck. Meet the forest road at a sharp bend* Go straight across the road and along the blue route. Hallgarth Ponds are across the little valley to the right.

* To visit the Hallgarth Ponds.

The ponds were made in 1978 as part of a planned nature reserve which was not developed further.

From the bend follow the road down to the bridge, cross it and turn L on a narrow path between the stream and the pools. A seat on the bank between the pools allows you to enjoy the tranquil

atmosphere. To return to the blue route go back over the bridge and a shortcut path turns immediately R going up to rejoin the blue route.

The path climbs a little away from the ponds then descends to a viewpoint at the old breached dam. A little further a bridleway is joined. Turn R, leaving the blue route, cross another bridge and descend to a forest road. Go straight across to a path signed Thornthwaite which is narrower now but gives a good view of the cascading beck. The old Thornthwaite mine is passed, hidden in the trees, and the path leads to the forest gate at Thornthwaite.

Go ahead to the surfaced lane through the village. Ignore a right turn and keep ahead then at the next fork bend L along a quiet lane past Thwaite Howe Hotel to a minor road. Turn L for 200m then branch L on an old road. Keep straight on and soon the 'Bishop of Barf' will appear, tall and stately, on the hillside ahead. Pass behind the farmhouse and join the outward route. Fork L and cross the road to the car park.

The Bishop of Barf

The white painted stone is reputedly the site of the demise of the Bishop of Derry who in 1783 took a wager to ride his pack pony up the steep front of the fell to Lord's Seat. The stone marks the spot where his mount staggered and fell, killing both rider and pony. It is painted annually by the Keswick Mountain Rescue team.

Whinlatter Forest Park

This is a prime example of how forestry work and tourism now go hand in hand. The Visitor Centre is always popular and a network of marked trails for walkers, mountain bikers and orienteers radiates through the forest. Many of the paths have been made more user-friendly by making walkways across the boggy bits and stiles can be passed by dogs.

A useful map showing the trails is on sale at the Centre.

Thornthwaite Mine

Most of the surface evidence of this once important mine now lies buried in the forest, but in its heyday in the 1800s Thornthwaite was a busy lead mining community. The vein rain north-south and is a continuation of that through Barrow. The entrance to Ladstock, the oldest mine worked before gunpowder, is passed near the beck whilst opposite lies a fenced shaft.

The mine was successful enough to warrant a smelt mill in the village. Various remains of water leats can be spotted along the beckside.

The site of a dam, made originally to provide a head of water for the pumps to drain the mine shaft, can be seen just below the present lake on Comb Beck.

WALK 18: Wythop and Sale Fell

The 'welcome gate' into Wythop Woods

SUMMARY: When the weather is grim in central Lakeland it is often far better on the northern fringe. This walk is an excellent choice for such an occasion especially as its figure eight configuration allows choice of an early sheltered return or to include Sale Fell, more open to the elements.

It is, however, a walk to enjoy in any weather. Stately Douglas fir, tightly planted Sitka spruce, delicate silver birch and traditional woods of oak are just some of the varied trees seen on this walk.

		Short Return
Distance:	6¾ miles (10¾km)	3¾ miles (6km)
Grade:	Moderate	
Height gain:	1325ft (404m)	
Terrain:	Woodland and low fell. Smooth paths.	
Summit:	In forest 1344ft (410m)	
Map:	OL4, HSW-NL	

Sale Fell is a complete contrast, with grass like a bowling green to walk on and a panorama to enjoy of blue Scottish hills over the silvery Solway Firth, and the bulk of Skiddaw to enjoy close by.

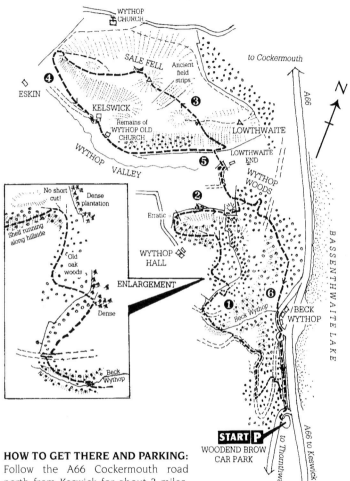

WYTHOP CHURCH

SALE FELL

Ancient field strips

4

ESKIN

KELSWICK

Remains of WYTHOP OLD CHURCH

LOWTHWAITE

3

to Cockermouth

A66

N

LOWTHWAITE END

WYTHOP WOODS

WYTHOP VALLEY

5

No short cut!

Dense plantation

Shelf running along hillside

Old oak woods

Dense

ENLARGEMENT

Beck Wythop

2

Erratic

WYTHOP HALL

1

Beck Wythop

BECK WYTHOP

6

BASSENTHWAITE LAKE

START **P**
WOODEND BROW
CAR PARK

to Thornthwaite

A66 to Keswick

HOW TO GET THERE AND PARKING:

Follow the A66 Cockermouth road north from Keswick for about 3 miles. Where the dual carriageway comes close to Bassenthwaite Lake there is a sharp turn L to Thornthwaite (note: do not take the earlier signs to Thornthwaite). Woodend Brow parking is immediately on the left.

THE WALK: From the Woodend Brow car park turn R, cross the road and go along the old road for 50yds. Branch L on the public footpath to Wythop Hall, an old right of way survivor, upset in places.

The path treads through a bank of old sycamore, beech, oak and Douglas fir, gradually gaining height. At a forest road turn R and in 50yds go L on an unsigned path into the plantation. Keep up the gently rising path to a steep exit onto a forest road. Turn R and after half a mile look out for waymarked steps on the R. *As you walk up the road there is a fine view over the lake to isolated St Bega's Church in the Mirehouse park.*

Descend the narrow path into the little ravine of Beck Wythop. The echoing road noise has given way to the gurgling of the beck as you cross the footbridge and walk by the stream. Climb the bank to meet a forest road. Turn R, then almost immediately L on a signed path, which runs through young trees to enter a break in the dark forest. Enter the gloom and go up a needle-cushioned rise then fork L (waymark), then L again to reach a stile on the edge of the Forest Enterprise plantation.

Go over into an old oak wood. The right of way path is not much walked but its way is clear and its tread green. Keep ahead a few yards then slightly downhill and a fraction left. Beyond the wood's edge lies Wythop Hall Farm below. Bear R along the fringe of the wood on an ascending path which widens and has makeshift shooting butts to either side. At a junction (care is needed not to overshoot) turn L following a shelf 100yds or so below the top of the hill. (The continuing path amy seem like a short cut over the ridge but it leads into a difficulty and is not a right of way.) In 50yds go diagonally L on a gently descending line. The way of the path can be seen by its overhead gap in the oaks. The path becomes clearer as you pass above the farm and follow it round the end of the ridge and come out of the wood with Sale Fell seen across the valley.

Pass a large boulder, an ice-borne erratic, through the gate ahead into a pasture. Keep by the fence, pass a small oak wood and a redundant stone gatepost of the old path. Carry on to a gate in a cross fence by the wood corner (left). Note: right of way path wrongly marked on the OS map. Keep ahead and over a stile in the Forest Enterprise fence. Turn L and go over the rise to a major path and 'welcome' gate on the left.

SHORT RETURN from this point.

THE TRAVERSE OF SALE FELL: Go over the 'welcome' stile and along the vehicle track, through a gate, ahead at the next gate/stile and just before approaching Lowthwaite End turn L and up past a little quarry, with interesting rock-fold features, to another gate. Carry on past wind-bent hawthorns and through the fell gate in the intake wall.

Wind-bent hawthorns

The character of the walk changes once more. Turn R 50yds then zig-zag back L on a diagonally rising path through the low gorse. A mere twist of the neck will give you a brilliant panorama of the Lakeland mountains as you progress up the green path, to join one along the ridge. Keep L through the gap between low interlocking spurs (pile of stones). The summit is ahead and looking north Higham Hall can be seen in the forested valley below. Go through two colourful walls, noticing the ridges of old strip cultivation between them, and along to the summit cairn. *There is a wonderful view from here looking north to the Galloway hills, west out to sea and the rich green valley and white*

Ridges of old strip cultivation on Sale Fell

houses of Embleton and its quarry behind at the foot of the fell. The broad Embleton valley was once drained by the River Derwent; now the river takes a loop to the north.

Turn half L (NW) on the green path towards the next cairn and descend into a dip. Turn L to pass scree below a small rock face and descend to the next shelf. Fork diagonally L towards grey rocks and white stones and along the ridge of Dodd Crag. The trig point ahead is on Ling Fell. Descend the end of Dodd Crag bearing R towards a wall. At the wall turn L and in approx 100yds turn L again on a high balcony path to Wythop Old Church, up the Wythop valley with the farmsteads of Eskin across the beck. At Kelswick Farm ignore the onward footpath, drop down onto the surfaced lane, turn L and pass the house and its shelter of trees (ignoring stile to the right) and turn R by a seat to resume our right of way signed public footpath through a stile.

Carry on to Chapel Wood and pass ruins of the old 14th-century chapel, built in the reign of Queen Mary and demolished when St Margaret's Church was built on the other side of the fell. Go through the gate and the oak wood to a path fork. Keep L on the upper rising path through trees, once coppiced, until the wood ends and the gorse bank heralds the return to the fell gate on the right. Turn R along the hawthorn path and follow it back to the 'welcome' gate.

SHORT RETURN: Go ahead down the forest track and round a bare rock bend which reveals the violent folding of the rock strata. At the forest road go straight across (C to C bike route and blue arrow). Soon the noise of the main road is heard and the waters of the lake seen below. Join the old road at Beck Wythop. Go R crossing the stream and along the old road. Pass the dual carriageway and bus turning area to continue ahead along the old road. *Traffic is out of sight but not sound, however the contorted rock of the cuttings and the encroaching plants of the verges are endeavouring to give pleasure.* Pass the outward footpath and arrive at the road and parking.

The Wythop Valley

This gently sloping rural valley is unusual in having no head for it has been chopped off by passing ice which formed the flat valley now occupied by Bassenthwaite Lake. Perhaps a tongue of ice lapped westwards to create the Wythop valley, broader at its head than foot, dropping erratic rocks here and there as it melted. Wythop Beck drains gently to the west, whilst Beck Wythop drops steeply to the east.

Ridge and Furrow

During the Napoleonic Wars much more marginal land was cultivated and the resulting ridges and furrows are still in evidence.

The summit of Barf with Skiddaw looming large behind (Walk 17)
Reflections in Hallgarth Ponds (Walk 17)

Above:
In its mining heyday
Roughten Gill was
crossed here by a
bridge (Walk 26)

Left::
Back o'beyond at
Blackhazel Beck. Few
people walk here, for
there is no bridge
across the River
Caldew (Walk 24)

CHAPTER 3
The Northern Fells and Dales

This area has become one of our favourites; away from the crowds and with a breadth of unbroken scene unusual in the Lake District. Again, there is a rich history of mining with its legacy of well graded tracks, some still velvety green underfoot. Once on top, even where paths are sparse the walking is generally easy. Starting points are fairly high which makes walks to the fell tops relatively easy, where views extend to the blue hills of southern Scotland above the glinting arm of the Solway. 'Back o'Skidda' has a quality of remoteness even on a good summer day when many cyclists pass through.

Avoid the higher walks in mist when the featureless nature of the fells could cause confusion. Don't get complacent on these predominantly gentle fells - the scrambling ascent of Roughten Gill is probably the most adventurous in this book, whilst the crossing of the River Caldew on Walk 24 is only recommended in low water, preferably in summer.

Old clapper bridge over Roughten Gill, Glenderaterra

WALK 19: Skiddaw House and Lonscale Fell

Lonscale Pike from the ruins of the miners' cottages

SUMMARY: Only a few miles from bustling Keswick and Borrowdale is a haven of tranquillity, a broad moorland basin at the 'Back o'Skidda', surrounded by bleak, rounded hills of heather and grass unbroken by walls. The home of grouse and skylarks. The heart of this haven of peace is Skiddaw House, once a shepherd's lonely residence, now one of a diminishing number of basic youth hostels. Our approach path, starting at the Latrigg car park well above Keswick, rises gently across the steep flank of the Glenderaterra valley. It is part of the Cumbria Way and is a popular mountain bike trail.

Both return routes are attractive. Over Lonscale Fell gives widespread views to reward the effort but the old mine track on the east side of the Glenderaterra is not just a poor weather option.

Distance:	Return over Lonscale Fell - 6¹/₂ miles (10¹/₂km)	By Valley Return - 7¹/₄ miles (11¹/₂km)
Grade:	Moderate	Easy
Height gain:	1500ft (456m)	1016ft (310m)
Terrain:	Valley and medium fell. Hard on the knees when the Skiddaw path is joined.	Valley
Summits:	Lonscale Fell - 2443ft (745m) Lonscale Pike - 2306ft (703m)	Skiddaw House - 1542ft (470m)
Map:	OL4, HSW-NL	

HOW TO GET THERE AND PARKING: From the A66 roundabout at the western end of the Keswick bypass turn on the A591 Carlisle road. Immediately turn R to Ormathwaite and Underbarrow. Continue ³/₄ mile to a junction and turn sharp R for ³/₄ mile to a parking area at the road end.

THE WALK: *Before leaving the parking take advantage of its position to orientate the local valleys on view. To the west is the Derwent valley with Bassenthwaite Lake and the white point of the Bishop of Barf on the wooded hillside beyond. Over the fence southward is the popular little hill of Latrigg (368m) and the River Greta in its wooded gorge at its feet; to the east the Glenderamackin valley with the two rounded humps of Great and Little Mell Fell on the horizon.*

Go through the gate and turn L along a fenced pathway. At the second kissing gate fork R on a less obvious level green path. (The unmistakable path up Skiddaw forks left and a stone cross can be seen above on the grass bank beside it.) Our path traverses the side of a deep valley of Whit Beck. The cutting on the left-hand side shows thin friable beds of the Skiddaw Slates.

Cross the ford of tree-lined Whit Beck, its waters enhancing the colours of the multicoloured rocks. The path now makes a steady climb across the bracken-clad shoulder of Lonscale Fell with much interest in the outlook as you go. *No prizes for spotting the old Threlkeld Quarries and the coach road winding around Threlkeld Knott on its way to Dockray and Patterdale, little Tewet Tarn and St John's Vale, the Castlerigg Stone Circle and a dark profile of Iron Crag, Shoulthwaite.*

View of St John's Vale and lower Borrowdale separated by moorland rising to Bleaberry Fell. (Walk 28)

Round the corner into the valley of the Glenderaterra Beck and the scene changes. *Evidence of mining lies in the valley floor and in Sinen Gill (the second deep gill on the east) the dome of granite, which donated the heat and minerals, reaches the surface.* The bracken gives way to heather and bilberry which fringes the rocks of Lonscale Crags above and below. The path cuts through the crag on a rock shelf - no problem for walkers but it tests the nerves of cyclists who often ride this part of the Cumbria Way. *Look carefully at the texture of the rock. It is more massive due to being metamorphosed (cooked) by its proximity to the granite and the major fault line, running the length of the Lake District from north to south and along which we are walking.* Continue to rise gradually passing over the waves of the fellside. Across the valley the bland end of Mungrisdale Common interleaves

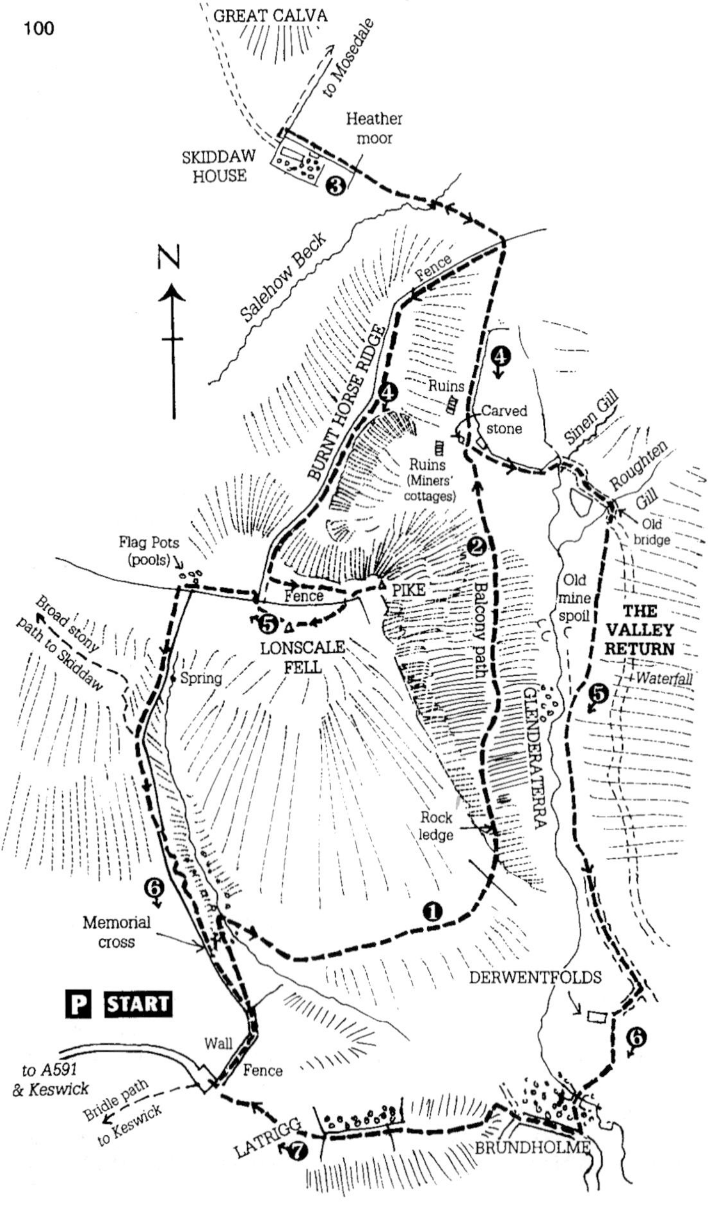

GREAT CALVA

to Mosedale

Heather moor

SKIDDAW HOUSE

③

N

Salehow Beck

Fence

④

Ruins

Carved stone

Sinen Gill

④

Ruins (Miners' cottages)

Roughten Gill

Old bridge

Fence

BURNT HORSE RIDGE

②

Balcony path

PIKE

⑤

Old mine spoil

THE VALLEY RETURN

Flag Pots (pools)

Broad stony path to Skiddaw

LONSCALE FELL

Spring

GLENDERATERRA

⑤

Waterfall

Rock ledge

①

⑥

Memorial cross

DERWENTFOLDS

P START

to A591 & Keswick

Wall

Fence

⑥

Bridle path to Keswick

LATRIGG

⑦

BRUNDHOLME

the Blencathra ridges, astride the valley head a dark moor appears and downstream the valley tunnels the view up Thirlmere to the U-shaped pass of Dunmail Raise. Our path descends a stony section. Ignore a right fork to the valley floor and carry on. From here our return route over the peak of Lonscale Fell is on the left-hand skyline. Cross a footbridge where old ruins stand like a huge plant pot to an elderberry tree. Ignore the path right towards a sheepfold and wall (the Valley Return via Derwent Folds) but as you go up the brow look out for the Guide Stone beside the path. *The head of the valley is now dominated by shapely Great Calva and the dark moor has spread into the long body of Great Knott with Carrock Fell to its right.* Walk on to meet a cross wall/fence.

Note this gate/stile, the 'watershed gate', in the cross fence/wall which runs from the watershed, the Stake, between Glenderaterra and Mosedale. Go through and along to the footbridge over Salehow Beck. *Notice the rock on the path. It is tough and rough textured for here the proximity of the underlying granite dome has hardened it into crystalline hornfels.* The next stretch of path still has a few of the set stones remaining and here we are at Skiddaw House, a remote yet popular youth hostel where the song of the wind in the surrounding larches is seldom hushed and the piquant atmosphere is slightly daunting. The building to the left of the hostel is open as a shelter as this can be an inclement spot. (The continuing access road runs to White Water Dash and the A591. The Cumbria Way turns right and runs down Mosedale before turning north over High Pike to Caldbeck.)

Return to the 'watershed' gate and go through.

RETURN VIA LONSCALE FELL: Turn R up Burnt Horse Ridge on a trod by the wall - a steady plod. The wall collapses into a line of stones but the fence carries on, the surrounding mountains diminish and the valleys are spread map-like below. *The camaraderie of the valley path has given way to silence leaving a circular sheepfold at the foot of Sale How and a hog-hole, still standing in a totter of small flat stones, to cheer the climb.* Bend right with the fence and cross the top of the crag to a gap. Still keeping close to the fence (many have used it as a handrail) go up the steep bank until the gradient eases and the fence angles left again. Turn L and make your way across the fell towards a cross fence, noting the stile, to find a path about 50yds below it leading on to twin pools. (If caught in mist continue along the fence to a junction with two gates, a wooden one and an iron one. Turn R by going through the wooden one and back through the iron one.) Turn L to the summit of Lonscale Pike where there is a modest cairn, a great view and a few yards beyond, **a long drop down Lonscale Crag so TAKE CARE.**

Return on the path past the pools to the stile in the fence, go over and up the dome of Lonscale Fell to the cairn at the summit. (A stone 20yds to the left gives an improved view of Derwentwater and a vast panorama of the central Lakeland mountains.)

From the cairn continue over the summit, veering right towards the fence and Skiddaw. Pass a doughnut pool and, keeping the same direction, follow the fence to the two-gate junction. Through the iron gate turn L to use the path on the opposite side. Go down past the wall corner to the pools of Flag Pots. Turn L through an old iron gate on a narrow path lined with the distant Jaws of Borrowdale. The emerging gill left with a gushing spring is the head of Whit Beck. Descend the hillside on the old grooved way past an upright sleeper at a wall end, and eventually merge with the 'motorway' from Skiddaw. Carry on to stiles with gate and after a slight welcome uphill pass the cross seen earlier, a memorial to Lakeland shepherds. Go through the kissing gate to the fenced path and parking.

VALLEY RETURN VIA DERWENT FOLDS: From the watershed gate continue ahead returning to the Guide Stone. Turn L towards the wall with a gap and sheepfold. Ignore the trod through the gap and keep following the prominent diminished old road by the wall. Cross a stream and a ladder stile then over a wooden footbridge with side extensions for a farm vehicle. *Some of the original paving stones are still in place standing proud of the eroding pathway. At the next bridge over Sinen Gill look in the stream bed where there are a number of granite boulders identified by their rough textured surface speckled with white and cream feldspar, brown and white shiny mica and glassy grey quartz.*

The road now rises over a slight hummock with ruins, their feeble walls giving us some welcome shelter from horizontal driving rain on one occasion, when the fine view down the valley was cancelled. *There is a large boulder to the left of the road carrying hammered scars where geologists have confirmed its origin on their expeditions to Sinen Gill, a favourite venue.*

The next bridge is one of the highlights of the walk; the splendid stone slab bridge over Roughten Gill (see p97). *Stripped of its surface, the construction is there for all to see and you have to take your hat off to the skill and strength of the road builders. The stone is the hardened hornfels, apart from one rogue slab of green volcanic slate.* Keep ahead on the road and round the next bend, pass a concrete marker by a Welsh AB grid then in about 25yds branch down R on a green path encumbered with rocks. Just before it becomes wet and invaded by rushes, aim for a ruin with tree in the valley bottom. Well before reaching the valley stream a path develops and turns across the slope and over a slight ridge, a good vantage point for the complex remains of the Glenderaterra Mine. From here continue a diagonal traverse down the fellside to where a bridge once crossed the stream, identified by its remaining side buttresses, and gain the road by a narrow traversing path just above the water. (*If you wish to inspect the mine ruins **exercise caution**.*)

Set off down the valley, the gentle gradient speeding the passing of a plantation where the view along the wooded valley to St John's Vale is continually enhanced until emerging from its arms. Pass a major rebuild of the road at a landslip then look back up the Glenderaterra for a last glance of conical Great Calva at the head. Go through a gate, across a splash and through another gate onto a surfaced lane.

Turn R to Derwent Folds Farm (the road left leads to Wescoe and the A66). Before the first building turn L, signed Skiddaw, and through a gate into an old sunken pathway. The path is shaded by mature oaks and forms a gentle contrast with the austere upper valley as you walk down to an old ford, between verges, colourful with delicate yellow cow-wheat and ruby foxgloves with over-burdened heads, to a road. Turn R, signed Keswick and Latrigg, and in a few yards arrive at a triangular junction.

Take the left fork, go through a gate and immediately turn R to Skiddaw and Underscar. Keep on the main path, the right branch, and climb the broad ridge with views south over the Greta valley to Borrowdale and north to Lonscale Fell and Skiddaw. The latter view becomes blocked by forest of mainly coniferous trees. Go through a gate by a sheep shelter and on to another gate at a bend in the forest fence. The southern view is now obscured by the rising pastures of Latrigg. At the next gate leave the forest behind and progress to a stile over the left-hand fence. Ignore this, unless you want to visit the summit of Latrigg, and amble along the path to the car park gate.

Skiddaw House

Skiddaw House

This row of old shepherds' cottages was used as an outdoor centre in the 1970s then became a youth hostel, seen by many as an ideal use in such a remote spot. Unfortunately a row over lack of planning permission forced closure for a while, happily now resolved, although passers-by cannot buy refreshments. The surrounding heather moors were managed for grouse shooting until the 1950s.

Skiddaw Slates and the Underlying Granite

The Skiddaw Slates were formed by alternating bands of mud and sand laid down on the edge of a shallow sea, then pressured into stone. You can sometimes see the fossil remains of the tiny creatures, graptolites, trilobites and molluscs, which lived in the sea. Later, the horizontal rock was uplifted, folded, faulted and tilted. You can see the folds in many places. Beneath the slates is a dome of igneous rock, once the molten interior, which partially melted the overlying rock where it thrust against it. When they cooled they had been transformed to a much harder consistency, well seen in the walk up the Glenderaterra. To see the changes look first for small white crystals of chiastolyte in the slates. The nearer the granite the larger and more numerous they become, sometimes over an inch. Then the rock becomes darker with dark oblong spots. These were the hornfels rocks used by Peter Crosthwaite of Keswick in 1765 to make a set of musical stones for the stone rings when struck. Other local men followed his example, and formed a popular show act which toured Britain.

WALK 20:   Below Blencathra

		Alternative
Distance:	7½ miles 12km	6½ miles (10½km)
		avoiding Scaley Beck
Grade:	Easy - but there is a short exposed rock	
	scramble across Scaley Beck.	
Height gain:	524ft (160m)	
Terrain:	Valley	
Map:	OL5 & OL4, HSW-NL	

SUMMARY: This low level walk, ideal when the fell tops are covered in cloud, allows a glimpse into the five deep gills of Blencathra with a gentle return along green riverside paths to join the old railway where it passes through an attractive wooded valley. The sting in the tail is the climb back to the car. There is a difficult, and in wet conditions, potentially hazardous crossing of Scaley Gill which requires a little rock scramble in an exposed position. It is just the sort of place where, in Alpine countries, there would be a fixed hand wire. The National Park authorities did fix one, but it was removed by vandals. It is unlikely to be replaced. The descent into and out of the gill is no problem to agile walkers but the path has eroded and the scramble down its earthy exposed side is steep and when wet, potentially dangerous. It is not suitable for the timid or young children.

The Alternative provides a safe and slightly shorter route.

HOW TO GET THERE AND PARKING: Parking area behind the Blencathra Centre, reached from Threlkeld along Blease Road. *The centre was a TB sanatorium in 1904, now it is a Field Studies Council Centre operated in partnership with the National Park. The FSC is a charity which runs courses throughout the year aimed at increasing environmental awareness.*

THE WALK: Leave the car park on a path just above the cattle-grid, which runs above the fence side. It follows the intake wall all the way to Scales

Green and needs little description, so we will just draw your attention to the main features as they occur. At once there is a fine view over the Glenderamakin valley to St John's Vale and its surrounding mountains. Where the fence ends look for a prominent path and blue stone sign to Gate Ghyll. Go up L to the intake wall where the path traverses once more. *Above Blease Farm is a 'welcome' notice on a gate inviting guests to stay, and if the splendid vistas*

Blencathra

across to the Dodds are anything to go by it would be a memorable stay indeed. Cross a small stream followed by the crossing of Blease Gill with its show of multicoloured Skiddaw Group rocks. Go straight on - the path branching up left is up Knott Halloo and Blencathra - until reaching the next deep ravine of Gate Gill. Just through the downstream gate is a seat for you to sit and decide your onward route.

WARNING - Half a mile ahead is Scaley Gill with its hazardous crossing.

ALTERNATIVE ROUTE AVOIDING SCALEY GILL: Go down the gill and through a kissing gate into the farmyard and bend R to a three-way signpost. Go through a gate and turn L crossing a flat spoil heap where your approach will stir the Blencathra hounds into chorus. Turn R down a narrow path above the ochre gill which is hurrying the erosion of the spoil and exposing its stone-arched tunnel below. Go over a stile, ahead on the track to the old road. (An old green ROW path cuts diagonally L across the pasture to meet the old road.) Ignore a public bridleway on the right. Turn L along the road which gives fine views over the valley to Combe Head and the line of the old coach road from Keswick to Matterdale. At the road end go through a gate and down the left-sloping path to the A66. Turn

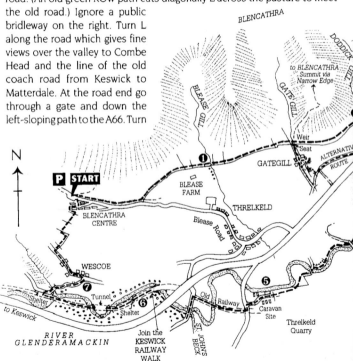

yards, crossing when convenient - do not underestimate the speed of the traffic on this straight downhill stretch - and make a R short-cut onto the Guardhouse lane below. Walk along the quiet lane (ignore a public footpath right over a footbridge) past a cottage and two field gates, and between the last gate and the river bridge find a stile and walkway to join the longer route via Scaley Gill.

TO CONTINUE CROSSING SCALEY GILL: Cross the gill and carry on. (The path up the hill to the left is the popular way to Blencathra via Narrow Edge and Hall's Fell.) On reaching Doddick Gill the unfolding panorama extends east to Mell Fell, Little Mell Fell with their grand neighbours the Helvellyn Range to the right. *Across the main valley is the disused Threlkeld Granite Quarry, now a quarry and mining museum.* Pass Doddick Farm followed by the clamber into Scaley Gill, with care. The wire fencing has been used as a makeshift continental style hand line but it is insecure. The exit at the opposite side is

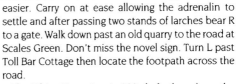

easier. Carry on at ease allowing the adrenalin to settle and after passing two stands of larches bear R to a gate. Walk down past an old quarry to the road at Scales Green. Don't miss the novel sign. Turn L past Toll Bar Cottage then locate the footpath across the road.

The White Horse Inn is 100yds further along the main road if refreshments are required. Bar meals are served but dogs are not allowed inside.

Cross the road and go over the footpath stile into a field. Straight ahead to the next stile then turn R. Cross a brook between a wall end and a large tree then bend L and down to a stile/gate in the lower right-hand corner of the field. Now turn diagonally R and steer towards an electricity pole. Go over the stile nearest to it and follow the fence ahead then R to reach a road at Guardhouse Bridge. Here we meet the River Glenderamackin.

Do not cross the bridge but turn R for 50yds then L over a stile onto a wooden walkway.

THE SHORTER ROUTE AVOIDING SCALEY GILL JOINS HERE.

Continue along the delightful riverside path. *Watch for a dipper skimming the crystal clear water and the primroses safe down the riverbank from grazing sheep.* Go over a gated bridge and the path, now on a raised floodbank, gives an uninterrupted view of Blencathra and our outward route. Across the river is the immaculate Keswick Golf Course. The river makes a long meander, its far bank now steeper and wooded and our side made more intimate by clumps of gorse. Soon the wood ends and the greens and clubhouse are seen across the water. Pass a bridge and lane leading to the golf course and continue on the riverbank footpath which is followed for about ¹/₂ mile.

Go through a stile into an enclosed pathway and along to a sleeper bridge. Cross it and turn R through a kissing gate. Keep to the left-hand fence side as the river swings away on a meander and cross a stone slab bridge over a ditch. Carry on to a gate in a wall, old sleepers bridging a stream which hurries to join the river returned from its wandering and turn R. *The presence of the sleeper bridge indicates the old railway is near.* Cross it, turn R and go straight on through a gate past the farm and through the caravan site then along the road. Pass Station House and some walls of massive stone which almost retain the whiff of steam. At the road go straight across and through a wicket gate waymarked by white arrows, mount onto the Keswick Railway, felled in 1972 by the Beeching axe and now a footpath and cycleway.

Freewheel along the old track bed. Look out for the old stone road bridge over St John's Beck before we leave the railway, go up to the road level and turn L across it. Turn R into Burns Wood and along the shady path under the new road viaduct over the River Greta. On joining the railway again turn L along it. Pass through a cutting and just beyond is a railman's shelter. *The information board inside is fascinating reading but it was the cartoon of the navvie taking tea with the local gentry that amused us.* Cross the river and go through a tunnel, brick-lined with sandstone edged arches, and over the river again. Cross Naddle Beck and then the river once more near its confluence with the Glenderaterra Beck. Immediately over this bridge turn R signed to Keswick via Latrigg and Blencathra.

Go to the picturesque old stone bridge over the beck and turn R over it and up the steep lane to Wesco. Turn L through Far Wesco. As you clear the cottages there are enticing views over Keswick and Borrowdale. Watch out for a R turn as the stile and its yellow waymark are up in the hedge. The way up the fields to the Blencathra Centre is well waymarked. On leaving the last field go up the enclosed lane into the centre and turn R to Skiddaw House and Blencathra. Go between the buildings and turn L up a gravel path to the cattle-grid at the parking.

From below Blencathra

BRAM CRAG   CASTLE ROCK   ULLSCARF   HIGH RIGG   RAVEN CRAG   TEWET TARN   BLEABERRY FELL

Gategill Mines
An ancient mine established before the days of gunpowder producing mainly galena (lead ore) and blende from two highly productive veins, the Woodend and Gatesgill. It was worked by the Saddleback Mining Co. and later the Threlkeld Mining Co. The mine closed in 1901 and during its last 20 years gave employment to an average of 100 men and boys.

WALK 21: Dodd Wood and The Watches

SUMMARY: A low level walk which is enjoyable when higher fells are shrouded in cloud. A pleasing path traverses the attractive lower reaches of Dodd Wood to emerge on the open fell where the scattered rocks of The

Distance:	5½ miles (9km)
Grade:	Easy
Height gain:	764ft (233m)
Terrain:	Valley and low fell.
Summit:	The Watches - 1092ft (333m)
Map:	OL4 and PF576, HSW-NL

Watches makes a fine objective. In clear weather the views from here are memorable: into Southerndale with the bulk of Skiddaw's screes on one hand and shapely Ullock Pike on the other. Turn around and beyond the end

Dodd Wood. The bridge over Skill Beck above Sawmill Cottage

of Bassenthwaite Lake you see the Galloway hills of Scotland across the Solway.

Return is through the gentle parkland of the Mirehouse estate, past historic St Bega's Church. A diversion along the lakeshore is possible if, before you start, you have bought a ticket to visit the grounds (only available between April and October).

HOW TO GET THERE AND PARKING: From the Keswick bypass take the A591 to Bothel and Carlisle. In 3 miles park at the Forest Enterprise

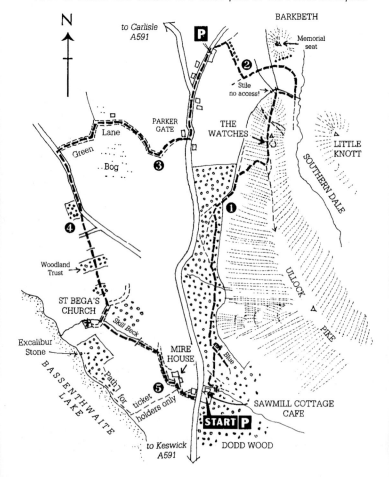

Mirehouse car park and the Old Sawmill Tearoom (refreshments, interesting artefacts and a very informative leaflet on Dodd Wood. All are recommended). NOTE: the parking gate is closed at 7.00pm.

THE WALK: Cross the bridge over Skill Beck, which was dammed to power the sawmill, and turn L on the Blue Route. *The forest comprises a variety of trees of mixed ages including tall Douglas fir planted in 1927. They shade the valley path and the whole is enclosed by young fir plantations.* Turn R at a forest road then L immediately on a rising path with a hint of Bassenthwaite Lake glinting through the branches. At the top of the rise turn L leaving the Blue Route along a path cut from solid bedrock, the Skiddaw Slates.

The path through the young trees is delightful, especially in autumn when the silver birch foliage makes a golden foreground to the sombre forests across the lake. The path narrows to cross Sandbed Gill.

Descend to a fork then branch up R on a lesser path which levels and passes through a more mature plantation, the Rabbit Warren. (The left-hand branch descends to the road.) Above, the slopes of Ullock Pike can be glimpsed through the larches. Go along to join a path coming steeply from the road (short return) and turn R along it for 100yds then fork up R to go through a gate onto the open fell. The path works its way steeply up the fenceside and turns the corner with it. *From here look back for an expanded view of Barf with the higher ridge of Lord's Seat behind and the Whinlatter Forest.* Then continue up the path over the rise until 50yds from the forest corner. Branch R at a collapsed little cairn, on a good path up the fell to the shoulder ahead and the views north open. Keep going up to the ridge, ignoring the many trods to either side and stop at a whorl of flat stones where we can see the deep valley of Southerndale cut by its straight drove path and the screes of Skiddaw behind.

Leave the main path as it turns away right to Ullock Pike and Skiddaw and turn L on a green path north along the wide ridge. Pass over the first little

Walk 21 from near Bassenthwaite village

Pinnacles of hornblende picrite on the summit of The Watches

heather-clad hump and ahead is the cairn on The Watches.

Go along to the summit cairn passing pinnacles of the grey rock, hornblende picrite showing the true colour, olive green, where geologists have obtained samples. There is a small quarry on the eastern side. *North is a distant view to Criffel in Scotland and nearer, the clock of St John's church, Bassenthwaite, measures the progress of the walking day with its chimes. Beyond the village is the dome of Binsey and to its right is the prominent transmitting aerial on Sandale Fell.*

Carry on over the top and drop down the steep end of the ridge to a ladder stile in the wall (do not go over). Turn R (blue arrow markers) and follow the wallside to the old quarry road which allows a look into Southerndale before turning L down the valley on an old green path. Pass by, or scramble up and sample a hump with an excellent seat for viewing Skiddaw, then go over a ladder stile in the left-hand wall, cross a pasture to another ladder stile and just beyond find a marker pole where you turn R. Pass to the L of a line of hawthorns to another marker pole. Turn L to the access gate into a surfaced lane.

Turn L and go along the lane to a road junction. Turn L, ignoring the public footpath opposite, and walk 300yds along the road to Parkergate. Just beyond the house turn R into the public bridleway which is a path on an old green lane. The character of the walk changes once more. Pass through a gate into the lane shaded by trees and holly bushes and running downhill by a chattering brook which falls into silence as the lane bends right to run along the edge of a boggy scrubland. At a farmhouse, Moss Side, keep straight ahead and in 100yds through a gate where the lane continues as a rough track. At a junction turn L, the way underfoot becoming drier as the lane begins to climb. Ignore a stile left and keep on over the rise to a gate.

Go through the gate at the green lane end and turn L along a road. Cross a bridge, ignore a public footpath on the right, and just beyond a patch of woodland turn R over a stile on a public footpath. Proceed across stile-linked fields with pleasant scenes of rough wetland adjacent to the lakeshore, to the Woodland Trust wood. A little path winds through the wood to an exit stile. Cross a field and another narrow strip of woodland to reach the stile at its edge. Enter into the parkland of Mirehouse. Go ahead to a track running below a bank of ancient oaks and turn R towards St Bega's Church. Cross the Skill Beck and turn L along its bank. Go through a gate with a rising hinge (unless you have purchased a ticket and intend to walk the lakeshore path and visit the house), and along the drive. At the house fork R and carry on to the cobbled yard. Turn R, run the gauntlet of the bee flight path and as the drive turns left keep ahead to the road gate. Turn L and cross to the parking area.

Mirehouse and Dodd Wood

Mirehouse is a stately home open to the public between April and October. It was here that Thomas Storey in 1790 planted the lower slopes of the Dodd to create one of the first commercial forests in the Lake District. Some of the original trees are seen around the old sawmill and have grown to an impressive height. Dodd Wood was leased by the Forestry Commission from the Spedding family of Mirehouse during the 1930s. The objective then was to grow plenty of timber to use as pit props in trenches during any future war, which resulted in very close planting of spruce. Much of the worst of the forest has now been reaped and new planting follows more enlightened thinking with regard to the landscape. However the lower parts of the wood still retain a good variety of trees from earlier days, including many fine Douglas fir which is easily recognised by its cracked orange bark and citrus smell of its freshly crushed needles. Seeds of the fir were brought from America to Britain in 1827 by David Douglas. Whilst they do not approach the 400ft of their native western America, their height is still outstanding.

Alfred Lord Tennyson stayed at Mirehouse and was inspired to write *Morte d'Arthur*, the well known piece about Excalibur, the sword flung into the lake, Bassenthwaite.

St Bega's Church
In an isolated position by the lake many of its parishioners would arrive by
boat. The interior of the church contains a fine 10th-century chancel and
nave. St Bega was the daughter of an Irish chieftain who fled to St Bees priory
in the 7th century. Her story proved an inspiration for Cumbrian novelist
Melvin Bragg in *Credo*.

WALK 22: Great Sca Fell via Trusmadoor

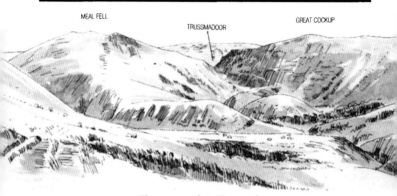

MEAL FELL   GREAT COCKUP

                            TRUSSMADOOR

The approach to Trusmadoor

SUMMARY: A surprisingly easy walk on the grassy fells of northern Lakeland.
The first objective is the ice-cut little pass of Trusmadoor, then the fine
summit of Meal Fell, which raises the questions as to its history. Are the
summit ramparts natural or man-made? Thence a gradual climb to the
plateau with its fine views to the Pennines and over the Solway. Return is
made along an old green bridle track, alongside the deep-cut Charleton Gill.

Distance:	6 miles (9½km)
Grade:	Moderate
Height gain:	1538ft (469m)
Terrain:	Medium fell on grassy paths.
Summit:	Meal Fell - 1804ft (550m)
	Great Sca Fell - 2135ft (651m)
	Little Sca Fell - 2046ft (624m)
Map:	OL4, HSW-NL

**HOW TO GET THERE AND
PARKING:** From the Caldbeck
to Bassenthwaite road, which
runs around the rim of northern
Lakeland, take a minor road,
signed 'Orthwaite and Mirk-
holme'. In one mile at Longlands
descend a short steep hill and

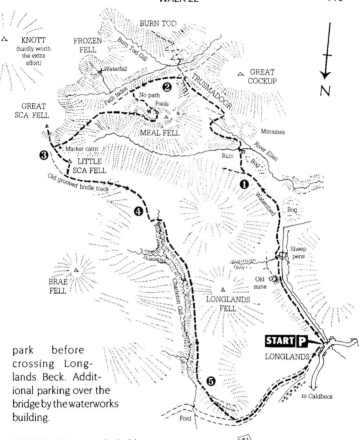

park before crossing Longlands Beck. Additional parking over the bridge by the waterworks building.

THE WALK: Go over the ladder stile by the parking and turn R on the path which crosses a stream and runs through a boggy patch beside the wall. Follow the wall up the deep-cut little valley of Longlands Beck, its waterside lined with a mixture of straggly trees. *Looking up the valley you see the dark steep cragside of Trusmadoor, the pass to the east of Great Cockup, with the bleak slope of Burn Tod behind.* Cross a dry streambed on the right, the drain of a locked and fenced copper mine adit above the adjoining spoil heap. Continue by the wall, to a group of sheep pens where you can examine the wheels and undercarriage of the hen hut, relics of the mine. The intake wall bends away west taking with it the green pastureland

and leaving us on the harsh moor. Carry on along the open shallowing valley on the path which has taken on the guise of an old green track. Keep ahead ignoring branching trods into a wilderness of moorland with smooth domed mountains ahead, a direct contrast to pretty Castle How with its two plantations forming an artistic silhouette against the western sky. Almost imperceptibly cross over a little watershed 296m, into the valley of the River Ellen. *From here note the onward route. Moraine humps lie in the valley, behind them is Trusmadoor with Meal Fell to its left.* Go ahead for 100yds and branch R, still on the green path, to cross a boggy stream and arrive at a ruin by the river. *Glance left up the river to its gathering ground on Little Sca Fell and downstream where the water is causing rapid erosion of the soft glacial moraine.*

Step over the river and go on the continuing path which mounts and bends between the moraines, where sheep shelter from the harsh winds, and cross the depression below the 'door. Gain the upper path on the slope ahead and turn L along it up the dry valley of Trusmadoor. *The screes show the amber and grey of the Skiddaw Slates with chunks of white quartz here and there. The weathering crags above, which mirror the mood of the sky, look foreboding. In the gap the wind rushes over the 'door and mingles with the draught funnelling up Burn Tod Gill.*

At Trusmadoor gap turn L at a cairn up the slope of Meal Fell on a green rising path above Burntod Beck progressing above the tributary valley of Frozenfell Gill in its deep-cut channel overhung with steps of soil creep. When you have made sufficient height on the path and can see the summit shelter on Meal Fell, turn L (north) up the pathless fellside for 500yds (grass and odd patches of very short heather) to the summit where a cluster of pools, a windshelter cairn, and minor cairns await from which to examine the extensive panorama. *The view from the west cairn over the Solway to the hills of Galloway is particularly impressive with the lone peak of Binsey and shining Overwater at its foot, to the north-west. Could the summit be the site of an ancient hill fort? There are some semi-circular ramparts which look remarkably man-made.*

Set off from Meal Fell via the east cairn on the path leading along the ridge. Cross the broad col, admiring the long ribbon waterfall in the black ravine opposite, and climb up the spur, gradually bending left, to the col between Great Sca Fell right and Little Sca Fell with a triangular cairn on the left. *There is a fine retrospective view of Meal Fell and Great Cockup. Also note the transmitters to the north which will aid our later direction finding.*

Reach a marker stone then a cross path just beyond. Turn R up the 250yds to the cairn on the summit of Great Sca Fell which is rather insignificant, but not so the view east to High Pike, Carrock Fell, the Eden valley and the Pennine horizon. *(The path continues south to the dome of Knott 710m but with no extra rewards to justify the effort.)*

Return to the marker stone col and carry on to Little Sca Fell with its fine view north and west, cairn and low windshelter. From here spy out the return

*South from the
hollow way below Little Sca Fell*

route which uses the Cumbria Way descending beside Charleton Gill dividing Lowthwaite and Longlands Fells from Brae Fell and to the west of the left-hand of two transmitters (noted previously).

Set off diagonally right towards Brae Fell and the large right-hand transmitter to meet a hollow path, the Cumbria Way. Turn L and stroll easily down its green groove looking left to Skiddaw and the mountains beyond Bassenthwaite. Descend towards the ice-worn U-shaped valley with a V-shape cut in its floor by the later stream which we cross at its head. Keep on the path, pass a quartz boulder and a glance back shows Little Sca Fell important at the the valley head.

Continue one mile to pass the end of Longlands Fell until the picturesque hamlet of Norman appears below and a track with ford is seen at the bottom of the gill. Keep on through a patch of rushes and bend slightly L on one of the three splinters of the path to join the track.

Turn L and go along descending gently past a plantation to Longlands at the stile and start.

WALK 23: Glenderamackin, Scales Tarn & Bannerdale Crags

SUMMARY: A quiet walk amongst lonely fells whose steep bracken-covered slopes run like interwoven braids into the furrow of the Glenderamackin valley. The long valley approach on an old mine track gains height easily, and reveals a sudden breathtaking view of Sharp Edge, a dramatic feature which dominates the scene for a couple of miles.

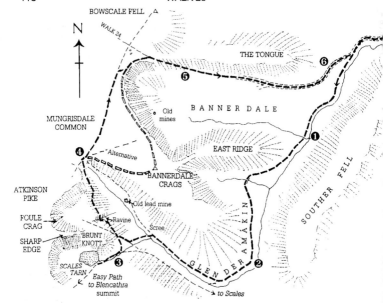

The excursion to Scales Tarn is the most strenuous part of the walk, but well worth the effort to soak in the dramatic atmosphere of the combe.

In mist the traverse of Bannerdale Crags requires expert navigation, in clear weather the immense views across the trackless rolling fells of northern Lakeland are invigorating. The walk continues along the rim of Bannerdale before dropping ever so gently back to the valley on a well graded old track so typical of these fells.

HOW TO GET THERE AND PARKING: Park at Mungrisdale opposite the village hall or a little further up the road on the second turn left opposite the telephone box.

Distance:	6¾ miles (10¾ km)
	7½ miles with summit of Bannerdale Crags
Grade:	Moderately strenuous
Height gain:	1732ft (528m)
Terrain:	Valley and high fell. Mainly on good paths.
Summit:	Bannerdale Crags - 2240ft (683m)
Map:	OL5, HSW-NL

THE WALK: Set off along the public footpath to Mungrisdale Common past Bannerdale Cottage. *The little building to the right contains a datestone of*

*Bannerdale Crags from
the path up Glenderamackin*

1734 *set in an odd position suggesting that it was probably salvaged from another building but indicating also many centuries of occupation of this remote Lakeland valley.* Negotiate the walled track, gated for use as a sheepfold, and walk on into the open valley. A scene of deep valleys with smooth overlapping symmetrical slopes stretches out in front of you. The Tongue stands in the centre with Bowscale Fell to the right and Souther Fell to the left. The scale of things is not as vast as at first appears and soon you have reached the footbridge at the junction of the River Glenderamackin and Bullfell Beck. Cross the bridge and in 50yds leave the old miners' track (our return route) to turn L on a narrow footpath following the Glenderamackin River.

The banks of the stream give a chance to see the underlying assortment of boulders captured in the glacial clay. Eroded ones were gathered for building in bygone days but now lie unwanted in the stream bed where the water enhances their varied colours. The

*Sharp Edge from the Glenderamackin.
Scales Tarn lies hidden behind the hump of Brunt Knott*

path rises gently up the Glenderamackin valley through a spread of bracken, its verges brightened by tormentil and foxgloves, and underfoot now and then, a palette of dazzling colours from streaks of oil oozing from the peaty soil. At a sidestream an old wall supports the path. This is the first hint that the narrow trod was once a major path to the Blencathra mines.

As you progress a feeling of remoteness grows. *Bent grasses sweep down the great slopes of Bannerdale Fell high above on the right while on the left the slopes of Souther Fell fall in folds to lock the lower valley behind.* A fine flake of rock shows that we are now on the Skiddaw Slates. As we turn the bend of the valley ignore a path branching down left to a footbridge which leads to Souther Fell.

Continue up the valley. The path is now green underfoot with an old ruin by the stream below. The sides of the valley are massive, empty and foreboding until suddenly a stunning view of Sharp Edge peaking in Foule Crag changes the mood. Sharp Edge is one of the most popular scrambles in the Lakes.

Follow the path until opposite the stream descending from Scales Tarn and where the path reaches an area of scree. (The path across the valley is from Scales.)

1. VIA SCALES TARN: Branch L down to cross the beck and make your way up the spur beside the outlet stream past the remains of an old bield towards the main path. Cross the line of an old water leat and an old narrow trod. Keep up the slope to a green path (our onward route), turn L along it a few yards and join the main path on our side of the stream. The climb continues past a suspended rowan and beside the water spilling down a staircase of velvet moss. Soon Scales Tarn is reached, a typical glacial corrie scooped from the mountain walls of Blencathra where the lap of the water pierces the cold silence and the bleat of a herdwick rises in a stampede of echoes.

Retrace your way to the point where the path turns across the stream. Do not cross but bend L on the narrow green path, touched briefly on the approach, and traverse to join the old miners' path now rising gently. Across the valley remains of the old mines can be seen with the line of the shorter

The north side of Sharp Edge and Foule Crag from the col at the head of the Glenderamackin

path 2. Ignore an old path which branches off left, the line of its edging stones rippling across the fellside to the back of Foule Crag.

As you progress up the valley take a look back where the valley sides blank the Dodds bringing insignificant Mell Fell to prominence. Swing suddenly into a great gash and cross the stream under the looming north face of Sharp Edge above. Rise gently to the col.

2.   DIRECT VALLEY ROUTE: Continue along the mine track. Take a R fork to climb steadily to the col at the valley head.

The lone reaches of Mungrisdale Common now stretch before you. **Warning - if mist or adverse weather approaches retreat down the valley.**
    Turn R along the ridge path for 50yds to a branch of paths.

1.   TO BANNERDALE CRAGS SUMMIT from the col: Turn R (east) up the fell to the summit cairn. Now turn L (north-west) and follow the path along the rim of the combe to join 2.

2.   SHORT CUT TO RETURN ROUTE from the col: Branch L on a gently rising path heading into the back of beyond and making for a stone where you can sit and unravel the details of the sweeping panorama. Continue and soon Bannerdale Crags come into your view. Ignore a left fork (unless you are going to the summit of Bowscale Fell, 702m) and keep ahead tending R until the ground becomes strewn with boggy pools. Trek R across the grass to gain the path from Bannerdale Crags running along the rim of the combe - what a view!
    Turn L on the rim path which bends with the edge and soon joins an old bridle track.
    Turn R down the track. As you go look into the combe on the right to the ochre spoil heaps of old lead mines.
    It is now an easy descent on the widening track through the bracken belt to a cairn at the junction with the mines track. Keep leftish down the valley until the valleys merge and you encounter the outward route. Cross the bridge and retrace the outward route to the car or the Mill Inn for refreshments.

Looking over Bannerdale Crags to Blencathra

WALK 24: Bowscale Tarn & Mosedale

PATH

DRYGILL HEAD

HIGH PIKE

Bowscale Tarn

SUMMARY: Bowscale Tarn was a popular venue in Victorian times; its deep turquoise waters holding the schelly, a freshwater herring, a relic of the Ice Age. It is one of the best examples in Britain of a glacial moraine held tarn. Today it is still a popular short stroll and on a hot summer day it attracts many picnickers and bathers.

Continuing onto the grassy fell tops brings a glorious vista over the lonely 'Back o'Skidda' country. If you want an easy return, then take the gently graded, smooth, old grass track to Mungrisdale. For a more adventurous, but still relatively easy return we follow the line of a long vanished path to Blackhazel Beck, an isolated valley of great charm. There is no bridge and you have to wade the stream. No problem in summer low water levels but after rain it can be difficult or impassable. Join the unfenced road for a pleasant, rapid return to the car; the river with its bed of boulders and pools a lively companion.

Distance:	8¼ miles (13km)
	Short return: 5¾miles (9¼km)
Grade:	Moderate
Height gain:	1561ft (476m)
Terrain:	Medium fell. Good path to the tarn, then virtually pathless. Road return.
Summit:	Bowscale Fell - 2303ft (702m)
Map:	OL5, HSW-NL

HOW TO GET THERE AND PARKING: From the A66 take the minor road north for miles through Mungrisdale to Mosedale. Park on the right just before the hamlet of Bowscale, or just before the river bridge.

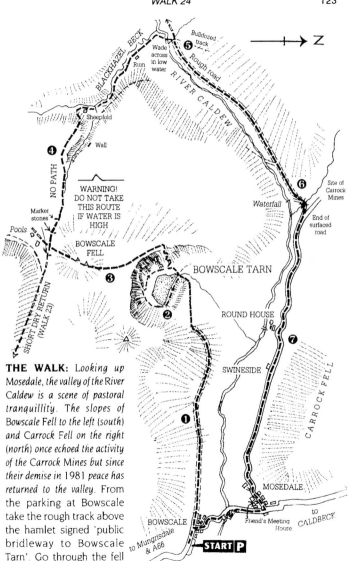

THE WALK: *Looking up Mosedale, the valley of the River Caldew is a scene of pastoral tranquillity. The slopes of Bowscale Fell to the left (south) and Carrock Fell on the right (north) once echoed the activity of the Carrock Mines but since their demise in 1981 peace has returned to the valley.* From the parking at Bowscale take the rough track above the hamlet signed 'public bridleway to Bowscale Tarn'. Go through the fell gate and walk up the gently rising track with no route-finding problems. *Whilst you walk along glance at the river to assess the water level because if the Blackhazel Beck circuit is chosen the river must be forded in the upper valley. The smooth sweeping slopes above us contrast sharply with the rough craggy hillside opposite. The reason is the underlying rock structure; we are walking on the Skiddaw Slates, but across the valley, which runs along a fault line, the rock is dark gabbro and pale granophyre.* In ¹/₂ mile cross the stream, Drycombe Beck, and continue up the traversing track watching the swallows on the slope below skimming for insects.

As the path bends towards the ice-scooped combe of Bowscale Tarn look carefully at its steep western flank for the onward route. A series of paths fan from the tarn outlet leading to the west ridgetop. Our route takes the zig-zags mounting a smooth, grassy section between outcropping rocks.

At the end of the track go on the path diagonally R which shortcuts an unused bend to join the old track, now green and pleasant, once more. *Lines of glacial moraine can be seen looking down Tarn Sike towards The Round House in the valley bottom. Carrock Fell with its summit-sited Iron Age fort, Round Knott with its prominent cairn and High Pike feature on the skyline beyond.*

Arrive at Bowscale Tarn, a beautiful blue-green water captive in a deep glacial combe. *Hot from the ascent there is nothing better than to paddle in the shallows or stretch out on the short turf enjoying the trenchant atmosphere whilst the leader decides on the route to be taken.*

1. DIRECT FROM THE TARN OUTLET: Cross the outlet stream, Tarn Sike, and go straight up the grass slope to the first zig-zag.

2. TOUR ROUND THE TARN: To walk this path a steady foot and head for heights are needed as the narrow path crosses steep slopes but is visually highly rewarding.

Go clockwise round the tarn on a path rising gradually with the bedding plane tilt of the Skiddaw Slates. When just over half way round, the path has edging stones, relic of mining activity, then it fizzles out. Keep going on a trod now, staying above rocks as the line of the path appears to be heading for a perched scree. To the right a tree peeps round a rock. Do not be tempted onto the scree which runs all the way down to the water. Follow the trod which gradually bends R, crosses the top of this scree then descends slightly to run below the rocks ahead, level for a while then descending. Continue over a rock slab, with extra care if wet, and when opposite the tarn outflow meet the direct route 1.

Turn uphill allowing the winding path to lead you to a sudden view west from the ridge. *The valley of Mosedale and the vast open slopes of Skiddaw, not a wall to be seen except for the plantation walls surrounding Skiddaw House, with Great Calva to its right and Blencathra on its left and left again is our summit Bowscale Fell.* Turn

L up the ridge, keeping away from the edge of the combe, and make your way over the short turf (ignore the cairn to the left beyond the combe which is on the end of the ridge as seen from the valley) bearing R as you gain height, to the cairn on the summit.

On top are two cairns, a wind shelter and an extensive panorama. *Before you settle down in the wind shelter let us warn you that we found it occupied by wasps. The summit is marked on the map as Pile of Stones so there are plenty of places to sit and enjoy the view.*

Set off in a south-south-west direction (from the back of the wind shelter towards Blencathra) on a spread path and after descending the initial slope look for a cairn at a path junction (if you have reached some pools you have gone too far). The cross path is the old bridle path from the Glenderamackin to upper Mosedale.

3. RETURN VIA BLACKHAZEL BECK AND MOSEDALE: WARNING - This route involves a wade across the River Caldew. Impassable in high water. Turn R on the narrow path with marker stones first to one side then the other. Take care of an ankle-turning water runnel which is hidden by the pathside grass. The right of way path, now more in the imagination than underfoot, bends L across the top of a tributary gill, a peaty area with cusp-shaped overhangs serving as windbreaks for the sheep, then leaves us to fend for ourselves in the back of beyond. Bend R keeping the line of the gill on your right and finding the easiest ground to suit your descent. Pass a section of wall seen across the gill and finding that the going gradually gets easier until you make a steeper drop to a sheepfold near the junction of the gill with the Blackhazel Beck. The old path shows its face briefly again, even with the odd marker stone, but it takes a visionary to look back up the fell and pick out the bold green line on the map and here the feeling of remoteness is complete.

Cross the tributary stream by a beautiful crystal pool and turn L down the bank of the Blackhazel Beck (do not be tempted onto an uphill sheep track through the bracken) passing an old ruin with a bit of roof, a carpet of nettles and occupied by a wren. Pass another sheepfold to reach a stile and the confluence of the streams. Turn R down Mosedale and paddle across the shallow Caldew before Burdell Gill adds extra water then scramble up the bank to join The Cumbria Way near the head of the track vehicle turning circle. Don't walk further downstream as it is very rough and crossing is more difficult.

It is easy walking down Mosedale alongside the river, a scene of merry family relaxation on a hot summer's day. Pass Wet Swine Gill and looking over the river a new track can be seen making its way from a ford, the next downstream crossing place. Gainsgill Beck on the left is the next feature, site of the extensive Carrock Mines, and here the road becomes surfaced.

Walk on down the valley passing The Round House, with Bowscale Tarn above, hidden in its mountain eyrie (footbridge over the river) and after a slight rise in the road arrive at the hamlet of Mosedale. *The Friends' Meeting House 1702 is open for refreshments in the summer.* At the main road turn R, go over the road bridge or the old bridge to reach Bowscale and the parking.

4.   SHORTER RETURN VIA BANNERDALE AND MUNGRISDALE: Turn L on the the old bridle path with marker stones and descend soon to be joined by Walk 23 from Mungrisdale Common. The views across Bannerdale and the Glenderamackin valley to Souther Fell are impressive for the sheer vast wild expanse. The path runs gradually down the northern side of the Bannerdale with ochre spoil heaps in the combe which indicate mining activity . Go through a belt of bracken to be joined at a cairn by the track from the mines. Keep L down the valley to the confluence of the Bullfell Beck and the River Glenderamackin. Cross the bridge over the beck and turn R through the pasture with the deep valley of Bullfell Beck pushing into the massive body of Bowscale Fell behind. At the intake wall continue ahead as the track is walled and gated to form a sheepfold. Go through the hamlet to the main road.

At the main road turn L (the Mill Inn is 100yds down the road to the right, bar meals and refreshments) and walk north along the road for ¹/₂ mile to Bowscale, Mosedale bridge and the parking area.

WALK 25: Carrock Fell and High Pike

Carrock Fell

SUMMARY: Two grand fells of great contrast provide a good short day, with surprisingly easy walking once on top, and the high start point gives a good lift. The ascent of Carrock Fell is rough and steep in parts, even a little exposed if you take the more interesting alternative. Very easy walking ensues, along a broad moorland ridge, wet in parts, to join old mine tracks for the rest of the walk. Unusually for northern England, no walls or fences are encountered on the walk.

A sense of history pervades these fells, with the Iron Age fort which crowns Carrock's stony summit; ancient grassed over tracks now grooves in the fells, and more recent mining scars in the steep sided gills.

HOW TO GET THERE AND PARKING: A minor road runs north from the A66, passing Mungrisdale, and Mosedale becoming unfenced below the unmistakably craggy front of Carrock Fell and the Apron of Stones boulder field. Immediately past the farm of Stone Ends a rough track left leads towards a shallow quarry below the crags.

THE WALK: Set off up the quarry track. Before the quarry turn R then L rising in an obvious upward traverse across the face of the fell. On reaching an area of scree, step and slide up, taking care to gain the continuing upwards traverse path, now a firm little trod. On entering Further Gill choose your onward path to the top of the gill.

1.   THE DIRECT WAY (VERY STEEP): Go up the right-hand side of the gill then continue up a grassy gully to the heather moor at its top and a cross path junction.

2.   THE EASIER WAY (LESS STEEP): Cross Further Gill and keep to the upward traverse path. Pass a silver birch on the right then up more steeply on an old zig-zag path with traces of the stone edging still intact. As soon as the gradient eases bend R towards the gully. Pass a cairn just below overhanging boulders which form a good sheltered viewpoint over the Caldew valley to the Pennines beyond. Make your way up the heathery slope on a trod which passes between two stones just before a tiny stream to the cross path junction at the head of the gully.

Now choose your onward route.

Distance:	6¹/₄ miles (10km) or 6³/₄ miles (10³/₄km)
Grade:	Strenuous up Carrock Fell, then Easy
Height gain:	1535ft (468m)
Terrain:	Medium fell, rough at first, then smooth walking along old mine tracks.
Summits:	Carrock Fell - 2165ft (660m)
	High Pike - 2159ft (658m)
Map:	OL5, HSW-NL

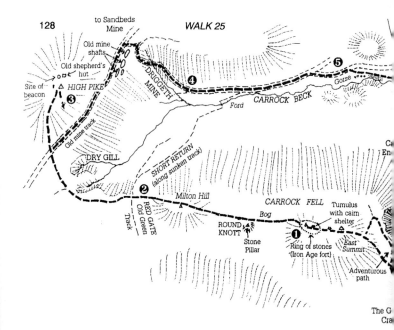

WALK 25

1. THE DIRECT WAY CONTINUED: Keep on the obvious path up the moor until joined by Route 3 at a cairn.

3. THE ADVENTUROUS WAY: This path runs along the crag edge and is a bit airy in places. It is not suitable for children.

Go straight on (north) from the junction on a path, up through heather, towards a cairn on the skyline. On approaching, the path runs above this cairn and on to pass a larger cairn. There are spectacular views down the crag face to the valley. Care is needed until reaching the next cairn where a L turn is made. Bend R round the following cairn and continue along the rim gaining height interestingly to a rock topped by a small cairn. *You may see paragliders who enjoy this venue at certain times in the summer.* Immediately beyond the rock take the upper branch of the path, cross the top of a gully with care (snow lingers long in its crevice) and once more keep to the upper branch. The path now bends away from the crag and the East Peak of Carrock Fell comes into view above. Meet a path in a more open area and turn L up it making a rising traverse to join the wide path of the Direct Route. Just before a cairn, turn R.

Continue up the moor passing cairns to a boulder field and the East Summit. Go straight on along the broad path towards the main summit which appears ahead. Look out on the right of the path for remains of a wall, part

of the old hill fort, and a large pile of stones, thought to be a tumulus. *This has been hollowed out to form an excellent wind shelter and today a variety of lichens peep from the lower stones at huddled, hungry figures muttering words of gratitude to the Iron Age navvies.* Just beyond the shelter is the summit cairn with a wonderful view of Bowscale Fell to the south and over Caldbeck to the Solway and Border hills beyond. If caught in mist check your direction of descent almost due west. Leave the summit by the West Gate on a spread path which descends a broad ridge. Pass on your left the summit of Round Knott 603m, with its distinctive finger-like cairn. Skirt a few boggy areas then on to the Pile of Stones and the guiding cairn on Miton Hill 607m. From here you can look south into the hidden corrie containing Bowscale Tarn (Walk 24) and to its right the deep trough of Upper Mosedale. Keep to the line of two cairns to reach the lowest point of the ridge. Here the Red Gate track, an old sunken path, crosses the pass.

*Summit cairn on
Carrock Fell*

SHORT RETURN: Turn R and follow the green hollow way down the fellside.

TO HIGH PIKE: Go straight across the Red Gate track on a good miners' path up the slopes of Drygill Head. The walking is easy and the views extensive. Just before turning across the valley head ignore a branch left. Go straight on for ¼ mile until meeting the Caldbeck Mines road (Cumbria Way). Cross straight over the road and with little effort walk up to the summit of High Pike 658m. There is plenty to see both on and from this beacon viewpoint. *The summit is arrayed with a great cairn, stone seat, triangulation point, a ruined shepherd's hut and a flat area used as a beacon platform from which spread warning across northern Cumbria from the Pennines to the Solway and the Galloway Hills beyond.*

Return to the mines road and turn L. As you walk along, the Driggeth Mines (lead and copper) draw nearer and the return path can be seen on the spoil heaps in the dry valley. Pass a pond, turned to a gelatinous soup by the local frogs in spring, and down on the left and parallel with the road the line of the ore vein is seen. Pass the ochre spoil then fork R on a path to cross the line of the vein (which carries on north as the Sandbed Vein to the barytes mines on Birket). Go down as far as the spoil just before the head of the dry gill then fork R down a sunken path with the dry gill to your left. Lower, the path crosses the gill and continues its descent on the other side, down the colourful spoil we viewed previously. Carry on down the Carrock Beck valley where the only fork in the path is just a loop. The Red Gate track can be seen across the valley and the SHORT RETURN joins here.

Continue for $1/4$ mile to a fork in the path. Branch R and as you approach the mouth of the valley look towards Carrock Fell. The intervening two tiny knolls are the Rospow Hills. Notice where the stream leaves its wandering way and cuts a shaped ravine in the valley bottom. A path which we intend to take runs above its gorse-clad bank. On approaching turn R off our mine path onto this one and make a pleasant short-cut down to the road at a ford.

Turn R over the footbridge and along the unfenced road. Keep ahead at the junctions for $1/2$ mile passing the remains of Carrock End Mine on the right to the parking area.

Carrock Fell Iron Age fort

Well visible from the surrounding area, the extensive defensive rampart covering five acres surrounds the double summit. The gateways, south and west, are still easily seen. Recent study indicates that it may date even earlier to Neolithic times for its construction is similar to other ritual sites in southern England. A nearby flint mine in the gabbro was a source of axes in the Stone Age. The whole area is an extremely sensitive scheduled site and visitors must be careful not to disturb anything.

WALK 26: Roughton Gill & High Pike

SUMMARY: A walk of contrasts. Most of it is very easy going on old mine tracks, apart from the ascent of Roughton Gill, which is steep, rough and scrambly in places. Stick to the described route and you will be alright; dangerous places abound off-route. The whole walk is entrenched in mining history. You can imagine the scene a hundred years ago when hard won minerals were carted down to the valley. At that time the Caldbeck Fells were one of Britain's richest mining areas. Today the most obvious relics are the countless tracks which criss-cross the fells. Some are still stony, but others, now grassed over, provide gentle walking both up or down. High Pike on the northern fringe of Lakeland's fells gives fine views over the Solway to the distant hills of southern Scotland.

Roughton Gill from near the old grindstone

HOW TO GET THERE AND PARKING: A lane bypasses Caldbeck to its south, linking Hesket Newmarket to Parkend. From this lane, another goes south to Fellside. Park in a side lane just above the farm.

THE WALK: Leave the hamlet of Fellside behind and go up the road to the fell gate. Follow the rough mines road, signed footpath to Roughton Gill and Caldbeck Fells. *Ahead lies the valley of Dale Beck, to the right (west) the little heather-clad peak of Binsey peeps over the sweeping flanks of Brae Fell, the outlier of Great Sca Fell, and over the northern horizon roll the Scottish Border hills.* Keep straight on at the Hay Gill Water Treatment Works, an imposing title for this modest

Distance:	6 miles (9¹/₂km)
Grade:	Moderate with one steep section up the gill.
Height gain:	1367ft (417m)
Terrain:	Valley and medium fell. The steep, rough scramble up Roughton Gill requires care.
Summits:	Unnamed top above Roughton Gill - 1997ft (609m)
	Great Lingy Hill - 1976ft (616m)
	Hare Stones - 2056ft (627m)
	High Pike - 2158ft (658m)
Map:	OL5, HSW-NL

sandstone building. As you enter the valley, old miners' paths can be seen on the opposite hillside making their way up to Ramps Gill. *Look out for the relics of an old smelt mill. Below the road are the remains of a brick-lined furnace and above the road the line of the flue. If you like poking around ruins the loadbearing stones of gritstone, their surface patterned by tool marks, and their relative positions will shunt your imagination back to a scene of fumes, toil and sweat.*

Cross Hay Gill and continue up the road. Cross Dale Beck ford by the footbridge and as you pass the lone larch notice the ledges of soil creep in Birk Gill. From here look right at the groove in the opposite hillside. This is probably the best example in Lakeland of a hush. The miners diverted water into a makeshift dam, then let it out to create a flood which hopefully exposed any mineral veins.

The road gradually gains height and at the valley head Roughton Gill with its

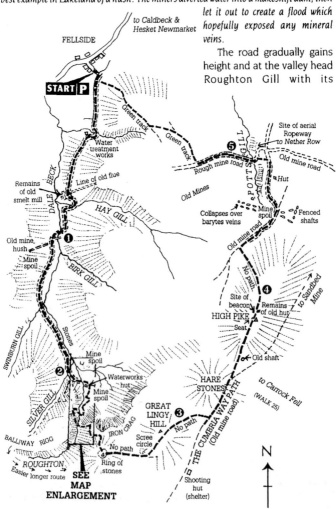

cascading water comes into sight. On its right is Silver Gill and the spur between is quilted into a design by the old green paths across its face. Step over Swinburn Gill where it crosses the road and on to the valley head. *A bleak area of stones bound the stream but in the wake of the mining desolation there is beauty to be found. Springs feed vivid green gardens of moss and the spoil contains many coloured stones, white quartz flecked with green copper, yellows, oranges and browns. At the workings a broken granite grindstone stands pointing its jagged edge to the sky but its grooves still hold a perfect arc and glide smooth to the touch.*

Now the route divides.

EASIER PATHS TO THE RIDGE VIA SILVER GILL: Cross the bridge over Silver Gill and turn R up the green zig-zag paths onto Balliway Rigg and the moor. You will need to contour across the head of Roughton Gill to regain the onward route.

ROUGHTON GILL (STEEP WITH SOME SCRAMBLING)**:** Keep along the road crossing Roughton Gill at the mine workings. Turn R at the spoil to a safety building then up L on a narrow path rising across the spoil above the gill. In a short distance you can see where the old track on the opposite flank meets the gill but no trace remains of the bridge. Turn your back on the gill and go L along the dent of the track for 25yds then R rising parallel to the gill once more. Stop a while by a waterfall and opposite an old mine level. *We advise you* **not** *to enter but cross the stream to see the entrance, an old coffin-shaped level, hand-tooled and a relic of the early days of mining. For those waiting on the path the folds of the valley embrace a view over the Solway.*

Map enlargement of Roughton Gill

Stones
Ruin
Old Grindstone
Spoil heaps
Hut
Old track
Fall
Spoil
Site of Bridge
Old level
SILVER GILL
Easy way
Old Path
Fall
Scramble
Escape
Danger! collapsed path
Do not scramble into upper ravine

The path ahead is now a bit of a scramble and keeps to the left side of the gill. Do not be tempted onto other paths which may seem more appealing. Pass two falls and a mossy cascade. Arrive on a little rock bluff where you can cross the gill downstream of a pretty angled cascade. Go behind a boulder and onto the slope of the grassy spur. Work your way up the grass to a cross path and turn L back to the gill. **Do not attempt to scramble up the gill** but cross it and go up the bank of brown earth and spoil by the foot of the rock. On reaching the grass spur turn R and wind your pathless way up the slope to the hilltop avoiding an eroded area. Over to the north-east is

High Pike and ahead, unseen yet, the cairn on the unnamed top. Cross a prominent sheep trod and conquer the final slope of short heather to the summit circle of stones and cairn. *Looking south you can distinguish the white memorial cairn on Atkinson Pike at the back of Blencathra, Sharp Edge being its black left-hand skyline. To the east is Bannisdale Fell, Bowscale Fell, Carrock Fell, Great Lingy Hill, our onward route, and High Pike.*

Turn L (east) and aiming at Carrock Fell set off across the moor. You may be able to raise a path from your imagination. Stride along it keeping to the highest round for ¼ mile and pass to the right of a patch of scree-like stones to reach Great Lingy Hill. From the summit looking west Great Sca Fell has come down in the world and rising behind Knott stands the lofty ridge of Skiddaw.

Proceed in the general direction of High Pike (north-east) through gaps in the beds of peat to meet the old mines road, now The Cumbria Way. Turn L on it (a short distance along the road to the right is an old stone shelter/shooting hut) and make your way over Hare Stones, in an atmosphere of spacious vistas, to the skylarks' song. Go over a rise (cairn) and in a few yards branch L at a cairn. Cross the line of an old path and a working then make your way to the summit of High Pike where there is a seat for still days, a wall shelter for windy days and an uninterrupted view round the compass.

Set off from the north cairn in the direction of Caldbeck village (north) over grass and in a few minutes the spoil heaps of Potts Gill mines can be seen below. Keep on down the turf and a sunken path appears and descends to meet a major path at a col. Turn R on it and progress to the mines.

IT IS IMPORTANT TO STAY ON THE PATH AS THERE ARE MANY WORKINGS UNSEEN AND CLOSE UNDER THE SURFACE. THE FENCED AREAS ARE SHAFTS.

Arrive by a flat-topped spoil heap and you are now on the line of the barytes vein. Up to the right are the shafts and across the gill a line of subsidence where the underground workings have collapsed. Carry on down the track and where the many spread paths join at a gap there is a shelter building a few yards on the right. In 25yds turn L down to the flat area site of the Potts Gill Mine complex and the top of the now removed aerial ropeway to Nether Row. Turn L, pass an adit drain and cross the gill. Go uphill and onto the brow of the hill. Turn R on a green track with a view over the Solway to Criffel behind the transmitting station mast. At a fork keep straight on and as the path becomes indistinct meet another path descending Fellside Brow and turn R along it. Go down to the wall, turn R and you will see the L turn through the gate into the parking area.

Roughton Gill Mines

One of the most productive and earliest mines in the area. A large smelting mill was built in 1794 but soon fell into disuse and became cottages. The oldest workings, cut before gunpowder, are extensive. A great variety of minerals were extracted, notably lead, copper and zinc. The hush seen on the walk is an impressive example, dating to around 1750.

WALK 27: Around Caldbeck and The Howk

Old mill and drying shed at The Howk, Caldbeck

SUMMARY: The Howk, a beautiful limestone gorge, with its old mill is worth an hour of anyone's time, and coupled with a stroll around delightful Caldbeck village makes a visit worthwhile. Our recommended longer circuit within the National Park continues up the pleasing streamside above The Howk to gain the foothills of the Caldbeck Fells. You could refresh yourself at the lovely old village of Hesket Newmarket before continuing down the Caldew valley to join the Cald Beck and a woodland return to the village. A good walk for a crisp winter's day, or

Distance:	8¼ miles (13km)
Grade:	Easy, but relatively long
Height gain:	512ft (160m)
Terrain:	Valley walking on green paths.
Map:	OL5 and OL4, HSW-NL

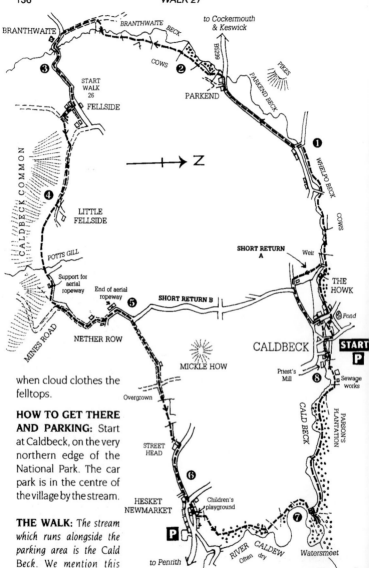

to Cockermouth
& Keswick

BRANTHWAITE

BRANTHWAITE BECK

COWS

PARKEND

PIKES

PARKEND BECK

B5299

START
WALK
26
FELLSIDE

CALDBECK COMMON

LITTLE
FELLSIDE

N

WHELPO BECK

COWS

POTTS GILL

Support for
aerial
ropeway

End of aerial
ropeway

SHORT RETURN B

NETHER ROW

MINES ROAD

MICKLE HOW

SHORT RETURN
A

Weir

THE
HOWK

Pond

CALDBECK

START
P

Priest's
Mill

Sewage
works

PARSON'S
PLANTATION

CALD BECK

when cloud clothes the
felltops.

**HOW TO GET THERE
AND PARKING:** Start
at Caldbeck, on the very
northern edge of the
National Park. The car
park is in the centre of
the village by the stream.

THE WALK: The stream
which runs alongside the
parking area is the Cald
Beck. We mention this

Overgrown

STREET
HEAD

HESKET
NEWMARKET

P

Children's
playground

to Penrith

RIVER CALDEW
Often dry

Watersmeet

because on leaving its parent valley as Roughton Gill the stream changes its name to suit the neighbourhood through which it is passing until joining the River Caldew at Watersmeet. Leave the parking by the exit road. (Straight ahead, yet hidden from view by a grass bank, is the elevated village green and pond, worthy of a visit in its own right to see the resident ducks.) Turn L to a T-junction and ahead is a signed footpath to The Howk. Go through kissing gates and as you progress along the path look left across the field and over Whelpo Beck to see the short, squat chimney of Lord's Mill which is passed later on Short Return A. *The white stones and gorge of Whelpo Beck identify the rock as limestone. In the narrowing gorge stand the ruins of The Howk Bobbin Mill, still impressive in its ruined state. The first building is the old drying shed for the coppiced wooden poles. Notice the datestone 1857 over the arched doorways faced with pink sandstone and, moving along the path, the huge water-wheel pit on the gable end of the building from which you can trace the water inlet above the overshot wheel by its remaining supports.*

Just beyond the mill go up steps and along the path which utilises the line of the old leat. *Across the gorge, through which the water struggles, a resurgence empties from a small cave fissure and beside the path clumps of primroses, celandine, the delicate pink notched petals of the moss campion and dog's mercury add their own delicate touch of brightness.* At the bridge carry on a few yards to see the leat head. *A pole now spans the beck where a small dam raised the beck level and the water entered the leat.* **(Short Return A leaves the route here.)**

Go over the step stile and along a pleasant streamside path, where fish can be seen in the clear water and swallows with aerobatic skill hunt for flies, to a stile on the left in the pasture corner. Go over into a wide avenue between the stream's alder and an old laid hawthorn hedge. Ignore a bridge on the left and find a stone stile in the wall ahead. Continue on this permissive path to a stile by a gate on the left and along the streamside with the road now seen across the water. Easy walking soon leads to a road.

Turn L over Whelpo Bridge then R along the road for ¼ mile. *Away to the right is the low, hilly ridge of Pikes while on the left the edge of the Caldbeck Fells occupy the horizon.* At the Fellside road junction keep straight on towards Keswick. In 100yds ignore a public footpath leading left. Pass the Parkend Restaurant & Country Hotel (lunches), and on the left between the antique GR postbox and the bridge turn L through a kissing gate into the hotel garden. Follow the yellow waymark arrows and wooden stepping-stones across the immaculate lawn with due respect to a stile in the bounding fence. Go straight ahead to another stile taking care as you step down the far side as grass hides uneven ground. Look up diagonally L for the next waymark, gain its higher level and make your way to the top right-hand fence of the pasture turn R through a gate and make for a stile in the next cross fence then the next ladder stile over a wall can be seen ahead. From the stile the line of the Parkend Beck can be traced leading to the fells with High Pike 658m the prominent peak. Keep

Farm dogs at Branthwaite

ahead with the line of an old wall on the right and cross the pasture to a clump of trees and stile to the left. Go over and descend diagonally R to the small flat flood plain of the meandering Branthwaite Beck. Stay at this level and walk upstream crossing a tiny sidestream spanned with stones to a stile over a fence and a footbridge. Go diagonally L to a stile in the corner. Turn L along the gated track to the road at Branthwaite. Turn L and pass through a cluster of farmstead building to the bridge. Here we say "Cheerio" to Dale Beck and "See you later", as we go up the rise past the old school house 1875 to a seat at the top and the hamlet of Fellside (telephone box).

At Fellside Farm turn R. Notice the old datestone, WS & A 1618, built into the barn. *The stone originated at the Old Hall at Middinstead which was destroyed by fire.* Pass the parking area (start of Walk 26), go through the fell gate and turn L. The old miners' track makes a slightly rising right bend then levels for a short distance. Where the track veers right and uphill keep ahead to merge with the semi-surfaced track coming from the farm below and continue smoothly along it. *The aspect looking north over Caldbeck in its tranquil, rural setting is delightful showing little hint of the prominent industrial centre it became in the 18th century, based on mining the minerals in the underlying volcanic rocks.* Eventually the concrete treads swing left into Low Fellside Farm. Go ahead keeping on the path diverging R away from the garden wall and running fairly level through a spread of rushes. It gradually improves and tracks across the fellside to Potts Gill, hub of the mining activity as the skyline edge of the spoil indicates. From the level platform above, an aerial ropeway conveyed the ore to Nether Row. Cross the gill and track running down to Potts Gill Farm and continue on the path passing an old support of the aerial ropeway until the left-hand wall turns a corner. Just beyond meet the mines road and turn L down to Nether Row. Go through the gate at the Caldbeck Commons notice and on to the surfaced road at Claybottom Farm. *There are remains of the mine ropeway buildings behind Potts Gill Cottage but only a dedicated enthusiast would seek them out.* Go along the road for 100yds to the first bend. **(Short Return B leaves the route here.)**

To continue, branch R on a hedged track. *Down to the left is the knoll of Mickle How and further right the Newlands wind turbines cannot be missed. A barn beside the path incorporates volcanic rocks and more easily trimmed limestone in its walls indicating the nearness of a change in the underlying rock structure.* Pass a pine plantation, cross a track and go over a stile ahead into an enclosed pathway. In high summer the lush grasses tend to encroach the path but it soon comes to an end where a stile leads into a field. Head straight across to a farm gate. Go through into the track and, ignoring three adjacent stiles, carry on through two gates to a road at Street Head. Turn R to a T-junction with the main road at Hesket Newmarket (shop with refreshments, inn, telephone).

Turn R down the village green with seat and shelter in the old Market Cross. Pass Smithy House and turn L on a public footpath between the playground and a picnic table area and through a kissing gate into a field. Go ahead to a bridge and kissing gate which opens onto a fenced path along the edge of a wooded ravine. At the next kissing gate turn L (yellow waymark arrows) on a narrow fenceside path through another kissing gate and along a strip of woodland above the River Caldew. The path has guard rails where the river has worn into the limestone leaving steep edges to its gorge. At a fork keep ahead and continue through the lush vegetation to a kissing gate at the end of the wood. Locate two waymark poles showing the direct route over an adversely sloping pasture whilst the river makes a lazy meander and we arrive at a kissing gate above on its return.

Keep to the fenceside path and on down a flight of steps to emerge from the woods at a kissing gate. A few yards into the field is a view over the valley to the plantations of Parson's Park. Turn R down the edge of the field almost

to Waters-meet. *The path and next stile stand on a rib of hard rock which diverts the River Caldew on our right from joining our familiar stream, now the Cald Beck on our left. The Cald Beck*

Jersey cows near Caldbeck

is about to enter a square-cut gorge and after going through the gate turn L crossing the footbridge and National Park boundary, for an impressive view downstream.

Turn diagonally L on a path through the streamside woods to a gloomy iron gate. Go through and into the pasture keeping on its right side maintaining direction upstream as there are no guiding waymarks outside the National Park. Ignore a bridge on the left and go over a stile tucked in the right-hand corner of the field and into the wood again. Turn L walking upstream alongside the gurgling beck. At a fork keep ahead through an open glade and, as the trees close in once more, a path joins in from the right. Keep ahead to a gate at the edge of the forest and civilization once more in the form of the local sewage works.

Go past the works and along the stony drive through a gate and into Caldbeck village. In 100yds turn L over the old packhorse bridge by St Kentigern's church (turn L to visit Priest's Mill). Turn R along the beckside walkway to the road B5299. Cross the road and the bridge and turn L into the parking area.

THE SHORT RETURN A: Return to the bridge, with a Wagnerian view into the gorge. (*A natural arch spanned the gorge but it collapsed in* 1860.) Cross and go up steps to a kissing gate (yellow waymark). Cross the pasture heading for a clump of pines and a refreshing view of High Pike and Caldbeck Fells to the south then find a ladder stile onto the road. Turn L and ignoring roads to the right go down the hill. *Interesting features of the buildings catch the eye; an old barn and a fine weather vane on Shire House.* Turn L at a junction to the old brewery, once a wheat mill built in 1760 but changed to a brewery in 1810. *The next mill with the fine stone chimney is Lord's Mill, a corn mill dating back to* 1670. *Look over the bridge where you can see the remains of the tail-race where it emerged from the water-wheel, its power spent.*

Do not cross the bridge but turn R at a public footpath sign passing a stone trough into a field. Cross the field (the car park can be seen across the beck) to a narrow slit stile and through a garden to the road. Turn L to the car park.

If you do not want to end the visit cross the road and continue on a riverside path to an old bridge by St Kentigern's church, burial place of John Peel. Just beyond is the Priest's Mill Craft Centre, once a corn mill, and sawmill (1702).

SHORT RETURN B: Continue straight along the road, down the hill into Caldbeck.

Caldbeck

Once a small pastoral village gathered round St Kentigern's church, Caldbeck expanded to become a busy mining community, its heyday peaking in the 1850s. Copper, silver, lead and later barytes were mined in the fells to the south. The beck powered eight mills and the accompanying service industries expanded. The workshop of the clogmaker is still there by the toilets. As the mining declined the village gradually returned to the rural community we see today. The last mine to close was Sandbeds in 1956.

The Howk Bobbin Mill

The water-powered mill was built in 1857 but was closed, like many of its sister mills, when the textile industry went into decline in the 1920s. It was burned down in 1958. The coppiced wood, ash, birch, hazel, oak and alder was dried in the tall barn-like building before being turned into bobbins. The mill was driven by a huge 42ft diameter, overshot water-wheel named 'Red Rover', the head of water, fed by leat from a take-off point above the gorge. Conservation work is in progress.

John Peel and Mary Robinson

You can see huntsman John Peel's grave in the churchyard and the inn, the Oddfellow's Arms, where he drank with Robert Graves, who immortalised him in the well known song. One of Caldbeck's mills made Hodden grey cloth which was so finely woven it was almost waterproof. This was John Peel's 'coat of grey'. Also buried in the churchard is Mary Robinson, better known as the 'Beauty of Buttermere'. She tragically married a bigamist and forger who was hanged at Carlisle. Later she settled down happily with a Caldbeck farmer and died in 1887.

Moss campion at
The Howk

CHAPTER 4
Thirlmere and St John's Vale

Thirlmere is often scorned by its detractors who see only rows of gloomy conifers above an unsightly shore. Others, with an unbiased eye, see a deep set valley of Norwegian fiord proportions flanked by majestic forest.

At times of low water, the shoreline is undeniably artificial, yet when the lake is near full it is very attractive. See it in autumn when it is completely still with rich-hued reflections of stately Helvellyn. View its forested length from one of the unforgettable viewpoints reached on our walks and you will know it is something special.

Walkers were once unwelcome here and the dense woods held its secrets. In 1980 strainers and a further chlorination plant at Dunmail Raise enabled an increase in public access. Now there are many paths which can combine to give good walks.

New thinking in terms of environmentally friendly forestry has resulted in thinning the dense spruce, the retainment of older native trees and new planting of mixed woodland, particularly near the shore, which has always had a varied tree-fringe. Here the native oak is regenerating.

Elephantine Helvellyn, framed by trees, is a feature of many walks here. Thirlmere is a working forest and some paths may be closed or diverted when felling is taking place. Midges can be troublesome at times. The forest can provide interesting sheltered walking when strong winds make progress in open country a battle for survival.

Thirlmere was originally two lakes, Leathes Water and Wythburn Water, the old coach road running between them, using a fine old packhorse bridge from Armboth to Wythburn. The site was chosen for a reservoir to satisfy Manchester's growing needs in the Industrial Revolution. The height of the lake enabled water to run by gravity to Manchester. Work began in 1890 and was completed in 1894. In 1908 conifers were planted to minimise soil erosion and control water run-off. Today the timber is used for fencing, boxes, pulp and of course Christmas trees.

Wythburn church seen from across Thirlmere

WALK 28: Shoulthwaite and Bleaberry Fell from Castlerigg

Shoulthwaite Gill, with Iron Crag on the right and the rocky knoll of Castle Crag hill fort centre left

SUMMARY: One of the longer and more arduous walks in this book with a spice of adventure across the pathless moor linking Shoulthwaite Gill to Bleaberry Fell. Definitely a walk in boots for clear weather. The path up the

Distance:	9 miles (14½km)
Grade:	Strenuous
Height gain:	1443ft (440m)
Terrain:	Valley and medium fell. Some rough pathless walking and wet patches.
Summit:	Blaeberry Fell 1935ft (590m)
Map:	OL4, HSW-CL

gill requires care.

The walk starts gently up the Naddle valley, keeping well away from the busy road, to gain the little upper valley of Shoulthwaite Gill, a delightful spot with a cascading stream dividing the forest from steep crags. Then comes the crossing of the pathless

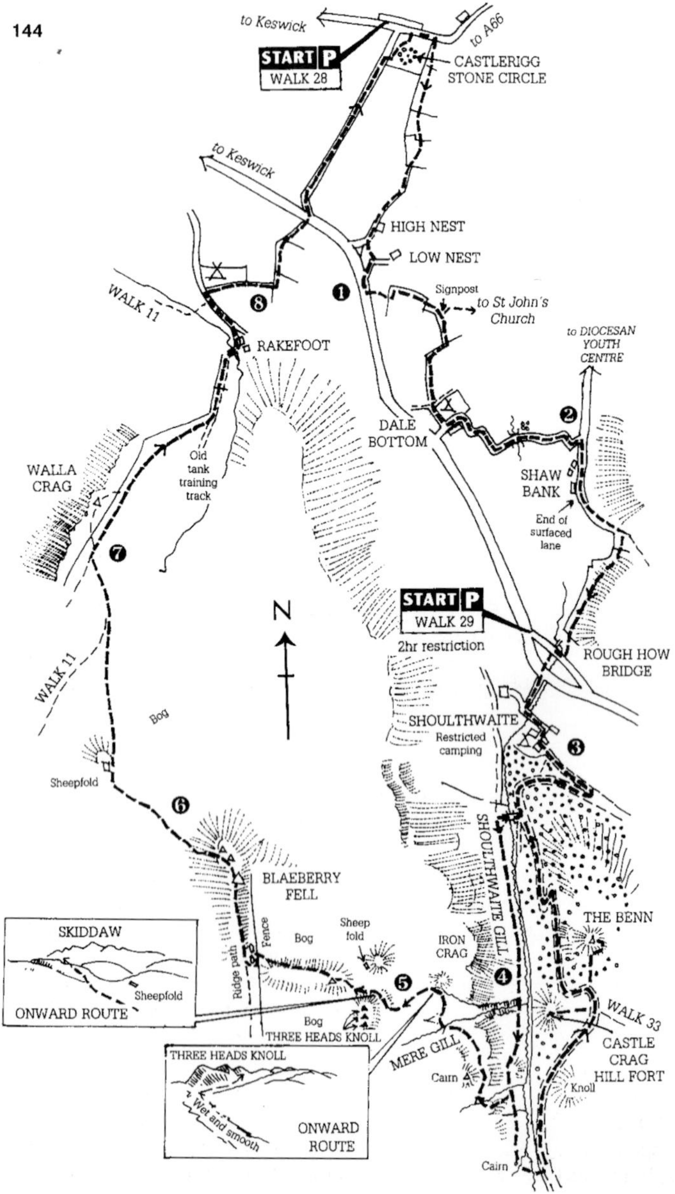

to Keswick

to A66

START P
WALK 28

CASTLERIGG
STONE CIRCLE

HIGH NEST

LOW NEST

to Keswick

Signpost

to St John's
Church

WALK 11

to DIOCESAN
YOUTH
CENTRE

RAKEFOOT

DALE
BOTTOM

SHAW
BANK

End of
surfaced lane

WALLA
CRAG

Old tank
training track

START P
WALK 29

2hr restriction

ROUGH HOW
BRIDGE

WALK 11

N

Bog

SHOULTHWAITE

Restricted
camping

SHOULTHWAITE GILL

Sheepfold

THE BENN

BLAEBERRY
FELL

Sheep
fold

Bog

SKIDDAW

ONWARD ROUTE

Sheepfold

Fence

Ridge path

Bog
THREE HEADS KNOLL

IRON
CRAG

Knoll

WALK 33

THREE HEADS KNOLL

Wet and smooth

ONWARD
ROUTE

MERE GILL

Cairn

CASTLE
CRAG
HILL FORT

Cairn

moor, interesting enough if you can follow our route which links several features. The wet moorland, with its numerous bogs, is a SSSI and walkers should keep to the driest route as indicated here. Once the ridge top path is gained the way over Bleaberry Fell is straightforward. If you are lucky you will finish past the stone circle glowing in the late afternoon sunshine.

HOW TO GET THERE AND PARKING: Park at Castlerigg stone circle, well signed from the A66 near Keswick. It may be busy at peak holiday times.

THE WALK: Set off down the road east (left when facing the Stone Circle), the ridgetop position giving an especially flattering view of Helvellyn summit. Helvellyn usually appears as a great grass mound above the forested Thirlmere trench from which the valley of Shoulthwaite branches. Looking further west of Shoulthwaite is the prominent peak of Bleaberry Fell. Turn R on the public footpath to The Nest. In front is spread the Naddle valley. Walk ahead over rough pasture to a ladder stile. Go straight on across two fields and stiles then along the fence to a gate at The Nest. Notice the agreeable blend of stone and brick as you pass the barn and walk behind the house to a gate and cattle-grid. Immediately over the grid step L through a gate and, with the fence at your right hand, continue in the original direction to a stile at Low Nest. Turn R and over the cattle-grid to the main road A591.

Turn L for 25yds then L again through a slit stile (public footpath, yellow waymark). Cross the field diagonally right facing the knobbly ridge of High Rigg (Walk 29) to a high stile. From here is a fine view of Blencathra to the north. On descending into the field turn L and follow its edge to the corner and right as requested to exit at a gate and onto a track. In a short distance is a little wooden signpost. Keep ahead to Dale Bottom and through a gate after which the track is enclosed. *The hedgerows are decked with dog roses in summer and a wide variety of grasses with descriptive names; cat's tail, cocksfoot and canary grass, sprinkled with the white and pink of flowers, yarrow and herb robert cover the verges.* At a lane go ahead through the caravan site to Dale Bottom Farm. Turn L and follow the lane which runs up the valley, heavy with the scent of meadow sweet, to the bridge over Naddle Beck. *Just beyond the bridge as you pass under an electricity wire look left along it. It leads the eye across the Glenderamakin and up the V-cut valley of the Glenderaterra between Lonscale Fell and Blencathra to Great Calva and High Pike in the distant Caldbeck Fells. It is part of the great fault line which cuts the Lake District from north to south.* Pass Broadstones dated 1660 and continue through a gate to a T-junction. Turn R and pass a rock cutting on the left exposing the Borrowdale Volcanics. Carry on, looking for the progeny of the red admiral butterfly we were privileged to meet as we walked, past Shaw Bank, Brown Beck Farm and cottages to where the surfaced road ends at a junction of ways. Continue by the wall and follow it round a bend to a gate with stile and bridleway sign. The bracken is not high enough to spoil the view as the way runs under High Rigg (ignore the ladder stile in the wall down right) and descend gently to a gate leading into a wood. At a signpost keep R to the road gate at Rough How Bridge.

SHORT WALK 29 STARTS HERE (See p149).

Glance downstream at the forlorn old bridleway bridge carrying only memories of the forgotten track. Cross over the old loop road to a stile and through a small field to a stile by an old ford. *Examine the stones re-used for the treads of the stile, shaped and decorated for some other purpose.* Cross the main road and proceed up the lane to Shoulthwaite Farm. Turn L over a bridge and enter the camping field by a barn where a L turn signed Keswick leads to gates and into the forest. Keep ahead on a small path through silver birches and just after the left-hand wall turns away find a small path branching up R to join a forest road. Turn R and plod up the road gaining height easily. *The impenetrable coniferous forest gives no view as it is planted in 'close canopy' formation to produce timber with straight trunks and a minimum of branches.* The road gradually bends into the Shoulthwaite valley. At a junction fork R, immediately R again to go through the tall kissing gate at the deer fence and enter the secluded valley of Shoulthwaite.

Cross the bridge over Shoulthwaite Gill, turn L and wander up the valley. There are no paths except for various animal trods which converge into a path then suddenly disperse, so as you go to Bleaberry Fell watch out for the red deer which roam the area. Walk along by the stream with the two-tier profile of Iron Crag dominating the right-hand skyline and Castle Crag, site of an ancient hill fort, on the left centre. Just beyond a group of holly trees find a trod leading to the crossing of a side stream then find your own way until you notice the wall on the opposite bank take a bend and run down to the stream. There is a narrow path on our side about 20ft above the gill. By now you will be below Iron Crag (*this is a popular crag with rock climbers with some hard modern climbs up the sections of clean rock*). Pass an old sheepfold and you are now abreast of the Castle Crag Hill Fort. Ignore the stile in the deer fence and continue to where Mere Gill tumbles into Shoulthwaite Gill below a neat waterfall. A narrow path leads into the gill. Negotiate the crossing with care (about 4ft below path level gives both hand and footholds) and scramble up the far side. Leave the path level and gain some height to avoid the outcropping rocks ahead then continue up the valley. On reaching a boggy area the trod disappears altogether. Go R up to the level of the bracken and along its edge to a flat bluff. Pass a small cairn and a boulder on each side of the path and in 100yds cross a stony stream. (Check your position - in the forest opposite, a rock knoll stands proud of the treetops and 500yds up the valley is a ladder stile into the forest leading to the forest road.)

WALK 29 leaves Walk 28 here and continues up the shallowing valley (see p149)

WALK 28 continued. Here we leave the security of the valley to cross the wild, rugged and unnamed fellside between Shoulthwaite and the High Seat to Bleaberry Fell ridge path. *You could set a straight course west uphill through moor, rock and mire but, if you carefully try to follow the route here described you will arrive satisfied with the adventure, so go for it.* Turn R steeply up the ridge to the left of the stream. The slope becomes easier as you gain height. At the top of the brow turn R. Cross the stream on a trod just above the first (or last) tree in its bed, a struggling hawthorn with a juniper and felled rowan, sending offspring from its roots, for company. Follow the trod across the slope gaining height to the next ridge (note a cairn far up on the left). Follow the trod along the shelf towards Iron Crag (north) and in the distance Bleaberry Fell peeps up as the highest point ahead and slightly left (NW). The ravine of Mere Gill now blocks our way at this level. Veer L below rock outcrops and keep up parallel to the gill on a trod which turns to cross the gill by two old iron fence supports. The trod runs level at first then disappears. Turn L uphill again and the next stream (a tributary of Mere Gill) comes into sight. We are now well above Thirlmere and a splendid view of the Helvellyn range is complete. Continue to the head of the diminishing stream then walk L along the remains of its green depression heading for a three-headed knoll (see sketch map). The grass is interspersed with short heather and moss. When 50ft below the rock at a scattering of stones and small cairn turn R on a level sheep trod then go past the end of the knoll onto a slight ridge which has an array of exposed rock which leads through a boggy area to a brow. To the NE should be a rock knoll with a sheepfold below it. Bleaberry Fell stands clearly to the NW with its cairn and a prominent fence running the length of the moor. Keep W along the highest ground passing colourful pools (or nasty looking bogholes), to reach the fence at a stile. Cross the stile and make your way round either side of the twin pools to arrive at the main ridge-top path beyond. Turn R and make your way up the slope to the first summit with a massive cairn. As Bleaberry Fell stands isolated at the end of a ridge there is a magnificent 360° view.

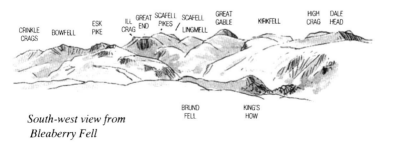

South-west view from
Bleaberry Fell

To descend go over the summit to a cairn in the direction of Keswick (NNW) and down the broad path to the next grand cairn with a bird's-eye view of Derwentwater. In complete contrast with the previous part of the walk you cannot go wrong; even when the path, after descending the steep north side of the fell, spreads into a soggy bog it continues on the far side. Pass a sheepfold and over a marshy moorland steering for the top edge of the walled Walla Crag woodland straight ahead. Cross a few gills, one with a pretty fall over a sill by a rowan tree, to a cairn at a path junction. Turn R and go up to the wall. (Ignore the stile unless you want to visit the summit of Walla Crag, Walk 11.) Turn R and keeping the wall to the left and ignoring stiles over it, go over the near rise and down the pasture to reach Brockle Beck. *The strange metal rods which appear embedded in the path are relics of tank training on the fell during the last war.* Go over the stile and the footbridge over Brockle Beck to turn L along the surfaced lane at Rakefoot Farm. A short way past the farm ignore the public footpath on the left but a few yards further on locate a path and turn R signed Stone Circle. Go along the sunken pathway past a campsite, over a stile in a cross fence then through fields along to a signed ladder stile. Turn L to a series of fields and stiles which lead to the main road. Cross over and along the signed lane Castle Lane for ¹/₂ mile to a stile R into the field with the Stone Circle. Exit by the north gate to the parking.

Castlerigg Stone circle

Likely to be between 3000 and 4000 years old, probably a late Neolithic or Bronze Age place of worship. Cumbria has 16 other locations of stone circles, but this is the best preserved and has the biggest stones, 48 in total.

WALK 29: Shoulthwaite Gill

SUMMARY: A shorter walk into Shoulthwaite Gill is described for it would be a pity to miss this hidden gem, but it does include some walking on forest roads, and the path up the gill needs care.

HOW TO GET THERE AND PARKING: Park on a loop of old road on the busy A591, opposite the lane to Shoulthwaite Farm. The parking is officially limited to 2 hours but this is to deter overnight stays.

THE WALK: See Walk 28 (p.146) for the description of the first part of the walk up Shoulthwaite Gill. Where Walk 28 turns right on to the moor (p147), continue up the shallowing valley to a cairn at its head. Here you will be able to cross the stream to a gate into the forest. Join the forest road (Walk 33) and turn L to commence the return. Ignore two forest roads which branch off R, keep straight on to a col with a clearing where forestry vehicles park. This is the junction where we can choose to visit the three little summits close by (see p.165). Return to the forest road and continue right down to meet the outward route.

Distance:	4 miles (6½km)
Grade:	Moderate
Height gain:	938ft (286m)
Terrain:	Some rough walking. Valley and forest.
Summit:	In forest 1344ft (410m)
Map:	OL4, HSW-CL

WALK 30: High Rigg and St John's Vale

SUMMARY: High Rigg is a modest fell sandwiched between loftier neighbours. Here, with little effort, you can savour all the delights of a higher ridge walk on a well trodden path which is pleasant underfoot. The knobbly ridge undulates for 1½ miles to culminate in a knot just a little higher than the others along the way. The return by St John's Vale is a complete contrast, for here we traverse a quiet valley with hay meadows and views restricted by the steep craggy sides to finish in woods by the stream.

Distance:	5¼ miles (8¼km)
Grade:	Easy
Height gain:	675ft (208m)
Terrain:	Low fell and valley. Good paths.
Summit:	High Rigg 1163ft (354m)
Map:	OL5, HSW-CL

HOW TO GET THERE AND PARKING: Turn off the A591 near the northern end of Thirlmere on the B5322 towards St John's Vale and Threlkeld. In ¹/₄ mile there is a car park on the left at Legburthwaite.

THE WALK: Leave by the gate at the back of the car park and either turn L along the old road to the A591, or begin the walk far more pleasantly by going straight over the old road to enter a riverside picnic area. Turn L and make your way along the gated path until, at a kissing gate, you branch L and regain the old road and the A591.

Turn R along the verge, cross the Beck Bridge and R again over a ladder stile fork L to a yellow waymarked path up the fell. In 100yds by an oak tree fork L (the other fork is our return path). Go steeply up the fell. *Castle Rock, very popular with rock climbers, is prominent on the right.* Soon you are looking down on the treetops and the valley parting, with St John's Vale to the east and Naddle valley to the west. The path levels then undulates giving a brief respite before climbing again. Pass hardy oaks and pines until reaching a shelf shaded by an oak, an inviting spot to take a break and enjoy the view up the Thirlmere valley. Continue with clusters of harebells and tormentil breaking the monotonous green of the bracken but soon the climb is over and you are at the long summit ridge.

There is a wonderful horizon with the peaks of Skiddaw and Blencathra (Saddleback) in profile. Reserve a little concentration for the path as the splendid view entices the eyes to wander. Descend to a gap in a wall and then up the rocky slope ahead. Skirt a knoll on its left and descend to a small tarn, its size dependent on the previous week's weather. The path is now wide and clear.

WHITESIDE — BROWN COVE CRAGS — PATH TO HELVELLYN — STEEL KNOTTS — GREAT HOW — ULLSC

View south from the climb onto High Rigg

Away down to the left is a shelf with a reedy pool. Turn L at a white waymark arrow and go over a stile in the fence. Keep ahead then bend round a knoll, descending then rising again. *Westward is the Naddle valley, wide and flat yet containing an inadequate stream for its size. It was an ice overflow channel gouged by glacial action.*

Enter a shallow valley between knolls and descend to a cross wall and a ladder stile. Keep beside the wall to Moss Crag. Circle

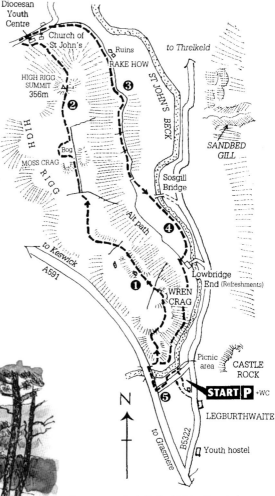

THIRLMERE

the moss on its left, the tighter the circle the wetter the boots, and continue to meet the wall again. Pass boulders scratched and abandoned by the ice then rise to the summit cairn. *Views are*

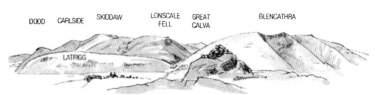

DODD CARLSIDE SKIDDAW LONSCALE FELL GREAT CALVA BLENCATHRA

LATRIGG

North from High Rigg

widespread across a plethora of shapely fells from Causey Pike in the west to Helvellyn eastwards but see if you can pick out the Castlerigg Stone Circle.

Regain the path and descend the steep north end of the fell to a kissing gate in a cross wall. Go round the left-hand side of the Youth Centre to the road. Turn R to pass St John's-in-the-Vale church and in 50yds turn R into the public bridleway to St John's in the Vale. The side wall of the bridleway is just below eye-level and allows views over the vale to Blencathra as you walk on soft green turf edged with foxgloves. Pass a ruin on a spur at Rake How. *Across the vale lie Bram Crag quarries and the deep-cut gash of Sandbed Gill, popular with scramblers. Above the quarries a zig-zag path with the intriguing name of Fisherwife Rake winds down the craggy fellside.* Approach a ladder stile at a wall corner where the bridle path descends towards the valley floor and a step stile at the next wall leads into a field. Go ahead to the wallside again and pass by a kissing gate in the wall where an old slot slate with five square holes for gateposts now rests unused. Our path is nipped between the wall and a raised bank. Go

St John's Vale with Castle Rock and Sosgill Bridge

through the first gate (the gate to the right on what looks like the continuation of the bridle path is not a right of way), and diagonally L across the pasture. Use the clapper stones to cross over the dyke, blue with tiny forget-me-nots, to Sosgill Bridge over St John's Beck. Admire the lovely old bridge but do not cross it. Turn R along the embankment in a delightful situation. *The beck is crystal clear and flows with a merry gurgle. Dippers skim the water and many water-loving plants thrive.* At Low Bridge End (tea garden) obey the signs directing you through a gate on the right and behind the cottage. The smell of wood smoke drifts across the path until at the next cross wall you are back on the familiar bridle path.

The wooded vale narrows, large boulders edge the path and across the beck the forestry woodyard appears. Take more care as the path narrows and rises along a ledge above the beck. *Through a gap in the oaks is a fine view of Castle Rock, now more renowned in climbing circles for its collection of brilliant overhanging face climbs. Literary buffs will know it from Sir Walter Scott's poem* The Bridal of Triermain. The path now contours round the southern end of High Rigg to join the outward route near the A591. Turn L, cross the bridge then turn L along the old road to the car park.

WALK 31: Threlkeld Knotts, Clough Head and the Old Coach Road

The tilted lava beds of High Rigg (Walk 30) are well seen from the path up Threlkeld Knotts

GREAT   WHITE   CLOUGH HEAD
DODD   PIKE

Clough Head from the A66

SUMMARY: This walk utilises a centuries old smooth, green path which climbs so easily you hardly notice it. Views are brilliant; from the deep-cut southern face of Blencathra to the skyline of Lakeland's highest fells, Threlkeld Knotts is a worthwhile objective for a modest walk, Clough Head rounds the day for the more ambitious by a path which cuts headily across the steep, ice-gouged northern slopes.

The return along the Old Coach Road proves swift and easy. For a walk so near Keswick it is surprisingly unfrequented apart from a few cyclists on the Old Coach Road.

HOW TO GET THERE AND PARKING: From the B5322 in St John's Vale turn west to Wanthwaite, Diocesan Youth Centre and Keswick. Cross Wanthwaite Bridge and park on the wide verge area to the left.

		Short Return
Distance:	6 miles (9½km)	4 miles (6½km)
Grade:	Strenuous but easier than you would expect	Moderate
Height gain:	1955ft (596m)	1164ft (355m)
Terrain:	High fell. A mix of good paths and trackless fell top.	Medium fell
Summits:	Threlkeld Knotts - 1624ft (495m)	
	Clough Head - 2381ft (726m)	
	White Pike - 2060ft (628m)	
Map:	OL5, HSW-CL	

THE WALK: Cross Wanthwaite Bridge over St John s Beck and stroll to the B5322 studying the slopes of Threlkeld Knotts, ravaged by quarrying, and the great scarp edge of Clough Head, ravaged by ice and weather, the vanguard of The Dodds. Turn R for 100yds then L to Matterdale on the Old Coach Road in company with the 'Coast to Coast Cycleway'. Here the climb, which will

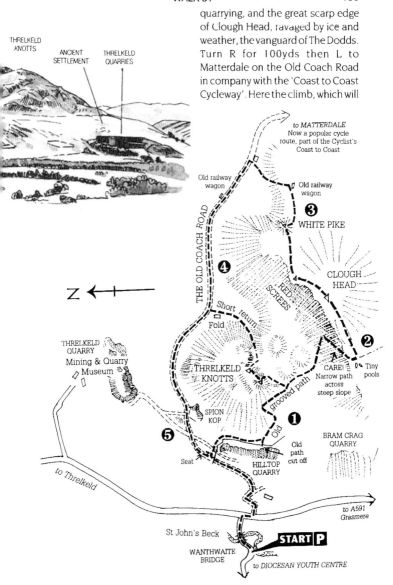

THRELKELD KNOTTS

ANCIENT SETTLEMENT

THRELKELD QUARRIES

to MATTERDALE
Now a popular cycle route, part of the Cyclist's Coast to Coast

Old railway wagon

Old railway wagon

❸
WHITE PIKE

THE OLD COACH ROAD

❹

RED SCREES

CLOUGH HEAD

Short return

Fold

THRELKELD QUARRY
Mining & Quarry Museum

N ←

THRELKELD KNOTTS

Old grooved path

CARE!
Narrow path across steep slope

❷
Tiny pools

SPION KOP

❺

Seat

Old path cut off

❶

HILLTOP QUARRY

BRAM CRAG QUARRY

to Threlkeld

to A591 Grasmere

St John's Beck

START **P**

WANTHWAITE BRIDGE

to DIOCESAN YOUTH CENTRE

prove less daunting than it appears, begins. Go through a gate and a mixed plantation, pass Hill Top Farm, which is off to the right, then bend L towards disused Hilltop Quarry. *The scar on the fellside where micro-granite was extracted is now, with a bit of help, reverting to nature.* Ignore a stile into the quarry. Continue up the Coach Road with a breathtaking view to the west with Crag Hill, Grisedale Pike and the green patchwork of Whinlatter Forest dominating the far horizon. Go through a gate by a memorial seat which gives its users a view of Skiddaw and Blencathra across the Glenderamackin valley. (The cutting on the left is the stone haulage road leading down to Threlkeld Quarry.)

Leave the Coach Road and turn R up very steep, pathless grass with the fence edging the quarry to your right. The angle soon eases. Cross a quarry road and continue by the fence. *The quarry edge, protected from nibbling sheep, is being colonised by heather giving a colourful carpet for the young trees. The quarry face reveals the almost vertical rock strata whilst across St John's Vale tilted beds of volcanic ash on the side of High Rigg show their form as shadows in the morning sunshine.* Follow the fence as it bends R and is replaced by a wall. Turn R at the wall corner and walk on a sheep trod running above the wall almost as far as a ladder stile. Turn L in the green groove of an old sunken footpath coming from a retired and buried stile in the wall.

Make progress on the friendly smooth path giving a steady ascent of Threlkeld Knotts against the dragging demands of the scenery. *Try to spot Castlerigg Stone Circle (see p148) for details [look west and beyond Tewet Tarn are the white buildings of Goosewell Farm. The circle is in the field above left beyond the strip of trees]).* The higher you go the easier it is to see. Pass a sheep-feed fenced area and continue to a cairn. Keep R on the lower path beneath stones. Pass a small shelter wall to the right and before an eroded patch of grey shale turn L on a slight path to Threlkeld Knotts. (Note the continuation of the grooved path to Clough Head.)

Go up the path to the rocks and 50yds further is the cairn at the summit where the view is brilliant. Walk along to the north-east cairn but halt 10yds short. *A stone of unknown intent is carved x d 1870 (maybe a miner staking a hopeful claim!).*

SHORT RETURN TO THE COACH ROAD: Turn R (south-east) to gain the shallow valley and follow it L and down on an improving path to pass right of Clough Fold, an old oblong stone sheepfold surrounded by fenced extensions. A short distance ahead is the Coach Road where you rejoin the route from Clough Head. Turn L.

TO CLOUGH HEAD (a route for fine weather only) from Threlkeld Knotts north-east summit cairn: Return to the first cairn. Turn L (south) towards Clough Head past traces of diggings to regain the grooved path without losing too much height. Do this by traversing to the R of the two intervening knolls, ignoring prominent sheep trods crossing your way. The large knoll is the highest of the Knotts and on rounding its neighbour the line of the grooved path will be seen ahead.

Get into the groove again and pick out the line of the old path as it zig-zags up and makes a rising traverse of the bare headwall. It is indeed a formidable sight but don't be put off - just be careful. Go along the green zig-zag cairned path. Keep a sharp eye on the cairns, especially for where the path takes a bend right and narrows. The path now approaches the scree where it is well used by sheep. **Care is needed on this section** but the path soon moves across the steep ground and the broad ridge is reached at a marker cairn. *From here is a wonderful view of Derwentwater and the Solway estuary to the north-west.*

Leave the old path to wind its way over the moor soon to be lost in the neglect of time. Turn L and make your own way directly up Clough Head. Pass a cluster of boulders and, as the turf becomes shorter the going improves, accompanied by a southern aspect over the little rock rooftop of Calfhow Pike to Great Dodd and the distant folds of Helvellyn. A tiny trod appears and leads to the trig point and wind shelter for small walkers on the summit. *The view east to the Pennines is extensive with the twin domes of Great (see Walk 49) and Little Mell Fell in the foreground.*

Continue over the summit on the broad ridge to a smaller cairn, just the location to view the Glenderamackin valley and study the line of the Old Coach Road as it uses the higher ground through the bog on its way to Matterdale. Now begin the descent on the path, continuing the same direction, to the rocky cone of White Pike - a mound of many cairns. The Coach Road appears just a stone's throw below. We recommend that you take the slope to the R (south) and head for an old railway wagon. At the wagon turn L and go easily down the grass (the many enticing sheep trods cutting the slope lead into trouble) to rejoin the road at sheep pens.

Turn L along the road passing another wagon, a reminder of the

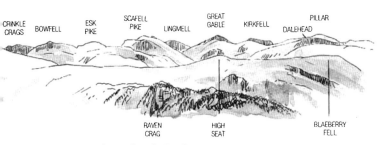

View south west from Clough Head

proximity of the old Keswick to Penrith Railway (see Walk 12), and in ¹/₄ mile meet the short route from Threlkeld Knotts. A further ³/₄ mile leads past quarries and on to join the outward route at the gate by the seat.

Retrace the outward route to the parking.

The Old Coach Road

This was the main Penrith to Keswick road before the present road was built.

The Threlkeld Granite Co

According to a 1913 advertisement in Postlethwaite's *Mines and Mining in the English Lake District* the company manufactured 'Granite-concrete Flags - never wear slippery, high crushing strain. 100,000 super yards of well seas- oned flags always in stock'. As well as 'Non-slippery paving sets' they also boasted 'granite macadam specially adapted for steep roads'. Much of the stone was used to build the Keswick Railway, and also used in the construction of Thirlmere. Their Hot Rolled Asphalt was used on many of Lakeland's roads.

Klondyke and Spion Kop were two quarries named after current events for they were opened when the Gold Rush and the Boer War were hot news. The quarries closed in 1937 but reopened when demand for granite rose after World War II, and a road built to link the three quarries. Granite sets were hand-cut. Lower grades of stone were used for railway ballast, intermediate for road stone tarmac whilst the smallest was used for concrete flagstones. The quarry effectively closed in 1982.

Threlkeld Quarry and Mining Museum

Houses a unique and extensive collection of original artefacts, plans, maps and other memorabilia, plus a collection of minerals and rock specimens, a narrow gauge railway and engine house, an excavator collection and shop. Open daily from 10.00am, Easter to October.

RAVEN CRAG   THE BENN   ULLOCK PIKE

St John's Vale

Looking down on St John's Vale you will see that the farms lie well above the flat valley floor and the river, although small, has built up protected banks. There have been cataclysmic floods here. In 1749 many bridges, houses and a corn mill were swept away. The isolated church on the northern end of High Rigg is centrally placed to serve both the St John's and Naddle valleys.

WALK 32: Thirlmere East Shore and Great How

SUMMARY: A well waymarked walk on good paths, at first by Thirlmere's shore with an optional ascent of Great How. The return is along the base of Helvellyn, passing the little ravine of Fisher Gill, where the path climbs sufficiently to give splendid views.

HOW TO GET THERE AND PARKING: On the eastern side of Thirlmere park at Swirls car park on the A591 3½ miles from Dunmail Raise. Toilets. Smaller viewpoint parking on the opposite side of the road, at Station Coppice.

THE WALK: Leave Swirls car park on a little footpath on the R, before the entrance, and cross the busy road to the Station Coppice parking from which there is an extensive view over the lake to the surrounding fells. Take the L-hand permitted path to Legburthwaite and Great How. *Immediately the traffic noise is replaced by rushing water as gills from the western slopes of Helvellyn, captured by a concrete leat, surge free in a boisterous leap down a natural ravine. The path allows views*

Distance:	4½ miles (7¼km)
Grade:	Easy
Height gain:	1029ft (314m)
Terrain:	Valley. Good paths.
Summit:	Great How 1092ft (333m)
Map:	OL5 or OL4, HSW-CL

Thirlmere and St John's Vale from the balcony above Swirls car park

SKIDDAW   GREAT HOW   LONSCALE FELL   GREAT CALVA   BLENCATHRA   CASTLE ROCK

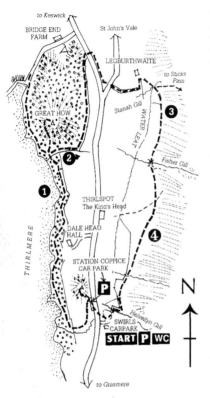

of the waterfalls before entering a larch wood at a kissing gate. Continue down to the lakeshore where the path turns parallel. *The shoreline, subject to constant variations in water level, is drear but the pleasant woodland path compensates.* Pass along a narrow strip of forest then bear L at a sign and go through a kissing gate in a fence. *Through the beech and oak, part of the old natural woodland, the vertical profile of Raven Crag can be seen across the lake.* Cross little footbridges as you pass a clearing below Dale Head Hall. At a wall corner join another track by a great redwood. *If you approach close you will notice that a patch is worn where people have knocked to test the spongy nature of its bark.* Go through a kissing gate and up the rise. *From the top the slender white falls of Fisher Gill and the pointed summit of Brown Cove Crags come into view on the right.* Go through a kissing gate just before an old wall and bend R up the slope. Between trunks of tall pines the shoulders of Brown Cove Crags rise towards Helvellyn. As you walk on, the shape of our more modest summit, Great How, can be discerned ahead.

At a four-way signpost there are three alternatives.

I.   THE ASCENT OF GREAT HOW: The path is easy and straightforward. Go straight ahead through gnarled oaks, part of the self-seeded natural woodland. The waymarked path narrows and zig-zags to the summit rock and cairn (1092ft). *The young larches planted on the summit have grown to restrict the view somewhat, but a fine vista to the SW shows Thirlmere and its surrounding fells and with a bit of neck-craning the distinctive shape of Blencathra is visible to the north.*

Return the same way to the signpost.

The golden glow of Helvellyn reflected in Thirlmere (Walk 33)

Harrop Tarn is renowned for its water lilies (Walk 36)

Intimate delights of forest walking on Thirlmere shore (Walk 35).

The old green path up Threlkeld Knotts makes uphill walking a pleasure (Walk 31).

Typical forest footpath

2. TO CONTINUE ALONG THE EAST SIDE OF GREAT HOW: At the signpost turn towards Legburthwaite. Through the beech wood Fisher Place and The King's Head can be seen on the main road. Descend to a track where you turn L and gradually move closer to and level with How Beck. Continue until reaching the kissing gate at the main road.

3. ALONG THE LAKESHORE: The lakeshore path continues through woods to the minor road at the 58ft high dams. Turn R to pass Bridge End Farm and campsite, R again at the busy main road to join Alternative 2.

Turn R along the hard shoulder for 400yds, cross the road and turn towards St John's-in-the-Vale and Threlkeld B5322. *From the section of old road look up the hillside and note the old pony path zig-zagging up the side of Stanah Gill to the Sticks Pass and Patterdale. Down the valley is the beetling face of the Castle Rock of Triermain, a crag well used by rock climbers.*

Just before the telephone box turn R on the bridle path to Glenridding via the Sticks Pass. Ignore a sign on the right to Stybeck and keep ahead up the lane, to a high ladder stile over the wall. Go up the broad fellside path to a gate by a big rock. The water leat which is collecting water from Great Dodd, Mill Gill, White Side and Helvellyn along the valley, enters a tunnel allowing us to cross without acrobatics and continue up the fell to the intake wall gate. *From here the views to the north and north-west are splendid with St John's Vale framing Blencathra and the lesser hills of the Naddle valley, High Rigg and Dodd Crag holding Skiddaw in its span.*

Turn R to Stanah Gill where you can pause on the bridge to admire the lovely falls and cascades. *In crossing the valley we have crossed a fault line and the volcanic rock is silken smooth, unlike the sandpaper textured rock around Thirlmere.*

Make your way up to the signpost where we leave the Sticks Pass path and turn R towards Swirls car park. The path traverses in the lee of the wall until the wall bends away downhill. Here take the L fork (sign), cross a major path which comes up the hill from Fisher Place and you are within earshot of Fisher Gill. Cross the footbridge over the gill which gives a favoured view of the tumbling water. Continue L upstream by the lovely cascades to the wall corner where the traverse continues above the intake wall. At the next wall corner keep straight on (sign) where the path from King's Head makes its climb towards Helvellyn. At a little stream the wall bends downhill again. *The path underfoot, like a narrow balcony across the steep fellside, is by courtesy of the young volunteers who spend their holidays doing such worthwhile work.* The intake wall rises up to the path level and tight under the wall the path begins its descent to a footbridge over Helvellyn Gill. Turn R to the forest gate and go through trees to the car park.

Sticks Pass

This was an important pony trail, the highest in the Lakes, named from the posts which marked the route. Ponies carried ore from the Greenside Mines to the Keswick smelter and to Stoneycroft in Newlands.

WALK 33: Raven Crag and The Benn from Armboth

View from The Benn. Two small figures are visible on a terrace below the top of Raven Crag. These are rock climbers who have just completed their climb. The low water level of Thirlmere reveals a pale edge

SUMMARY: This walk gains little summits in the forest by the moorland behind. Each top is worth visiting; Castle Crag for its sense of history, Raven Crag the highest, but first choice must go to The Benn for this is the finest viewpoint over the length of Thirlmere. The return is made along the well constructed shore path.

Distance:	4¹/₂ miles (7¹/₄km)
Grade:	Moderate
Height gain:	1052ft (320m)
Terrain:	Low fell, forest and lake shore. Some wet paths and rough walking.
Summits:	Castle Crag hill fort - 1400ft (427m) Raven Crag - 1512ft (461m) The Benn - 1462ft (446m)
Map:	OL4, HSW-CL

HOW TO GET THERE AND PARKING: Park at Armboth car park (toilets) midway along the western shore of Thirlmere.

Boulders above Armboth

THE WALK: From the car park entrance turn R along the road for a few yards then L up the public footpath to Watendlath. The cascades of Middlesteads Gill can be seen as the stream tumbles down a deep ravine. Cross the chunky little stone bridge and go through a gap in the wall. Now the serious climb begins up a green path to a group of angular boulders, perhaps removed from the crag by earth movements or more likely, erratics left by melting ice. *This is an area of faults (deep cracks in the earth) and dykes (rock, different to the main country rock where molten material from deep below the earth's crust, has been forced up the fault and solidified), which we intend to examine.* Continue by the edge of the forest and as height is gained the deer fence allows the noisy waters of Fisher Gill to be heard on the left.

When you reach a rock on the right of the path with an orange paint sign B2 Δ the path bends R. Note carefully your progress so that you do not miss the Dyke. Zig-zag past four cairns, pass an ash tree on the left, then halt at the next cairn. You are now on the line of the Armboth dyke.

The dyke is only to be seen on the right of the path. Its continuation on the left is displaced some yards away by fault movement. The dyke is of pinkish rock with little holes where quartz crystals have weathered out. The true colour can be seen where geologists' hammers have exposed the surface. The line of the dyke can be followed by turning right up the hillside and where the heat of the dyke has metamorphosed the country rock on each side, garnets can be found.

Continue along the path walking about 25yds on the line of the fault. The dyke is more obvious when seen from here. Carry on towards the wall then fork R to meet it. Go through an old gateway, turn R along the wallside

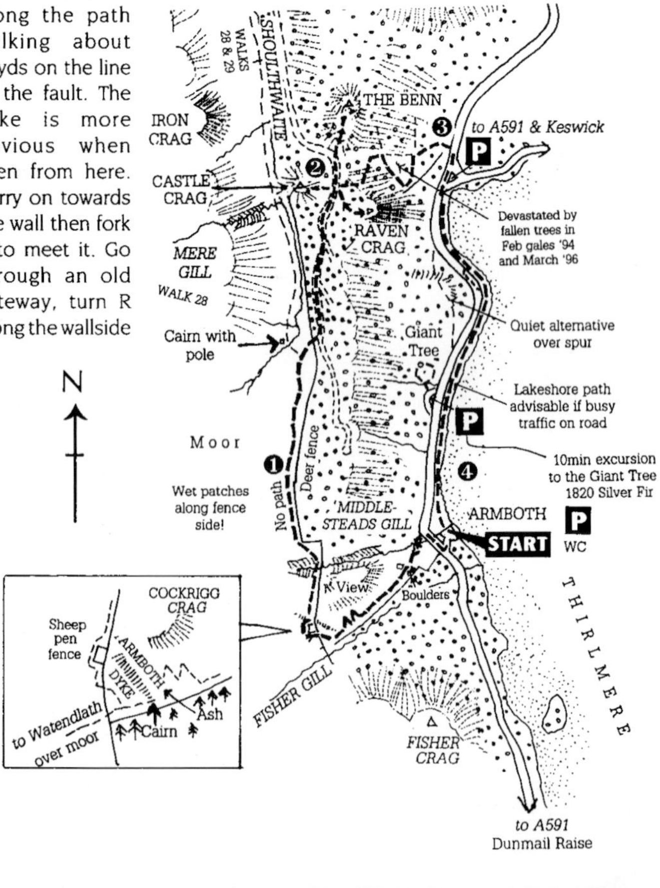

SHOULTHWAITE

WALKS 28 & 29

THE BENN

IRON CRAG

③ to A591 & Keswick

P

CASTLE CRAG

②

RAVEN CRAG

Devastated by fallen trees in Feb gales '94 and March '96

MERE GILL

WALK 28

Quiet alternative over spur

Cairn with pole

Giant Tree

Lakeshore path advisable if busy traffic on road

N

M o o r

P

Deer fence

No path

Wet patches along fence side!

①

④

10min excursion to the Giant Tree 1820 Silver Fir

'MIDDLE-STEADS GILL

ARMBOTH

START

P

WC

T H I R L M E R E

COCKRIGG CRAG

Sheep pen fence

ARMBOTH DYKE

to Watendlath over moor

Ash

Cairn

View

Boulders

FISHER GILL

FISHER CRAG

to A591 Dunmail Raise

and follow it to a distintegrating sheep pen. As you pass the end of the pen you cross over the dyke once more, its pink stones can be seen in the wall. Keep on until reaching the highest point of the wall and make a detour through a broken-down gap. The views of the Helvellyn range are majestic and with the main uphill walking accomplished, this is just the place for a break.

Return to the path and drop steeply down into Middlesteads Gill. Cross the gill together with two undetectable fault lines and climb up the bank for a few yards. On reaching a break in the wall on the right, fork L along the sheep trod leading from it. Forge on up the slope and head for the deer fence and a lone pine bordering the replanted forest. Keep on with the fence to your right and ignoring the high ladder stile. Where the deer fence takes a sudden bend go ahead past a rectangle of stones to a low rock shelf. This is the displaced dyke conveniently settled. Sit on it and enjoy the retrospective view south to Ullscarf and west over the feature-less moors of High Tove.

Walk on keeping within sight of the fence and forest border. Go through a broken cross wall and up a bracken covered bank using an animal trod. The height now keeps on drier ground above the fence side bog but within sight of the forest fence. Ignore a nailed up gate in the fence keeping on the higher slope until as you progress over a rise and an impressive scene appears. *The valley of Shoulthwaite, deep between Iron Crag on its western side and Castle Crag opposite leads down to St. John's Vale. Behind the slopes of Blencathra complete the picture.*

Look out for a kissing gate in the deer fence, descend to it, go through and onto the forest road beyond. Turn L and continue as the road runs along the slopes of Raven Crag to a col and clearing where forest vehicles park. This is the junction from which we can choose to visit the three little summits close by.

ASCENT OF CASTLE CRAG FORT: At the edge of the clearing a footpath sign L indicates a well made path. (There is also a signpost set well back to the right at a major path junction.) The path leads down to duckboards and a bridge then to a sign at the foot of the crag.

ASCENT OF RAVEN CRAG: A signed path branches east opposite the Castle Crag path and rises over a wooden walkway to the summit cone. Views are restricted.

ASCENT OF THE BENN: Continue along the forest road north past the clearing and look for a slight path branching R. The path crosses a wettish area and it is well worth persevering along its adventurous indistinct route until rising above the trees to the rocky cone of the Benn. Scramble up to a marvellous viewpoint.

Return to the col with the parking area and turn L (east) along a footpath into the forest. This soon descends steeply to a forest road. The path continues straight across but it is easier to turn right along the road. At the bend is an impressive view up to the steep rock face of Raven Crag. Look out for the footpath branching right down to the road. Turn R and pass the road triangle at the end of the lake. Just after this you find the start of the lake shore path which is worth following back to Armboth car park.

Castle Crag

This is possibly the site of an Iron Age fort or it may date from the Dark Ages. Visible remains are slight. Defences consisted of ditches and ramparts - here the craggy nature of the knoll provides a perfectly defensible site, although the living area is quite small. It is a scheduled site.

WALK 34: Behind the Forest to Armboth

Deergarth How Island, Thirlmere

Summary: A typical Thirlmere walk which visits the lonely country behind the forest. Dense bracken may be a problem in season. Dark dense forest to shy lily-fringed Harrop Tarn, then a delectable pathless passage over the knolls edging the headwaters of Launchy Gill where red deer are often seen. Views are restricted once the forest fence is joined but Fisher Crag pokes out of the trees to make a wonderful view the length of Thirlmere, and an almost aerial view of the islands below. Rough

Distance:	6 miles (9¹/₂km)
Grade:	Moderate
Height gain:	1092ft (333m)
Terrain:	Forest and medium fell. Trackless, wet and rough in parts.
Summit:	Stone Hause Knott - 1519ft (463m) Fisher Crag - 1394ft (425m)
Map:	OL4, HSW-CL

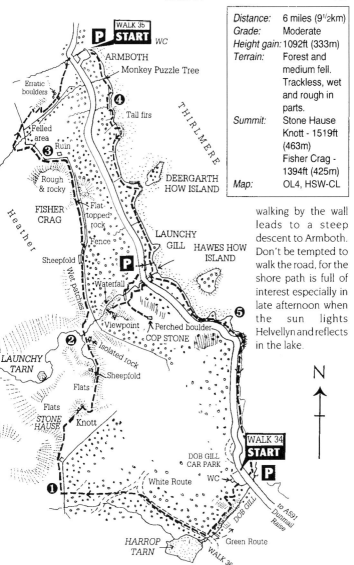

WALK 3b
START WC
ARMBOTH
Monkey Puzzle Tree
Erratic boulders
Felled area
④
③ Ruin
Tail firs
THIRLMERE
Rough & rocky
FISHER CRAG
Flat-topped rock
Fence
DEERGARTH HOW ISLAND
Heather
Sheepfold
LAUNCHY GILL
HAWES HOW ISLAND
Wet patches
Waterfall
Viewpoint
Perched boulder
COP STONE
⑤
②
Isolated rock
LAUNCHY TARN
Sheepfold
Flats
Flats
STONE HAUSE
Knott
White Route
①
WALK 34
START
P
DOB GILL CAR PARK
WC
N
HARROP TARN
Green Route
WALK 36
DOB GILL
to A591 Dunmail Raise

walking by the wall leads to a steep descent to Armboth. Don't be tempted to walk the road, for the shore path is full of interest especially in late afternoon when the sun lights Helvellyn and reflects in the lake.

HOW TO GET THERE AND PARKING: Armboth or Dob Gill car parks (toilets) on the western side of the lake.

THE WALK: From Dob Gill car park take the signed (blue/brown routes) footpath to Harrop Tarn. It rises steeply through the forest but is a good path with a three-quarter way resting place on the left in full view of the Dob Gill waterfalls. At the tarn turn R on the blue route along the forest track skirting the tarn. *The woodland fringe is not dense and allows you to enjoy the lily-clad water whilst giving protection from the winds which swirl around its basin.* At a junction fork L on the public bridleway to Watendlath. (The blue route returns through the forest to the car park.)

Go on the shortcut path a few yards then join another track bearing L along it. From here look back left for a view over the tarn to The Beacon visited on Walk 36. In about 100yds go R on a rising path, the ancient bridle path to Watendlath. Continue steeply to cairns. where the gradient eases, and on to the edge of the forest. Go through the double-gated deer fence and turn R into a different world. *The soft upland moor is a sharp contrast to the stone-pathed forest. The paths are animal trods, grasses, rushes and mosses cushion the ground and there are boggy patches to be skirted or wallowed in.* Keep along the forest fence side and go quietly as deer are often to be seen. Stay with the fence as it turns a corner and make your way between an old sheepfold and the smooth toe of a glaciated rock. From the rock look ahead on the left and the gap of Stone Hause is seen. The path leads towards it (do not

A spine of ice smoothed rock provides dry passage at Stone Hause

fork down right towards the forest) but bend L into the hause where the ribbons of rock hold linear pools. Beyond the gap is a basin and the wetland which gathers waters into tiny Launchy Tarn.

Turn R along the rocky spine of the hause and holding a parallel line to the forest edge find your way up Stone Hause Knott summit where the Ice Age deposited a stone erratic which makes an excellent viewpoint seat. To the north see Skiddaw, Great Calva and Blencathra and to the east the Helvellyn range. Go over to the poised erratic then into the gap before the next little hump. Turn R towards the forest and down 25yds to easy ground by shattered rocks. Bend L on a trod towards a perched stone then through a trough bounded by a stone-topped craglet on its right. Make your way ahead aiming for the valley of Launchy Gill seen between the interlocking folds of our developing rill. *The bright purple flowers of the carnivorous butterwort abound (as do the midges) in this area.* As you walk look left for the remains of an old sheepfold and a smooth-topped rock bluff protruding into the valley. Keep well right of the bluff and descend towards a bundle of spiky rocks with rowan trees on a trod which tracks dry along the edge of the bracken to Launchy Gill.

Cross the gill, go through the wall to an imaginary 'path' and turn R. As the stream enters the forest it plunges down the gorge explored by the Launchy Gill Nature Trail but we cannot reach this from here and are captive on the moor. Circle L along the fence and jump ditches and bogs to an old sheepfold. Keep between the fence and the wall then move L through the wall at a convenient hole sooner rather than later. The trees at the forest edge, toppled by gales, struggle to raise new growth from the remaining lifelines of their root systems and delicate rowans scent the air with their profuse blossom.

Keep by the fence up a bank and through a boulder and rock gap. At the highest point and 100yds to the right in the forest is Fisher Crag and from its cairn is a wonderful view of Thirlmere and St John's Vale.

Carry on along the fenceside and descend to a wall corner with an old roofless building in the felled woodland. Turn L and summoning your determination make your way up the wallside conquering a short rough passage to go over the brow to a ladder stile. Ignore the stile, it leads to trouble, just angle L to cross the top of Fisher Gill and turn R along the narrow path. Go along to the forest corner, through a gap in a wall and down the path past the Armboth dyke (see p.164 para.2) to the road. Turn R then L into the car park (toilets).

THE SHORE PATH: You could make a rapid return along the road, but views are limited and it is only worthwhile if you are short of time. *The shore path has much to recommend it; the road is hidden and the path winds in and out of intriguing* *coves, the tree fringe is varied and interesting, overgrown walls and ruins hint at a way of life in the dale before it was flooded.*

Armboth Car Park to the bridge over Launchy Gill via the shore path: see Walk 35 pps171/172

CONTINUATION FROM LAUNCHY GILL: Ignore the path right leading up to the road and Launchy Gill lay-by. Continue slightly left downhill through the coppiced silver birches. *A rise over a little promontory gives an exceedingly pretty view down the lake past Deergarth How island with Raven Crag rising to the western skyline beyond.* Pass Hawes How Island and soon a rising gradient brings awareness of the nearby road and the rising walls of Rough Crag looming above. Go through a gap in a wall among a stand of old pines where a divertion onto a headland provides a peaceful waterscape worthy of a picture. Carry on past a shining holly and soon the path rises to the road gate at Hause Point.

The gate and steps immediately left lead up to a seat which commands an impressive aspect over the upper Thirlmere valley.

Turn L on the road through the cutting and go L through the gate to find the continuing path. Cross Hause Gill, overhung by a fine holly. *Look across the lake where, between the plantations, Brownrigg Gill tumbles down its ravine past the dressing floor and spoil of the Helvellyn Mine.* Pass through a close canopy planting of fir. At a group of ruins with yew and rhododendrons an old track between the crumbling walls emerges and is used briefly by our path before homing its way to Wythburn beneath the water. Pass another old walled path on the right and go on through the forest until Dob Gill can be seen making an unmistakable entry to the lake between high stony banks. Little footbridges help the path over tributary streams and the path bends R up the hill to the road and Dobgill car park.

WALK 35: Launchy Gill Trail from Armboth

SUMMARY: (See sketch map p167) The Thirlmere lakeshore path runs through a mixture of trees, not all dense, not all conifer, with attractive views across the lake. The Launchy Gill trail is steep, stony, slippery if wet, but gives exquisite views of riotous cascades and visits

Distance:	3 miles (4¾km)
Grade:	Easy, but steep and rough in parts on the trail.
Height gain:	360ft (110m)
Terrain:	Forest and lake shore
High point:	951ft (290m)
Map:	OL4, HSW-CL

the remarkable Cop Stone, the Bowder-stone's little brother.

HOW TO GET THERE AND PARKING: Armboth car park on the west side of Thirlmere (toilets).

THE WALK: Go through the gate onto the shore and turn R. Immediately look for the remnants of a path, its set stones pleading for remembrance as the vegetation gnaws at the last traces of the hamlet. *There are wonderful views over Thirlmere in spite of the rough shoreline, even in winter when the streams are gushing and the clouds hang low over the fells.* Go into the coppiced wood and look for the giant monkey puzzle tree (Chile pine) on the right of the path recognizable at path level by the distinctive pattern on the bark of its towering trunk. If you reach the end of a wall go back 10yds, you have passed it. *The tree is a reminder of its earlier life in the grounds of now submerged Armboth Hall.*

Continue along the path, cross a wooden footbridge over Fisher Gill and on through the plantation. Keep leftish above the shore for best views over the lake. Pass slivers of old walls and onto a tiny headland. Birds call in the broadleaf woodland fringe where all hints of the road above are hidden by the denser coniferous plantation. Cross a bridge over a small stream then pass through a dark grove of mature fir and their offspring. Pass by two old walls to the next view looking along the lake to the dam. Keep L of the wall and descend to the next bay where Deergarth How Island stands in the lake. At the next wall gap look up right to see the shoulder of Fisher Crag.

The Cop Stone

Go over a footbridge and through a boulder clearing replanted with broadleaves to an area of silver birch. A few steps lead to a wall end then look for steps down left by a great boulder to the nearest point of the island.

If the 'tide' is out take a stroll onto the 'causeway' for an exclusive sight of the valley. The deep side valley on the near west is Launchy Gill, our objective. Return to the path and after crossing a wire-trod bridge, pass a recently felled area to a kissing gate. On approaching Launchy Gill bend R to cross the bridge (signpost) and turn R to the road. Across and a few yards left is the entrance to the Launchy Gill Forest Trail but it is worth going onto the road bridge to peer into the plunging gill.

LAUNCHY GILL FOREST TRAIL: We have always found the leaflet box to be empty so here is a brief description.

Go on the managed and fenced path up the left-hand side of the gill. Autumn colours in the gill are beautiful unless the wind has stripped the summer garment away.

At a path junction by a wooden handrail:

a)   Turn L up the steep path to reach the Cop Stone (a fine viewpoint).

Return the same way to the path junction.

a) Ahead up the slight path to the left of the gill for waterfall viewing. Return the same way to the path junction.

b) Turn R to continue. Descend to the bridge over the grill and wire-trod walkway then follow the path down the woodland to the road.

RETURN TO START: a) Turn L and walk along the road to Armboth car park. Not recommended in summer because of increased traffic.

b) Return by the outward shore path. The path opposite connects with the shore path.

Cop Stone

A shapely balanced erratic boulder left in its precarious position by retreating ice. **The Steading Stone**, which marked the spot where manorial courts were held, now lies under water where Launchy Gill enters the lake.

WALK 36: Harrop Tarn and The Beacon

The Beacon and Nab Crags from Birk Crag

SUMMARY: A short walk packed with interest and variety. A pleasing stroll by the lakeshore is followed by a climb through the forest on an excellent pitched path to beautiful Harrop Tarn; rather aloof and inaccessible.

Out of the forest we visit a couple of small summits with grand views along the trench of Thirlmere to Blencathra. The Beacon is a fine objective.

HOW TO GET THERE AND PARKING: Park at Steel End car park, west from the A591 main Dunmail Raise road near the southern end of Thirlmere.

THE WALK: Set off from the parking through a kissing gate and along the footpath leading towards the lake. *The pleasure is immediately apparent in the scent of the pines and the trickle of water as Wyth Burn flows towards the reservoir.* The path soon turns through a garden of mosses and head-high grasses to run parallel with the lake shore. Soon a gap in the waterside alders opens and you can look across to the deep-cut valley of Whelpside Gill and the tiny white Wythburn church. *In times of low water the line of the track to the old bridge can be traced, and the head of the lake becomes a green swathe.*

Waymark poles and duckboards ensure no problems in route-finding. *The view up the valley is of a sweeping U-shaped profile cradling the pass of Dunmail Raise.*

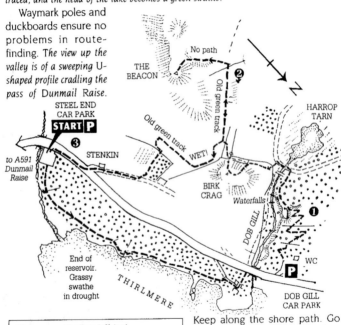

Distance:	3 miles (4¾km)
Grade:	Moderate
Height gain:	777ft (237m)
Terrain:	Low fell.
Summits	Birk Crag - 1170ft (357m)
	The Beacon - 1312ft (400m)
Map:	OL4, HSW-CL

Keep along the shore path. Go through a gate in a fence then onward to make a R bend by a gate and ruin then turn L to walk beside the wall for a short while. At an overgrown ruin turn L between dark walls and through a stand of stately pines to a kissing gate at the road.

Ignoring the footpath directly opposite, turn R across Dobgill Bridge and walk 100yds along the road to turn L into Dob Gill car park (toilets). Go straight through and on the path signed to Harrop Tarn.

The pitched-stone path rises steeply through a gate in the deer fence. Tall trees give a tranquil atmosphere to the climb until the silence is broken by the sound of falling water which beckons you aside to rest and admire Dob Gill falls. Continue up the less steep path to Harrop Tarn. Turn L to a channel lined with water lilies, which begins its flow between large stepping-stones before splashing under a footbridge and away to the valley. Choose your crossing and walk ahead for 100yds then turn L through the deer fence and R up a narrow path through the bracken parallel to the wall/fence. *As you climb do not neglect to look back at the tarn, beautiful in its sombre setting.* As soon as the angle eases, and a ladder stile at a meeting of walls is in view well ahead, turn L on a narrow path past a clump of juniper to gain the ridge of Birk Crag. Turn R to the summit cairn for a panorama of Thirlmere with Blencathra (north), Helvellyn (east) and the next objective The Beacon with its square cairn (south). Walk along the ridge then down towards the ladder stile to a gap in the wall and go over the step stile by the gate.

Turn R passing the ladder stile and follow the wall on the left over a hummock to find and go through a gap in this wall. A few yards ahead is the shepherd's pony path.

View over Thirlmere from The Beacon

SHORT RETURN: Turn L down the shallow valley which steepens and becomes wet. Keep down by the forest edging wall where old set stones still remain. At a fenced area turn R onto the old path again which takes a sharp bend at a scree gully to reach a strip of woodland by a wall. Turn R through the gate with the wood to your left and go steeply down the pasture to a track. Follow this R and cross a bridge made of recycled gateposts to Stenkin Barn. Go straight through the gates and yard to the road. Turn R and walk the short distance, with a view across Wythburn to Steel End, to the car park.

TO CONTINUE: Turn R on the green shepherd's pony path from Stenkin. Round a rocky rib to enter an open wide valley, a complete contrast to the forest scene. Pass a wall end and on to a gap in a broken wall. Leave the path and bend slightly L to mount a little bluff. From there pass to the left of some boulders and up the final slope of The Beacon to the top. *"What a con!" we hear you say when the solid squat Beacon cairn is not what you expected, but you cannot fault its plinth, which offers a seat with a backrest, or the spectacular view and the onward ridge that beckons.*

TO RETURN: Retrace the route to join Short Return.

It is tempting to continue the walk for another mile along the rocky summits of Nab Crags which stretch before you, but this is very rough and trackless. The reward is in negotiating the jumble of small craggy knolls and two tiny tarns. Do not go further as the moor becomes boring and there is no easy way into the Wythburn valley.

CHAPTER 5
Patterdale

One of Lakeland's most popular valleys, Patterdale with its numerous side valleys has plenty of variety to offer. There are lovely walks to combine with a sail on the lake steamer; there are walks so popular that the paths are visible on satellite photographs; and walks which include miners' and shepherds' paths which can still be walked in comparative solitude.

We select some modest summits which require a degree of effort to attain, but provide satisfying views and a mountain atmosphere. Unlike Borrowdale, parking is adequate and you will usually find a place even at busy times. An exception is the south-east shore of Ullswater where the narrow lane to Howtown may be overcrowded in high season. The walks here can be accessed less stressfully by steamer, but check the return sailings first!

Fell pony

WALK 37: Steamer Walk over Bonscale Pike to Pooley Bridge

ARTHUR'S   BONSCALE
PIKE   TOWER

The Ullswater steamer arrives at Pooley Bridge

SUMMARY: To combine a good walk with a lake steamer trip is a recipe for a memorable outing. There is a popular low level path, indicated on the map, but the route we describe traverses the fell rim above the south-eastern side of the lake. We feel that the extra effort incurred to reach the tops is so worthwhile, particularly as height is gained relatively easily on a long forgotten green path which zig-zags steadily up the hill. Once on top all the hard work is over and it is easy walking for the rest of the day. The cairns, or towers, were built as landmarks, now they serve as glorious viewpoints. You may meet many fell ponies on this walk; gentle, sturdy beasts, a joy to behold.

The steamers run from the end of March to the end of October and a convenient boat leaves Pooley Bridge at 12.00 midday or 12.35pm according to the season (refreshments).

HOW TO GET THERE AND PARKING: Riverside parking at Pooley Bridge at the northern end of Ullswater. For shops, toilets and information go over the bridge to the village centre.

Distance:	6¼ miles (10km)
Grade:	Strenuous
Height gain:	1410ft (430m)
Terrain:	Medium fell. Green paths.
Summits	Bonscale Pike - 1718ft (520m)
	Arthur's Pike - 1747ft (530m)
Map:	OL5, HSW-EL

THE WALK: Leave the car park at Pooley Bridge and approach the jetty either on a path running through adjoining woodland turning L at a junction to arrive at the road just beyond the jetty, or go along the road.

The sail to Howtown gives wonderful views and refreshments are available in the saloon.

KEAWASSA BEDA FELL HALLIN FELL PLACE FELL

From the Howtown jetty go along the shore path (ignore the footbridge to the right) to the road. Turn R for 50yds until, having crossed the bridge over Fusedale Beck, turn L immediately along the streamside public bridleway. The path passes an old stone bridge where we keep straight on through the hamlet on a rising road which follows the stream into Fusedale. Pass a neglected clapper bridge then look back over the rooftops where Hallin Fell thrusts into the lake, being joined by a 75ft deep underwater ridge to Skelly Nab on the opposite side, the general depth to either side being 125ft. At a junction go straight ahead signed public bridleway to Cote Farm. Go to the cattle-grid then turn L to Pooley Bridge. From here examine the northern daleside above. It is seamed by ancient pathways which we use for our onward route following the rising intake wall then a zig-zag line to gain the top of the gill easily.

Cross the clapper bridge and turn L to a stile leading onto the private drive of Mellguards house. Keep ahead up the drive to the fell gate with blue waymark arrow. Go through and, leaving the bridleway lower route to Pooley Bridge, turn R on narrow trods keeping close to the intake wall. As you walk, the lesser hills surrounding Fusedale take their turn to create the view: Steel Knotts and Pikeawassa to the south, Gowk Hill at the valley head and the slopes of Brock Crag in front of us. On nearing the highest point of the wall a sheep trod traverses a rising ramp. Follow the path as it diverges uphill from the wall. It may be partially obscured by bracken. Watch carefully for a little cairn on the L which indicates a turn L on the start of the zig-zag path. At a reedy bluff, with a scene across the lake to the round dome of Great Mell Fell (Walk 49) and Blencathra, turn R on the next leg. Continue to climb relatively easily up the very steep slope. Pass an area of scree (cairn) and continue the rhythmic plod broken only by stops enforced by the expanding vista of the higher mountains (cairns) until approaching a junction of old green paths at the gill. Ignore a groove to the right but go uphill a few yards to find a L turn and the continuation of the zig-zags to where the gradient eases and the gill fizzles out. The path tracks right with rushes now growing in its groove, so make your own way aiming up the slope a short distance to the saddle at the top of the gill and its ridgetop path.

The moor between Brock Crag and Swarth Fell is a featureless desolate spot, apart from the ridgetop path. Turn L along it and the splendid panorama will cheer your way along the 1/4 mile to the cairn on Bonscale Pike. Take care to hold your direction as the guiding cairn dips from sight as the path undulates. Continue along the rim of the fell to Bonscale Tower with its varied well-built, tall cairns, each a prominent landmark with a breathtaking view over Ullswater. Now continue on a narrow traversing path beyond the last built 'stone man' to overlook Swarthbeck Gill. Our next objective, Arthur's Pike, can be seen across the gill, but don't take a direct line to it. Bear right to traverse into the gill without losing too much height, and cross it by the site of a ruined sheepfold. Once more join the groove of an old path slanting leftwards across the hillside

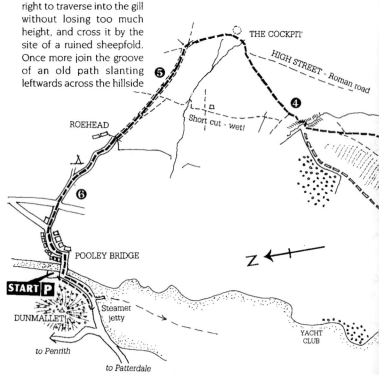

THE COCKPIT

HIGH STREET - Roman road

5

4

ROEHEAD

Short cut - wet!

6

POOLEY BRIDGE

Z ←

START **P**

DUNMALLET

Steamer jetty

to Penrith

to Patterdale

YACHT CLUB

to join a better path from the Roman road to the main valley at a multi-path junction (cairn). Turn L. Leave the well cairned main path to make a short detour left to visit the summit of Arthur's Pike. Shortcut back to the main path and turn L along it. It is now an easy freewheel down the broad path with widespread views over the Solway to Scotland's Border hills and over the Eden valley to the Pennines on the eastern horizon. Ahead and closer at hand is Heughscar Hill, its limestone slopes being the site of many prehistoric dwellings. As the descent steepens ignore a path to the right and keep straight on to meet a wall by a gill.

Turn R, cross the gill and follow a path which traverses the hillside to join the Roman road just before a ford over Elder Beck. Branch L along it to the Cockpit, a neolithic stone circle. Turn L passing a ford across a tributary of Elder Beck to a junction and cairn. Turn L on the dirt track and continue ahead until meeting the surfaced road at the Barton Fell Common gate. Keep ahead to Pooley Bridge. Cross straight over the Penrith-Howtown road to St Paul's church. Turn L into the village (refreshments, shops, toilets, information). Cross the river bridge to the car park.

The Lake Steamers

The *Raven* (1889) and *Lady of the Lake* (1877) are the two old steamers, now refurbished with diesel engines, which ply the lake.

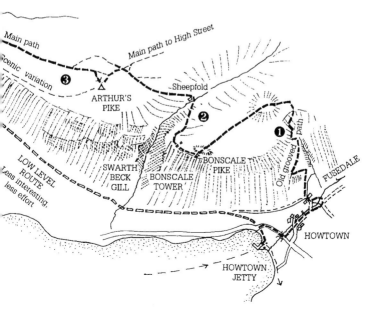

WALK 38: Hallin Fell and the Three Dales

Hallin Fell and Howtown Pier

SUMMARY: The short walk up Hallin Fell with its fine obelisk and panorama of Ullswater is an ideal introduction to hill walking for children if you return the same way. This walk continues over the top on a little known path to join the lakeshore. Dense bracken may be a problem in season. Thence an intriguing route visits Boredale, over a fine little col to Martindale, then follows an ancient track to the ridge overlooking Fusedale. The finish over Pikeawassa, with its striking summit rock, is along a rarity in Lakeland - a green ridge path.

HOW TO GET THERE AND PARKING: Take the narrow road along the south-east shore of Ullswater, from Pooley Bridge to Howtown,

Distance:	5 miles (8km)
Grade:	Strenuous
Height gain:	1804ft (550m) in four undulations.
Terrain:	Valley and low fell. Green paths.
Summits:	Hallin Fell - 1273ft (388m)
	Howsteadbrow - 852ft (260m)
	Pikeawassa - 1417ft (432m)
Map:	OL5,HSW-EL

and continue towards Martindale and Sandwick. Go up the hairpin bends to the top of the pass separating Steel Knotts and Hallin Fell. Park by the church of St Peter-in-Martindale.

THE WALK: Start directly up a broad green path up Hallin Fell to a wall corner and a spaghetti junction of paths. Keep ahead making straight for a pile of stones in a gap on the horizon. *The energy-burning gradient demands a rest to look left into picturesque Martindale, renowned for its little church which we visit later and its herd of deer which roam the lonely combes at the valley's head.* Go ahead over the brow on a continuing green path to the next gap. The extra height now allows you to see all three valleys of our walk, Fusedale, Martindale and Boredale. Bend R and in a few yards the summit is seen on the right. Note the little cairn just ahead then mount R to the summit obelisk and vantage point for a wonderful lake and mountain panorama.

Return to the little cairn and carry on a few yards. Our onward path can be seen below winding through the bracken on the Ullswater side towards the northern end of Hallinhag Wood. Now descend 25yds and turn L just before a patch of scree, cross the shelving grassy slope and turn R on a grassy rake with a gradually developing path. The path becomes clearer and

The monumental cairn on Hallin Fell

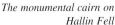

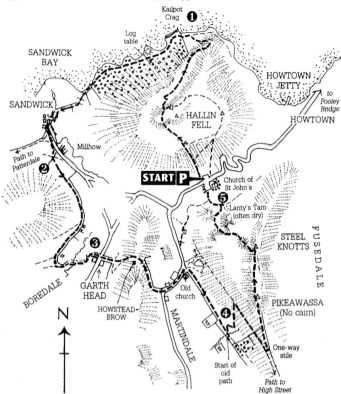

when approaching scattered, weatherbeaten hawthorns ignore all paths right. *At a small bluff a pretty scene shows the lake reflecting the far tree-fringed shore, the surface broken by the service launch and the air filled with cheeps, caws, chirps and quacks as the waterside woodland nears.* The path now bends left, steepens and tracks down right of an oak-decked crag to the shore path.

Turn L and go through the kissing gate at Kailpot Crag and into the wood. Pass ice-scored rock, a log seat-cum-table and leave the wood at a kissing gate by the sandy shore and short turf of Sandwick Bay. Carry on along the well signed path through the fields to Sandwick, turn L then R over the Sandwick Beck bridge to the road.

Turn L and up the road towards Martindale Hause. One hundred yards past a junction and footpath sign angle R by a tiny stream on a rising path to meet a wall corner. To the north is a fine profile of Hallin Fell. Ignore the path right to Sleet Fell and keep ahead close above the wall to make a gradual traverse round the end of the ridge into Boredale. Cross a small stream and keep by the wall. Ignoring the right of way path rising right to Place Fell, keep on the permissive path by the wall. Join a wider path, swing L to a stile and cross the Boredale Beck on an old clapper stones footbridge. Go up the track to Garth Head Farm. Keep straight across the surfaced lane and up ahead to a stile with public footpath sign. It is a steep climb straight up the wallside to Howsteadbrow but a sharp eye may spy some zig-zags to ease the slope and a single shapely pine makes a lovely feature in the view up the little frequented dale. Go straight over the brow to look down into Martindale.

Continue down the path and follow the left-hand wall to a surfaced lane at Winter Crag Farm. Turn L over Howegrain Beck to the charmingly situated old parish church of St Martin. *Look inside, then sit outside for a view up the dale to The Nab, a striking cone, and Rampsgill Head, the imposing rugged terminus of the valley.* From here either make a short return or continue to see Fusedale and Pikeawassa and Steel Crags.

SHORT RETURN: From the church turn L along the road for 500yds then fork R on an old green path. Carry on below a cottage and round the knoll to the church of St Peter and the start.

TO CONTINUE: Turn R on the public footpath above the intake wall. Examine the hillside above to pick out the upward traversing path which we aim to join. Pass a corner in the intake wall (a single barn in the field below confirms progress). Carry on to an ash tree 25yds before a small stream. Turn back sharp L on an old green path (small cairn) and mount its abandoned zig-zags up the fellside. (If the wallside path narrows and you reach the wood you have gone too far.) Meet the upper traversing path and turn R. This balcony

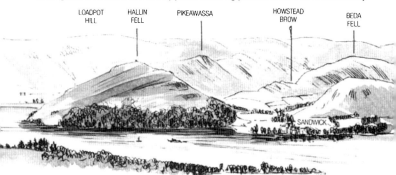

The route of the walk is clearly seen from the Gowbarrow Balcony Path (Walk 48)

path shows Martindale, split by The Nab into two upper forks, Ramps Gill and Bannerdale, a scene of wild splendour. Go through a gap in a cross wall and on to the pass with a ridge-top wall.

An old stile invites you to go over into Fusedale, but it is a con, with path and steps on one side, bare wall, deep heather and a rough plunging fellside on the other. Turn L along the ridgepath (leaving our traversing path to continue on its way to High Street) and as you go look into isolated Fusedale and the barely visible old path used by Walk 37 as it mounts towards High Street and the Roman road across the head of the dale. Go through a cross wall and up the steepled cone of Pikeawassa to its spiky summit. Carry on to the next cairned summit of Steel Knotts where there is a face on view of our route up Hallin Fell and the northern end of Ullswater.

Do not carry on along the ridge path which descends to Howtown. Drop down L into a shallow rushy hollow and the church by the start can be seen below. Cross the hollow and go over or round a tiny knoll on the left to find a narrow path which leads down keeping left of a series of outcrops and a lower crag with scree. Pass the last knoll on its right, past the usually semi dry puddle of Lanty's Tarn, to a wall and wide path. Go ahead to the church, road and the start.

The Old Church of St Martin

It was built in 1633 on the site of an earlier chapel of 1266. Some traces of the original chapel, from which the dale took its name, are visible on the south side of the building. In 1881 it was superseded by St Peter's as the parish church of Martindale. In the north-east corner of the churchyard is an ancient yew, around 700 years old, used by the renowned bowmen of the dale for making their bows.

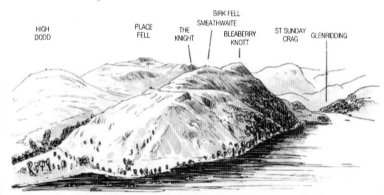

Place Fell from the Balcony Path on Gowbarrow Fell

WALK 39:
Steamer Walk -
from Howtown to Glenridding over Place Fell

Distance:	7 miles (11¼km) (Circuit from Sandwick 7½ miles 12km)	Summits:	Birk Fell - Smeathwaite 1574ft (480m)
			Birk Fell - Bleaberry Knott 1673ft (510m)
Grade:	Strenuous		
Height gain:	1892ft (577m)		Place Fell 2155ft (657m)
Terrain:	Medium fell with some pathless walking.	Map:	OL5, HSW-EL

WALK 40:
Steamer Walk -
from Howtown to Glenridding by the Shore

Distance:	6¼ miles (10km)	Terrain:	Stony, well walked paths.
Grade:	Easy	Map:	OL5, HSW-EL
Height gain:	426ft (130m) in undulations.		

SUMMARY: A steamer sail on Ullswater to Howtown with a walk back to Glenridding is a very popular outing. Most people opt for the low level path which undulates close to the shore (Walk 40) but with a bit more effort the rewards are so much greater. Our Walk 39 over Place Fell eschews the normal path (which traverses a viewless plateau) in favour of a little used route along the fell rim overlooking Ullswater. The climb over the twin summits of Birk Fell reveal a feast of views across the lake into a succession of valleys and peaks. Indeed the aerial view over Glenridding from Bleaberry Knott is particularly spectacular.

Although our route uses some indistinct paths the way is straightforward. At peak times when the steamer service is crowded an alternative circuit is suggested, from Sandwick where there is space to park. The steamer service from Glenridding to Howtown runs all year, with many more sailings from March to October.

HOW TO GET THERE AND PARKING:
1. The circuit of Place Fell from Sandwick
From Pooley Bridge take the road to Howtown on the narrow alpine-type road past St John's Church. Turn right to Sandwick and there is a parking area at the end of the road by the bridge.*

2. Patterdale to Howtown by steamer returning along the shore path
Park at the Pay and Display by the pier at Patterdale and board the steamer to Howtown (refreshments on board).

WALKS 39 & 40 HOWTOWN TO SANDWICK BAY
START: At the end of the jetty turn R over the footbridge, signed public footpath Sandwick, and go along the shore path, with the cottages of the hamlet clustered at the entrance to Fusedale on the left, east, through two meadows towards Hallin Fell. Turn L into an enclosed path by a new plantation and up steps to a kissing gate. Turn R and walk by the wall above a cottage. Over the wall the fell-slopes to the east of the lake now appear more interesting. Stone pillars on Bonscale Pike and Arthur's Pike point skywards and a series of old green paths criss-cross the steep slopes on their way to Brock Crag Moor (Walk 37) and High Street.

The gently rising path levels and traverses round the foot of Hallin Fell. The wall turns down left and leaves a magnificent view of the north end of the lake. *Sit on an iron seat, perfectly placed, to admire it.* Progress a short way to Geordie Crag, a rock buttress protruding into the lake, *where the fishermen of*

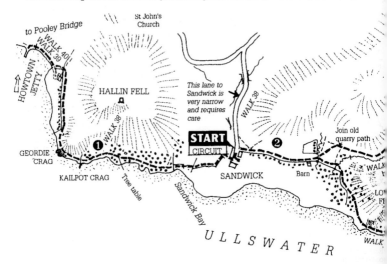

old strung a net across the shallow narrowing to Skelly Nab to catch the schelly, a freshwater herring which was once abundant. Descend steeply by oak trees to the shore at Kailpot Crag.

Go through a kissing gate at Kailpot Crag and into woodland. Pass ice-scored rock, a log seat-cum-table and leave the wood at a kissing gate by the sandy shore of Sandwick Bay. *This is a spot where children will love to play on the short turf. Ideal for a break.* Carry on along the well signed path through the fields to Sandwick, turn L then R over the Sandwick Beck bridge to the road.

Turn L and up the road (parking area, **Sandwick alternative Start***) then go R up the stony short-cut path alongside Townhead Cottage signed public bridleway and along the well-used path by the intake wall. *Ahead the cairn on Low Birk Fell distinguishes it from its multipeak skyline.* A peep over the wall across Ullswater reveals Gowbarrow where sharp eyes can see the traversing

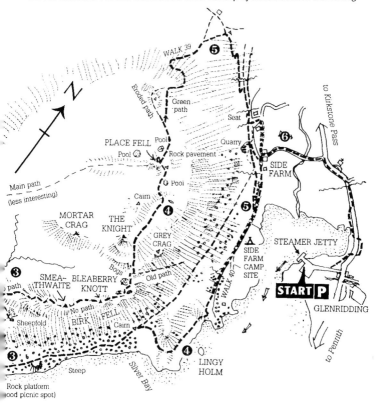

balcony path and viewpoint seat of Walk 48 above Yew Crag. *At a barn notice the red sandstone coping stones and carved corbels holding the copings in place. On the fell opposite, a walled enclosure sheltered by old pines*

PLACE
FELL

provides hay for the barn. Cross a gill. The routes diverge here.

WALK 39 VIA PLACE FELL: Leave the shore path and turn diagonally L up a path of barely dented grass which soon becomes recognisable as an old quarry track rising steadily across the hillside above a boulder and triangular stone. The angle eases and the track runs by Scalehow Beck

where birch-clad cascades clatter along before sliding over the ice-smoothed rock of Scalehow Force. *A wonderful view north of the lake curving round Hallin Fell is but a curtain raiser of things to come.*

When opposite the col between Low Birk Fell and Smeathwaite turn R to cross the beck easily 50yds above a line of alder trees and walk up the shallow depression on a slight trod through the bracken on turf starred with yellow celandine in spring.

As soon as the gradient eases (a rocky gap with a sprouting tree is seen in profile ahead) meet a cross trod and turn L along it for 25yds to gain a broad spur. Turn R and make your own way up wandering around to suit

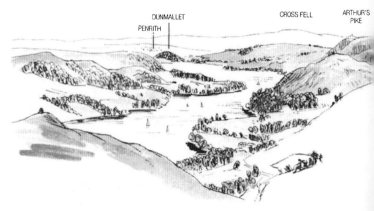

PENRITH   DUNMALLET   CROSS FELL   ARTHUR'S
                                            PIKE

GREY CRAG | ARNISON CRAG | DOVE CRAG | ST SUNDAY CRAG | DOLLYWAGGON PIKE | NETHERMOST PIKE | HELVELLYN | CATSTYE CAM

GLENRIDDING

View from Bleaberry Fell. The onward route is shown

yourself but always aiming for a pointed pimple, the highest point ahead. *Across the Scalehow valley to the east runs our old path, terminating at a quarry in the Borrowdale Volcanics, then continuing as the modern 'motorway' up Place Fell, which is hidden behind the bulk of Mortar Crag with the shapely pyramid of The Knight drawing the eye to the right. To the north-west Blencathra raises its ridge with Carrock Fell on its far right but the choice view is still down Ullswater.*

The final pull is quite steep but the view to the far side of Ullswater and the wooded valley of Aira Force offer compensation because on arriving at the pimple you discover it has disappeared. Carry on still towards the highest point where a cairn identifies the summit of Smeathwaite. *Sit down 25yds to the north-west where there is a plunging edge giving a remarkable view of the U-shaped valley of Glencoyne with Raise behind.*

Ullswater from the spur of Smeathwaite

Press on, now on an intermittent ridge path, towards the next cairned peak. Pass a hollow with a white quartz stone, little pools (or foul bog holes according to the season) then up the slope to the cairn on Bleaberry Knott. *The view is brilliant. Glenridding lies set in the green meadows of its dale with the grand mountains of the Helvellyn Range behind.*

Survey the route ahead from this point - beyond an area of glowing bog our path mounts a grassy slope to the right of The Knight, its shapely profile merged with Place Fell behind.

Descend the rock cap of Bleaberry Knott and follow the narrow path to the right of the upper bog. Turn L to cross between the upper and lower bogs and wind round rocks and through a gap to face the path previously observed. Cross the intervening ground keeping high to avoid the wet. Sheep trods will lead you to the foot of The Knight and a cairn at a junction with a path from the valley. Keep L up the path to The Knight col and look north for a pleasing view over Bleaberry Knott and beyond the dome of Great Mell Fell to the Scottish hills.

Follow the path past a cairn through an area of peat with pools off to the right and as you move towards Place Fell the widespread scenery is cut off. Pass a cairn on the left and shortly a view of Grisedale with St Sunday Crag on its left appears. *As you approach the final summit rocks look left where a collection of upright split rocks are a fine example of exfoliation (frost shattering on the cleavage).* Make the final assault on the summit, pass a small cairn and arrive at the triangulation pillar with a benchmark on its north side.

Go straight over the top, south, and down the summit rocks (wind shelter 25yds off to the right). Pass pools, now on a wide path and down the end of the summit plateau. The main path goes over a cairned knoll but fork diagonally R down the old green path and meet the main path again beyond the knoll. *Look back at the worn-out runnel we have avoided yet still retained the outlook over the head of Patterdale with Brothers Water at the foot of the Kirkstone Pass and the deep Hartsop valley to its east.* Go down the cairned, wide, worn path but halt occasionally to look ahead. *Erosion streaks pattern the steep valley sides of Boredale. Ahead on Boredale Hause is a rectangular ruin, the remains of an old chapel, with the continuation of the main ridge path, previously an old mine quarry track up Angle Tarn Pikes.*

On approaching the Hause and just before a cairn fork R down a shortcut green path to meet the path coming from a junction by the ruin and turn R at a large cairn.

Descend the fell enjoying views into Patterdale and on a zig-zag continue R where a small path joins from the left. The poor path does improve, passes a Victorian iron seat (Jubilee 1897) and joins a major lower path above the intake wall. Cross a small stream immediately before a path junction above Place Fell Cottage.* *

View south from the descent of Place Fell

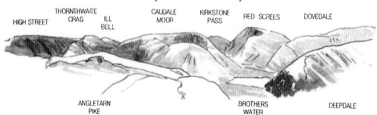

HIGH STREET THORNTHWAITE CRAG ILL BELL CAUDALE MOOR KIRKSTONE PASS RED SCREES DOVEDALE

ANGLETARN PIKE BROTHERS WATER DEEPDALE

Above:
The old clapper bridge
in Fusedale is still used
by local traffic
(Walk 37)

Right:
The tall cairn of
Bonscale Tower is a
striking landmark with
widespread views. The
conical hill at the end of
Ullswater above Pooley
Bridge is Dunmallet,
site of an Iron Age fort
(Walk 37)

Above:
The bridleway out of Swindale traverses the crest of a moraine at Dod Bottom (Walk 55)

Left::
The Old Corpse road, well graded, with rock cuttings, provides a fine way to the fell top. Behind are the waterfalls of Hopgill Beck (Walk 54)

WALK 40: THE SHORE PATH TO SIDE FARM AND GLENRIDDING:
Proceed by the wall on the broad path which descends to cross Scalehow Beck at a footbridge. Little instruction is now needed as the prominent path, often described as one of the most beautiful in the country, runs trapped between Birk Fell and Ullswater. Pass through light juniper, birch and holly woodland with the undulating path giving a succession of vantage points showing breathtaking scenery. When high above Silver Bay ignore a huge cairn which indicates a fork over Silver Hill to circle the crag on the lakeside (right). Carry on past the campsite with a fine stepped gable barn. The end of the lake can now be seen and the buildings of Side Farm. Go into the farmyard (refreshments) and turn R signed to Glenridding. (Join Return to Glenridding at ***.)

RETURN TO GLENRIDDING**: Turn L down the streamside, cross a wooden bridge and go through a gate at the end of a surfaced road. Turn R on the public bridleway access road to Side Farm (refreshments). Turn L between the farm buildings, signed to Glenridding***, and on the farm track through the meadow, landing place of the RAF Mountain Rescue helicopter. Go over Goldrill Beck Bridge to the main road (for toilets turn left 500yds then turn right just past the Patterdale Hotel). Turn R past St Patrick's church and along the road using the footpaths provided to escape the traffic (see ⚡p209) and through the park (toilets) to turn R to the start.

RETURN TO SANDWICK: Stay on the upper R fork, a slightly rising green path to a quarry above Side Farm (refreshments). Cross the flat dressing floor and take the middle one of three paths branching across the rid. At the next

junction fork L to walk under the boughs of larches and a great beech. Join the main farm track and carry on past a typical Lakeland barn with stepped gable.

There is no need for further details of the route, just stay on the public bridleway signed to Howtown, but a few pointers will help to indicate progress. Pass the campsite with another fine barn and an area of mature woodland. Soon the way is barred by the knoll of Silver Crag. We recommend to go round its left side for views over the lake and easier walking

The woodland path by
Ullswater shore

rather than the stony path climbing the nick between the Crag and Birk Fell. Pass a huge cairn above Silver Bay where the nick path rejoins. The next stretch of woodland, the dark green of the juniper and holly contrasting with the delicate silver birch, is rendered doubly delightful if you have lingered into the evening. The surges of walkers will have gone, the birds fill the trees and the gentle light reflected by the water takes on a magical glow. When Hallin Fell is in sight the path curves away from the lake and after crossing the footbridge over Scalehow Beck meets the outward route at the barn, a few minutes from the start at Sandwick.

WALK 41: Angle Tarn from Hartsop

Spinning gallery, Hartsop

SUMMARY: A walk which includes a pleasing stroll along the valley, a gradual climb to the heights and a fine little summit overlooking Angle Tarn, a popular picnic spot in summer.

HOW TO GET THERE AND PARKING: Close to Brothers Water near the foot of Kirkstone Pass, a lane branches east to Hartsop. Drive through the most attractive hamlet to a large parking area.

THE WALK: Leave the parking area and return towards the hamlet. Turn R at a public footpath signpost and up the concreted track confirmed as heading for Rathmore. Go through a gate and as you gain height the wonderful spread of scenery begins. *Just over the wall and across the Hayeswater valley stands Hartsop Dodd, then across Patterdale*

Distance:	6½ miles (10km)
Grade:	Strenuous
Height gain:	1590ft (485m)
Terrain:	Valley and high fell. Wet in parts. Some rough paths.
Summits:	Angletarn Pike south summit - 1853ft (565m) Buck Crag - 1869ft (570m)
Map:	OL5, HSW-EL

from left to right High Hartsop Dodd, Dove Crag and Gavel Pike with Red Screes putting in a later appearance at the head of the valley as you pass through the fenced end of a crosswall. Brothers Water, surrounded by rich green water meadows, fills a depression in the flat glaciated

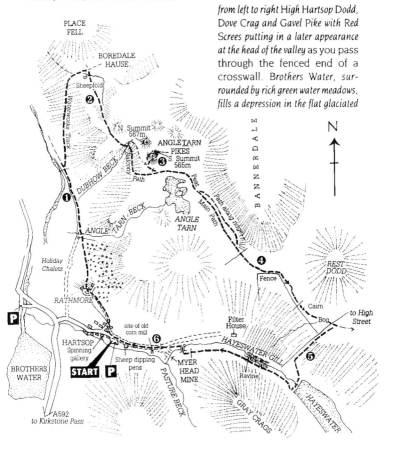

*Most of the route is visible from the
Hartsop above How ridge, (Walk 42)*

floor of the U-shaped valley. Pass a huge sycamore,
its roots flowing over the bedrock, their colour
merging with the weathered volcanic rock. Over
a rise and at a junction keep straight on (yellow
arrow waymarks) then bear R, signed Patterdale,
to a stile behind Grey Rigg cottage where a gate
leads onto the open fell. Views down Patterdale
are unrestricted by a stretch of light woodland as
progress is made along the line of the intake wall.
Go over a ladder stile by Angle Tarn beck which
comes leaping down the fellside from the tarn in
a spectacular display. Our longer route to the tarn is more gentle.

Join a bridleway coming from Hartsop at a lower level. Continue along
the path which is separated from the wall by Dubhow Beck in its short stretch
of leat. Pass a group of larches above a barn. This area is usually a winter
feeding station for the sheep and they stand their ground while you pass. At
a junction just before a cyclists' warning notice fork R and up the rough path.
*Above to the right buzzards soar across the craggy face of Dubhow, to the left lies Deepdale
and Gavel Pike takes on a prominence far beyond its stature.* The stony nature of the
path ends with the waterworks interest and becomes easier underfoot.
Ignore any paths branching off and just as you begin to turn away from
Patterdale with the curve of the path Striding Edge and Helvellyn come into
view on the western horizon. Do not be tempted onto a gentle reedy path

Angle Tarn

ANGLETARN PIKES   ANGLE TARN   REST DODD

branching left on approaching the last steep section. Keep plodding up, cross Stonebarrow Gill and up again to meet the path ascending from Patterdale and go along it a few strides to a cairn and flat area on a spoil heap, the redistribution centre for several paths.

Branch diagonally R and cross the stream taking a repaired path with your back to Place Fell. Make your way up the moor with your ears cocked; skylarks live hereabouts. Go through a narrow gap. This opens out at four large cairns which countdown to a view of Hartsop Dodd and at cairn zero the northern summit of Angle Tarn Pike 567m is seen on the left.

The path is now level. Fork R to cross Dubhow Beck and the fell on a fine balcony path which traverses the fellside. The cairned path uses a cut ledge to round a corner and Angle Tarn is in sight with the twin southern summit of Angletarn Pike 565m to the left.

TO ANGLETARN PIKE: Pass a flat-topped stone then in about 100yds look for a small path branching back sharp left and a meagre stone cairn hoping to identify it. The narrow path goes easily along to another larger cairn on a flat shoulder. Turn R and attack the steep grass to a gap with scree and pools. Turn L again and zig-zag up to the excellent summit 565m with extensive views. Return to the main path (see sketch map).

TO CONTINUE: Contour on the wide path above the tarn where, on its eastern side the peat is decorated with footprints and holes of all shapes and sizes and much jollity is to be had as you make progress. A more sober demeanour can be maintained by taking a parallel course on the ridge above. *Crows examine the terrain for remains of picnics and for those on the ridge, deer may be seen on The Nab of Bannerdale. The islands of Angle Tarn support a few trees which manage to survive the harsh weather and are safe from nibbling sheep.* The path

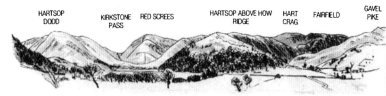

HARTSOP DODD — KIRKSTONE PASS — RED SCREES — HARTSOP ABOVE HOW RIDGE — HART CRAG — FAIRFIELD — GAVEL PIKE

Patterdale from near Hartsop

gradually becomes solid and you can either keep along it or, we recommend, look out just above the path for an old iron fence pole and supports shaped like a 'ban the bomb' sign on Buck Crags. Gain this and follow the line of the old fence which gradually angles away left along a broad ridge. At the highest point turn L for the summit. There is no cairn but the view down Bannerdale is impressive as are the crags at the head of the dale and our onward path along the top. (Note that the ROW path on the OS map is marked in the wrong place.)

Continue along the ridge gradually descending to rejoin the main path at a gate in a crosswall. Go through and onto the path seen from Buck Crag beside a broken-down wall. The path undulates and wriggles across the dale head then after passing pools and a wall corner makes a sweeping traverse by a fence for $1/4$ mile. The fence is replaced by a wall. Pass two large cairns and continue with the climb. The wall being followed now descends but keep on the level path and the best of luck in crossing the peat hags to Sulphery Gill and a gap in the cross wall. Hayeswater can be seen below and ahead is the path climbing steeply to The Knott and High Street. Turn R down the hill on a path parallel to the wall which gives an easy and scenic descent to the dam. Cross the footbridge and turn R down the valley on the wide waterworks path. Hayeswater Gill leaves the dam and splashes down through a series of falls, cascades and pools. *The Filter House building on the right indicates the line of the aqueduct which pumps water over Boredale Hause and supplies Penrith with drinking water.* Go through a gate in a cross wall and on past a barn and over a bridge. On the left is the deep valley of Threshthwaite Cove and at the confluence of Hayeswater Gill and Pasture Beck are the ruins of Myer Head Mine. *The walls of the wheel pit and the old dressing floor stand as a witness to the tragedy which befell the mine.* Go over a cattle-grid, note the remains of the old corn mill just below. The parking area lies just beyond the sheep pens.

Myer Head Mine

A very productive lead mine worked from an adit similar to others in the area. A 30-fathom shaft was sunk and this was always plagued with water which caused its demise. In 1877 water was struck and the miners fled with the flood lapping "at the heels of the last man up the ladder".

Hartsop

Once the major hamlet of the dale, it contains a wealth of lovely old buildings. There are houses with spinning galleries, where wool was spun in better light than inside, and an old corn drying building. Date stones, above the doorway, were common in the 17th century. The initials of the husband and wife's Christian names were either side of the surname initial above, with the date.

WALK 42:   Dovedale

Low Hartsop Hall

SUMMARY: This walk begins easily past tranquil Brothers Water, becomes more strenuous on pleasing grassy paths up Dovedale to culminate in an arduous stony gully which emerges on an ice-gouged shelf alongside the sombre Dove Crag. Return is easily made by the long undulating ridge of Hartsop above How, with its grandstand views; stunning with afternoon sun at your back and shimmering Ullswater in front.

HOW TO GET THERE AND PARKING: Between Patterdale village and Kirkstone Pass. Park at a loop of old road at the northern end of Brothers Water on either side of the river bridge.

Distance:	5¼ miles (8½km)
Grade:	Strenuous
Height gain:	1575ft (480m)
Terrain:	Valley and medium fell. Some rough paths.
Summit	Hartsop above How - 1902ft (580m)
Highest point:	In Houndshope Cove - 2132ft (650m)
Map:	OL5, HSW-CL

THE WALK: Leave the car park at the kissing gate by an information board and walk along the track leading to Hartsop Hall Farm. *It is a fairly smooth path rising imperceptibly through light woodland with delightful views of Brothers Water, edged by flat flowery pastures and the steep sides of the U-shaped valley rising to the rolling mountain tops. This path is suitable for families with a pushchair and toddlers (also wheelchairs if you can negotiate a few hiccoughs before reaching Hartsop Hall).*

Hartsop Hall is around 400 years old, the mullioned windows identifying the oldest part of the building.

(Note: Beyond the farm the path is rougher and eventually changes to the usual mountain footpath although it is easy walking as far as the bridge.)

At the farm the path divides. Ignore the public footpath to Kirkstone Pass and Scandale Pass and continue ahead past sheepfolds, barns and

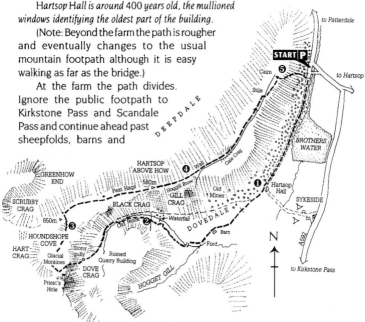

windbreak trees to a fork where we swing L to Dovedale. (The right-hand fork is a path slanting across the fellside at a higher level which does not allow the intimate views of the waterfalls.)

Our path follows the valley floor. The deep gill facing you is Hogget Gill, a popular scramble in dry weather. Level with the gill top and to its right is Dove Crag which our route passes to the right. Go through a kissing gate and continue. *The trees on the right are remnants of natural woodland and the ice-smoothed slopes opposite curve upwards to High Hartsop Dodd.*

On reaching the head of the valley go upstream, before the ford, 100yds to cross a little footbridge between a holly and an alder. Bend R where an intermittent path runs alongside the little side stream which you soon stride over. Continue up a green slope enhanced with scattered weather-torn trees and murmurs of falling water. The old footpath fallen into disuse rises straight up the slope and becomes a stony wet groove. Take care not to get on it but begin the serious climbing up the more popular streamside path. *The gradient is steep enough to warrant a breather so study the glacial legacy of Dovedale, the flat floor of Kirkstone and the uniformly rising contours of Hartsop Dodd.*

Keep up the narrow path alongside the ravine where the stream tumbles in sparkling cascades. Pass a slab of rock with a ribbon of quartz reminding us of a bit of geology to view a beautiful two-tier waterfall. Now mount steeply to join the old path and continue keeping on the streamside of a flat area unless you want to test the wax on your boots, to reach a ladder stile over a wall.

The ravine peters out into an upper valley. Continue until it is possible to turn R, jump over the stream and up the slope to join the high level path by a dead tree. Turn L and continue up the valley

Dove Crag now looms ahead and the 'mouth' high above the rock face is the Priest's Hole. The narrow path with its aspect of the V-shaped valley, the dominant face growing larger and the mouth grinning ever wider gives an interesting approach. Cross over a side stream, the excitement being proportional to the rainfall, then, as you walk along, view the way ahead. *Contain your horror as you see the cheery overtakers of 20 minutes ago reduced to ant-like proportions on the stony stalk of a path which rises sheer to the pass above and on the right of the crag.* Keep going and pass by a ruin to the right, the site of a small greenstone quarry.

Settle into low gear and using the tiny zig-zags which appear, mount gently. The last very steep bit is cairned as this is an important descent route from the tops. The gradient suddenly eases and the extensive bowl of Houndshope Cove opens out, complete with a large erratic boulder some 20yds away which will provide shelter from the ubiquitous breeze. *The Priest's Hole is gained by a narrow scrambly path up to the left. It requires a sure foot, a head for heights and if you go up do not forget that Dove Crag lies below.*

View from the Priest's Hole cave. The return along the Hartsop above How ridge is shown in the foreground

From the boulder look north (right) across the grass-covered humps of glacial drift to the broad ridge dividing Dovedale from Deepdale, which holds our descent path.

Keep in the same direction (NE) on the path which runs alongside a water-based peat hag to a spot where the path begins to climb left towards the main mountain ridge top. Here turn R and traverse the pathless wastes of the combe. Keep your navigation north and more or less level. A bit of an animal trod develops along a shelf. Work under a low crag then head for a cairn on the ridge. The cairn stands on the return path. The view from here is one of dramatic contrasts. Over the ridge plunges Link Cove forbiddingly shaded by the moss-hung walls of Hart, Scrubby and Hutaple Crags

North west aspect from the Hartsop above How ridge

terminating abruptly in the smooth summit slopes of the horseshoe walk of Fairfield.

Turn R and freewheel away down the broad ridge into fabulous views of the High Street fells. Make easy progress past peat hags to a brown bog on a col and on to Hartsop above How with its tiny cairn. Continue along Hoggill Brow and eventually the path meets a wall and runs alongside it. Carry on to where the path steepens at the end of the ridge and look for a ladder stile over the fell wall to the right. (The main path continues 1 mile down to the A592 at Bridgend, Patterdale 1 1/2 miles further.) Climb over following the path slightly L (it appears to be heading for Hartsop village), then bend L through a gap in a broken crosswall and along to a big bold cairn (with two lesser cairns for good measure). Turn R down the very steep hill taking care not to get out of control as the path bends L above rocks and down to the woods. From here Brothers Water is indeed a picture. Go through the gate and straight down to a stile in a fence. On down again to the gate at the car park.

WALK 48: The Elmhow Zig-zags and Arnison Crag

SUMMARY: A circuit which purposely avoids the stony paths of St Sunday Crag in favour of a smooth, green track which gains height easily up a remarkably steep hillside. Views across the valley to the combes of the Helvellyn range demand frequent stops. Once on top, again we eschew the worn out path to return over the grassy top of Birks, and the fine natural castle of Arnison Crag, where sparkling Ullswater draws the eye on the descent.

Distance:	5 1/4 miles (8 1/2km)
Grade:	Strenuous
Height gain:	1640ft (500m)
Terrain:	Valley and medium fell on old grassy tracks.
Summits:	Birks - 2040ft (622m)
	Arnison Crag - 1420ft (433m)
Map:	OL5, HSW-CL

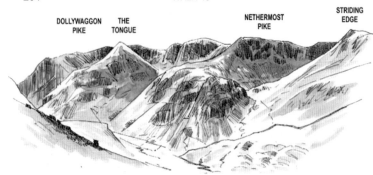

Across Grisedale from the Elmhow zigzags

HOW TO GET THERE AND PARKING: Car park opposite the Patterdale Hotel.

THE WALK: From the car park entrance turn L along the road for a few yards then R opposite the telephone box. Go up the lane (toilets) and after passing a building on the right turn L on a signed public footpath. There are pleasant woodland views as we pass Lanty's Pool and cross over its outlet stream to a kissing gate. Make a brief climb to a wall and go through the second (kissing) gate and on through the Glenamara Park to cross Hag Beck. *Patterdale Hall can be seen below, rising above its surrounding trees. Look down to the lake where the pier and adjacent parking area stand on a fan of gravel. This is a washout delta of debris caused by the breach of the Keppelcove dam in 1927.*

Our objective, Birks, rises directly ahead but our approach is more subtle than a direct frontal attack. At two large oaks ignore the stile to the right and the path left up the spur. Keep straight on by the fence and plantation wall. Across Grisedale note the old pine woods on Keldas (Walk 44). Follow the intake wall then through a kissing gate in a crosswall. Near sheepfolds turn R through a kissing gate and steeply down to join the valley road.

Turn L up the valley towards a fine mountain setting of L to R, St Sunday Crag, Dollywaggon Pike, Nethermost Pike and Helvellyn. Pass Elmhow to a small barn at the end of the wood. Go through the gate above the barn, singed 'Grisedale Tarn, Grasmere' then turn L by the wall to the upper corner of the plantation. Bend L with the wall, cross a stream bed, go along under a little rock outcrop and turn R up its side. You should find yourself on an ancient, smooth path mounting straight up the hill to the first rightward swing of the Elmhow zigzags. There are plenty of resting stones alongside the path from which to enjoy the scenery. Make a rhythmic pace, dictated

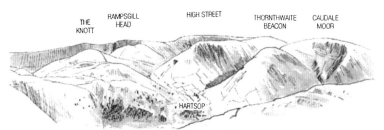

THE
KNOTT
RAMPSGILL
HEAD
HIGH STREET
THORNTHWAITE
BEACON
CAUDALE
MOOR
HARTSOP

View east from Birks

by the steep fellside yet eased by the wisdom of the path-layer. When the gradient eases and a bowl spreads out do not fork right (the scramblers' path to Pinnacle Ridge on St Sunday Crag), but keep ahead then bend leftwards looking carefully for the dent of the old path as the green zig-zag becomes less obvious. Head diagonally L to the left end of a patch of scree and onto a jutting spur with a small cairn. Here the path is more prominent again and there is a good outlook over Ullswater. Go through a trench then, if you will, sit on the big stone at the top. *Looking up the valley the profile of St Sunday Crag has a notch just below our level. This shows the line of a lateral moraine; debris left as the side of a melting glacier diminished, as are the humps of glacial drift on the valley floor.* Carry on up

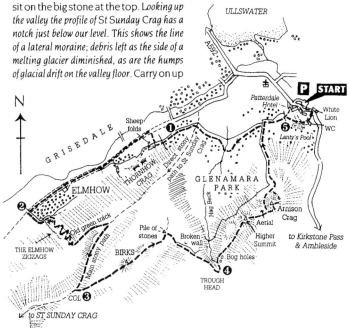

SHEFFIELD PIKE

GLENRIDDING DODD

GREAT MELL FELL

KELDAS

Ullswater from Arnison Crag

the path to another cairn where we meet the main stony path from Glenridding over St Sunday Crag to the summit of Fairfield. Turn R noticing the ice striations on the layered rock of volcanic tuffs as you go along. Keep up the path until the gradient eases and we arrive at the stream draining Gavel Moss (cairn). Turn L (the main path crosses the stream and continues ahead), up the grass for 25yds then L again up the hillside on a path which runs along the ridge top with views on the right (south-east) over Deepdale to upper Patterdale and High Street beyond. Go along the hummocky ridge of Birks on a clear path passing to the right of a rock outcrop and over a knoll (the highest point 622m). Carry on to the next summit with a cairn, an especially good viewpoint when the mountain gullies are highlighted by lingering spring snow. Go straight on and begin to descend to a group of cairns and stones. Here the line of an old path crosses. Turn R for 50yds down the imaginary line of the old path to find the broken end of a wall. There is a trod with cairns on the right-hand side of the wall. Descend to a gap in the wall at a level patch. A rock step is in front. Carry on down through the narrowing between the rock and the wall until you can see the wall turning off left into the Hag Beck valley. We are heading round the head of the valley, Trough Head, and the ridge of Arnison Crag beyond. Turn R and make your way diagonally down a slight basin and over a mossy bank and down to Trough Head. Cross the dip and turn half L onto the ridge leading to Arnison Crag. A path materialises passing unsavoury-looking bog pools and rises gently skirting little humps and more bog holes until a rock crag is on your right. Mount to a summit where you will find a meagre cairn and a magnificent view. Drop down L to regain the path and turn R to continue the direction of our walk. Descend to a gap then pass knolls to the left to reach the next gap with a television aerial. Note: we return to this point.

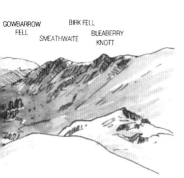

GOWBARROW FELL
BIRK FELL
SMEATHWAITE
BLEABERRY KNOTT

Go right past the rocks then up the rock finial of Arnison Crag, lower than the previous summit but in a splendid position. Return to the TV gap path and go over the right-hand of two gaps over a shoulder. (This can be gained by going over the summit and dropping down L to short-cut onto the gap.)

Carry on down the path and a wall comes into sight. The path traverses above rocks on a shelf then descends to the wallside and follows it. Enjoy a pleasant descent with the lake spread below. At a gap with a cairn keep straight on by the wall, it is steep but smooth, to pass below a crag. Down again until, under the branches of a majestic sycamore, meet the gate on the outward route. Turn R and retrace the path to Lanty's Pool and the start.

WALK 44: Keldas

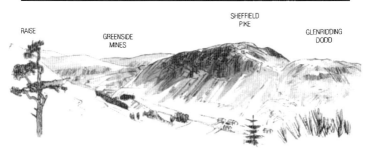

RAISE
GREENSIDE MINES
SHEFFIELD PIKE
GLENRIDDING DODD

Looking across Glenridding to Sheffield Pike from Keldas

SUMMARY: This very short walk is ideal for an evening or a rain-shortened day when the clouds have cleared. The small hill of Keldas is a magical viewpoint - through a fringe of stately pines you see Ullswater and its adjacent fells, or up Grisedale to the

Distance:	2¼ miles (3½km)
Grade:	Easy
Height gain:	538ft (165m)
Terrain:	Woodland and low fell, on good paths.
Summit:	Keldas - 1016ft (311m)
Map:	OL5, HSW-CL

Helvellyn range, Lanty's
Tarn is a tranquil place
and the descent around
the base of the hill is
full of interest. Paths
are generally easy
underfoot.

**HOW TO GET THERE
AND PARKING:** At the
main pay and display
car park in Glenridding
village. Information
centre with weather
report and toilets.

THE WALK: Cross the
river at the main road
bridge and turn R past
the shops. The track to the left leads past a cottage where a stealthy
approach may be rewarded with the sight of red squirrels. A waymarked
path splits off L and makes a brief alternative before rejoining the track.
Keep up the steep pitched stone path which quickly brings views over the
valley. At a junction keep L towards the tarn. When halted by a gate leading
into the woodland surrounding the tarn turn L over a stile and follow the
winding path by tall pines to the summit of Keldas.

*Spend a while here for there is much to see in the extensive view. Wander down to the
wall below the summit crag. The gap between the wall and the crag must have acted as
a wind funnel for just beyond stoops a giant pine, its roots firm and strong yet its trunk
twisted and splintered, with its noble head forced to the ground.*

Return to the tarn gate and go through to stroll along the broad tarnside
path accompanied by reflections of the plantation across the water. At the

Grisedale and St Sunday Crag from the tarn dam

dam a view of Grisedale and St Sunday Crag opens up. Continue down the main path ignoring other side trods and at the wall turn sharp L. Go to a stile by a gate then on behind the farm fork L past a three-way marker post to a gate in a wall on the uphill side of some yew trees. Go through the gate and turn R down the wallside. Turn R at the wall corner then L at Grassthwaite Howe. The path gradually develops as you walk on down through a pasture with groves of mature trees and sounds of cascades in the Grisedale beck below. Go through a gateway with a fancy iron gatepost then meet the driveway of Patterdale Hall. Turn R to the bridge where the delights of the rushing water can can be seen. Over the bridge a gate leads onto the road. It may seem superfluous but instead of just turning L for 100yds to the main A592 road cross to the double gates leading into King George's playing fields. *The gate post plaques with lion and unicorn are splendid in detail* and by entering the park and turning L a path leads past the pavilion to a children's playground. A little gate on the left will see you back at the main road.

Turn L across the beck bridge and before crossing over the A592 notice the fancy iron gate, here a complete sibling of the pasture gatepost. ⚹ Find the path in the trees and continue enjoying a lake view as you go. When the path ends cross the road where a few steps lead to a continuation path well above the traffic. This ends opposite the boat landings. Cross over the road again and go towards Ullswater a few yards before turning to follow a gravel path through the park to the road. (A path branching off over the grass to the right leads to toilets.) Turn R along the road for 100yds to Glenridding and the start.

Patterdale Hall is a 19th-century building on the site of an earlier hall. Once the home of the Mounsey family. In 1648 John Mounsey roused a group of dalesmen to defend against marauding Scots and routed them in an ambush at Stybarrow Crag. After that, the family were know as the 'Kings' of Patterdale. In 1825 the Marshall family bought Patterdale Hall and William Marshall was responsible for many of the good paths in the surrounding area. Patterdale Hall is now part of a holiday accommodation complex.

Lanty's Tarn is named after Lancelot Dobson who lived with his family in a cave nearby. He died aged 95 in 1865. The tarn is man-made.

WALK 45: Glenridding and Red Tarn

SUMMARY: The ice-scooped combe which holds Red Tarn is a dramatic objective with a sombre mountain atmosphere. The steep craggy wall of Helvellyn, which often holds snow well into the early summer, is bounded by the two ridge arms of Striding Edge and Swirral Edge, the most popular circuit of the mountain and a highly recommended scrambly extension if you have the time and energy. Our less ambitious circuit is still quite strenuous and the walking is on rough paths, a result of its popularity. Helvellyn is now an SSSI, for there are rare alpine plants which grow in its craggy combes.

Distance:	6½ miles (10½km)
Grade:	Strenuous
Height gain:	1870ft (570m)
Terrain:	Medium fell on popular paths, peaty in places. Some rough and stony.
Summit:	Red Tarn - 2362ft (720m)
	Birkhouse Moor - 2355ft (718m)
Map:	OL5, HSW-CL

Red Tarn with Striding Edge (left) and Swirral Edge (right) leading up to Helvellyn

HOW TO GET THERE AND PARKING: Park at the main car park, Glenridding. Information, weather forecast, toilets.

THE WALK: Exit the car park by the main entry gate, turn R over the main road bridge and R again along the streamside shopping street. Pass Eagle Farm with a stepped gable barn, circular chimney stacks and a forgotten old trough on the left of the track, its stone almost hidden by a garden of ferns and moss. At a fork keep R signed 'Bridleway to Gillside'. Across the valley of the Glenridding Beck are rows of miners' stone cottages backed by the slopes of Glenridding Dodd 447m (Walk 46) and the steep rocky wall of Heron Pike. Pass the campsite to Rattlebeck Bridge then turn L signed 'Greenside and Helvellyn via Miresbeck'. *Norweb's first hydro-electric scheme in the Lake District is at Rattlebeck Power Station. Water is taken from the dam on Red Tarn Beck above Greenside Mines and piped to the power station. It supplies some 500 local households with electricity.* Keep up by the wall to gates and stiles. go over the L-hand stile and up to a wall corner where our path forks R to 'Helvellyn via Mires Beck'. Mount the stony path to a ladder stile and gate. Here we leave

the Mires Beck path. Keep to the right-hand wall on a path which gives a pleasing retrospective view to the wooded knoll of Keldas, the village and over the lake to Place Fell. at a fork of green paths keep to the R and soon our path levels into a balcony which makes its way up the valley with no need of description. On the left rise the bare slopes of Blea Cove but it is across the valley that the interest lies. *The lower slopes of Sheffield Pike are smoothly stepped with replanted spoil of the Greenside Mine. The falls of Swart Beck, the buildings and works rest in uneasy neatness like a miner's rough hand forced into a kid glove by the necessity of circumstance.* On reaching a fork by a large flat-topped chunk of rock branch L and steeply up the bank to reach the level of a path running along the line of an old water leat now used by the hydro-electric pipe. Turn R and along easily to the gorge where our path leaves the leat and climbs above the dam. (There is a bridge over the beck if you want a closer look.)

The path has been repaired against erosion and the ground is being recolonised with the bright yellow flowers of the quatrefoil and the blue/white milkwort. The conical peak of Catstyecam dominates the walk up the valley until we reach a footbridge and an old sheepfold. Look beyond the walls of the fold up the valley into Keppelcove. *There were two dams in this valley and in 1927 the dam was breached sending a flood containing great quantities of earth and mine spoil down the valley. Bridges were destroyed and the debris was deposited in the lake to form the delta now used by the steamer pier. Also by the sheepfold is the concrete remains of a previous attempt to harness water-power. The line of the pipe supports can be seen on the southern hillside and an old leat tracking round the fell into Keppelcove will be passed later.*

Go over the Red Gill bridge and up the zig-zag path. The path levels into a neatly stoned walkway then over the next boggy area by a plank walkway and just beyond we can identify the old leat by its line of resident rushes. Continue the trudge up the valley. *To the right Catstyecam shrinks to a modest cone, to the north Sheffield Pike has been pushed aside and the huge bulk of Stybarrow Dodd rolls along the northern skyline. Striding Edge stands to the south and ahead the steep cragface of Helvellyn (950m) shades the dour waters*

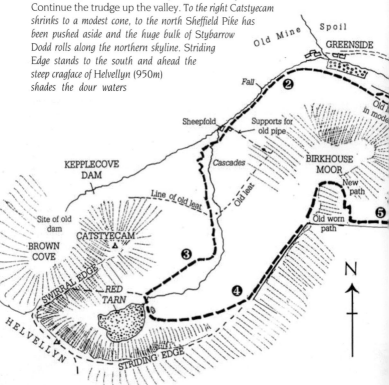

of Red Tarn. At a cairn meet the path descending from Helvellyn via Swirrel Edge then make your way to the tarn and cross the outlet stream. *Red Tarn's waters may look deep, cold and uninviting, as do most of the ice-gouged corrie tarns, but the waters are home to the skelly, a rare fish surviving from ancient times.*

TO RETURN: From the outlet walk south, towards Striding Edge, for a few yards and find a little tarn on the moraine. Turn L and go past boulders and a renovated path will gradually appear, leading across the fellside to a ladder stile on the skyline wall.

Do not go over the stile but turn L and follow the wall. *The view to the right is over Grisedale to St Sunday Crag and across Patterdale to High Street and the distant Pennines.* The path makes its way gently up Birkhouse Moor to a cairn where

you will need time to take in the spectacular mountain panorama forming the western horizon. Go to the next cairn where the path is diverted from the wall. Before the next summit cairn bend R and down the pitched stone path with thanks to the willing hands that laid them. Presently the diversion rejoins the wall, descends, then bends away from it to the left (cairn). A very steep descent on the Mires Beck set path, passing a sheepfold, gives a swift descent down to the wall and ladder stile where we join the outward route. Turn R and reverse the outward route back to Glenridding remembering to turn L immediately before Rattlebeck Bridge signed 'car park'.

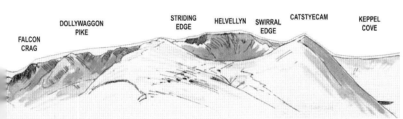

WALK 46: Glenridding Dodd

Looking across Ullswater to Silver Point and Birk Fell

SUMMARY: (See sketch map p219) An attractive lakeshore path, despite the proximity of the road, is followed by a steep but short climb onto Glenridding Dodd, one of Lakelard's minor summits which affords wonderful views of the surrounding fells. The descent by a rough path into Glencoynedale culminates at Glencoyne, one of Lakeland's finest 17th-century farmsteads.

HOW TO GET THERE AND PARKING: A592 just over a mile north of Glenridding at Glencoyne pay and display car park.

THE WALK: The footpath which runs between the lake and the busy road transforms the walk to Glenridding into a pleasure. Cross straight over the road at the car park entrance and turn R on the gravel path beside the Ullswater shore. This stretch is short-lived as you have to use the road to cross Glencoyne Beck. Look up Glencoynedale to the farm nestling in the shelter of Sheffield Pike (674m).

Distance:	3¾ miles (6km)
Grade:	Moderate
Height gain:	1132ft (345m)
Terrain:	Lake shore, medium fell, some rough walking.
Summit:	Glenridding Dodd - 1445ft (442m)
Map:	OL5, HSW-CL

Watch left for the gap in the wall onto the next stretch of path which runs through mixed woodland over a little spur **(if you have children with you be aware of the proximity of the busy road)**. At Hawkhow the thrusting face of Stybarrow Crag forces you back onto the road for a

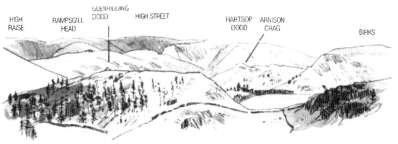

HIGH RAISE · RAMPSGILL HEAD · GLENRIDDING DODD · HIGH STREET · HARTSOP DODD · ARNISON CRAG · BIRKS

Glenridding Dodd from the path over to Glencoynedale

few yards. Just long enough for you to notice the rock-bolts which stabilise the face before branching down L onto the path once more to pass a seat on a belvedere. Carry on along the lakeside woodland path ignoring various paths turning up right to the road. Steps wind up to another seat on a belvedere and the road at the Glenridding village sign. Cross the road, turn R for a few yards then L (public footpath sign) onto a gravel track. Keep ahead past Greenside Lodge and through an iron gate. The track traverses the hillside with views across the rooftops of Glenridding, one with a weather vane of a deer, to Keldas (see Walk 44). At the Greenside road turn R and on as far as High Rake and Low Rake cottages. *In the 1860s the Greenside mine was expanding and the cottages were built and rented to the miners for £1.5s.0d a month.*

Go through the gate marked to YHA and branch R up to High Rake cottages. Climb the stony path which mounts diagonally right above a scree-slope to a shoulder then bends back left past a mine adit to the pass, or go straight up the grass (steep) to gain the pass between Glenridding Dodd and Heron Pike. *Across the valley stands Birkhouse Moor cut by the line of a leat, now used as a footpath, which brought water to the Rattlebeck Power House of 1928.*

Branch R before reaching the wall and follow it L across scree to its highest point. Turn R again passing an old boundary stone inscribed with the initial M (for Marshall) to the summit cairn and superb mountain view from Glenridding Dodd. It is worthwhile settling down to examine the panorama of Ullswater.

RETURN TO THE COL: Follow the wall ahead then turn R above the wall which runs along the head of the Mossdale Beck valley. The path is overlooked by the formidable face of Heron Crag. (Do not be lured to take a shortcut on the tempting path down Mossdale which abandons its users in steep, untamed woodland.) Follow the wall through a rock gateway and a view into Glencoynedale with the old miners' path to Dockray (used on the

Glencoyne Farm

return from Sheffield Pike) on its northern side. Continue by the deer-fenced
wall past a plantation to a cross track and gate in the crook of the wall. Turn
R on a green path below the wall which becomes stony and ends in a pasture
above the cottages of Seldom Seen, built for the increasing mines' force
shortly after the ones at High Rake. Head down the fell towards the cottages
and on the path below their wire fence. Cross the pasture passing piles of
stones gathered from the field to
Glencoyne Farm 1659. Zig-zag down
to the gate and turn R in front of the
house. Walk down the farm lane to
the road. Turn L to the car park.

WALK 47: Sheffield Pikc and Glencoyne Balcony Path

SUMMARY: A walk of contrasts and splendid views. The ascent of Sheffield Pike is steep and rough by its south-east ridge, onto a heathery plateau with boggy depress-

Distance:	7 miles (11¼km)
	4¼ miles by Glencoynedale short return
Grade:	Strenuous
Height gain:	2017ft (615m)
Terrain:	Very rough over Sheffield Pike, high fell
	Some wet sections of path.
Summit:	Heron Pike, Sheffield Pike - 2212ft (675m)
Map:	OL5, HSW-CL

ions. You could descend by Glencoynedale but we strongly recommend the traverse of the balcony path. This was an important miners' path and before that a way onto the Sticks Pass over to Thirlmere. It is now a gentle, smooth and grassy delight although a few deep-cut rocky side streams bite into the path. Ullswater, with its backdrop of Place Fell and the length of High Street, is a refreshing sight on the descent to Glencoyne Park. It is a pity there is no short-cut back to the car park, for return from the Aira Force road is on a little used right of way which could do with some refurbishment.

Glenridding with Sheffield Pike above

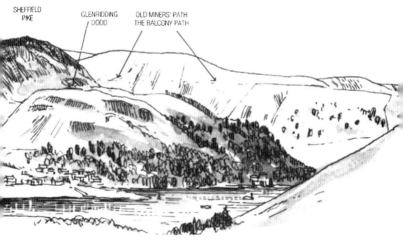

SHEFFIELD PIKE   GLENRIDDING DODD   OLD MINERS' PATH THE BALCONY PATH

HOW TO GET THERE AND PARKING: At the Glencoyne car park on the A592, 1¼ miles north of Glenridding, Patterdale.

THE WALK: Turn R along the road a short distance then R again on the Glencoyne farm road. *The farmstead, built around 1659, is a fine example of a Lakeland statesman's house, with typical cylindrical chimney stacks and fern-decked stepped gables.* As you pass in front of the farmhouse with eyes tipped to the roof and camera at the ready do not miss the L turn between house and barn. Go up the rising path and look back for a meaningful snapshot with the length of Ullswater in the background. Keep on past a gap in a broken down wall and hay meadows with stones in piles, cleared throughout the centuries. After passing the wire fence below the old miners' cottages of Seldom Seen, turn L up the fellside. The going is steep but the magnificent circle of mountains at the head of the dale beckons. Look for the line of a path from Seldom Seen traversing across the fell and when you reach it turn R along it. The path is stony as it approaches the plantation wall but soon becomes smooth and green as it runs below the wall to a hidden gate by a stream. Go through the gate and straight ahead up the wallside. (Ignore the stile on the left and the path to the right which is the short return from Nick Head.)

Continue up the fell following the intermittent path in line with the wall. A deer fence protects new saplings from high-jumping sheep and as you gain height beautiful old pines break the force of the wind which sweeps from the pass above. Turn and look over the U-shaped valley of Glencoyne where high on the north side of the valley runs the old miners' path to an old working then across the head of the dale. This is our balcony return. Arrive at a col where there is a wonderful view southward. Next is a short descent and a brief respite from the climbing. From here glance up right to the spiked summit of Heron Pike with its sheer face and save it at the back of your mind for later as you mount once more, still by the wall, to go through a gap in a crosswall onto

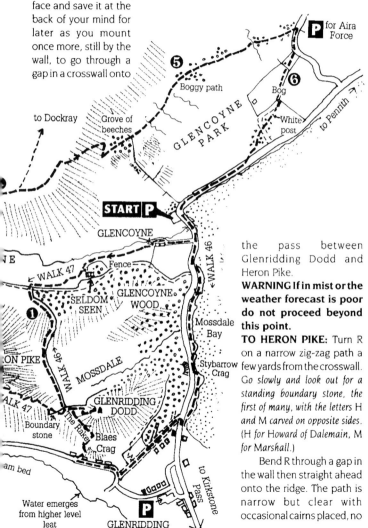

the pass between Glenridding Dodd and Heron Pike.

WARNING If in mist or the weather forecast is poor do not proceed beyond this point.

TO HERON PIKE: Turn R on a narrow zig-zag path a few yards from the crosswall. *Go slowly and look out for a standing boundary stone, the first of many, with the letters H and M carved on opposite sides. (H for Howard of Dalemain, M for Marshall.)*

Bend R through a gap in the wall then straight ahead onto the ridge. The path is narrow but clear with occasional cairns placed, no doubt by well-wishing fellow walkers. The path follows the wide ridge between clumps of short heather. *The Glenridding valley is on the left, its green fields punctuated with piles of stones and its flanks cut by functional tracks hastening commuters to and from the mines in times past.*

The ridge merges into the mountainside and the path continues to climb on a wide green shelf with extensive views. Make a sharp R bend through a break in a rock band then bend back to the original direction still following cairns to emerge on a lonely plateau strewn with little tarns. The spectacular summit of Heron Pike is the innocent light-coloured cairn with boundary stake on the bump 100yds to the right.

Note: *Remember the sheer face seen from below.* **This is no place for children to dash for the summit.** *The name Heron Crag comes from the Old English 'earn' - eagle.*

TO SHEFFIELD PIKE: Go between the pool where the path is indicated by white stones exposed by the weathering peat. Continue to ascend, more gently now, to the hummocky plateau of Sheffield Pike. The path passes a pool to the left and a livid green bog (which I understand is waist deep) on the right, then rises easily again to a large cairn on the escarpment edge. Turn L for a short distance to the wind shelter (note the ice striations in a rock by the shelter) and the summit. A superb viewpoint.

Leave the summit cairn in the opposite direction to your approach (west). The path which makes a good start may disappear in the squelchy ground but stay on the highest driest part of the wide ridge and make your way down past an iron boundary stake H M 1920 to the cross path on the pass of Nick Head.

SHORT RETURN: Turn R and follow the path down Glencoyne to the intake wall and the gate at the plantation corner. Turn L and retrace your outward route. (The path left from Nick Head descends to Swart Beck and Glenridding.)

TO THE BALCONY PATH: Go straight across the pass and on up the slope towards Glencoyne Head for 200yds. Watch carefully for the sunken line of the old miners' path crossing the slope. Turn R along it (in winter a deep snowdrift forms at this point). The path is narrow but sound underfoot and now crosses the steep slopes below Glencoyne Head making its airy way across the dale. Pass over a slab cutting and on to cross a stream with a mine and spoil heap just below. *The spoil, if examined, holds rocks heavy with galena, lead ore.* Continue along the 'balcony' passing cascading streams, worthy of named fame if nearer civilisation. The path gradually threads along the northern side of the glen descending imperceptibly. Across the valley our summit and route lines the horizon and after crossing deep-cut Wintergrain

Gill, Seldom Seen makes a rare appearance. The remains of an old dam can be seen in the valley bottom. At a stream and cairn keep straight on and level. The path forking up left is an old right of way path to Dowthwaite Head. Pass through a broken wall and over a slight rise where, on the flat top, ignore a path branching left with cairn. Keep straight on passing cairns and as the path approaches a wall look over for an aerial view of the length of Ullswater backed by an horizon of High Street. Turn L along the wallside and as the ground dips fork R to go over a stile at its lowest point. Go to the cairn and descend diagonally L to a group of gnarled larches then descend more steeply as the path seems to drop directly into the lake. Carry on down through a mature beech wood to a stile in a wall.

The car park is seen below and by turning R by the wall to the road you could be back in 10 minutes. (This is **not a right of way** but people have gone this way by keeping close to the wall in rough pasture. Halfway down there is a gate in a fence and a gate onto the lakeside road. The car park lies 100 yards to the right.)

The right-of-way path continues ahead through Glencoyne Park for 1 mile on a path which at one point disappears in mud and must be negotiated on wobbly stepping-stones. At the road turn R for 200yds then R over a stile into a field. Make for the electricity post and go through the gate beyond (ignore the gate to the left). Follow the line of the fence making enforced detours round boggy areas, to find a stile in the fence. Go over to gain a gravel track and follow white-topped poles with difficulty to cross the gravel track again and enter the wood at a stile. Follow the poles again across the wood to the main road stile. Turn R and go along the road to the car park.

The Boundary Stones

The HM carved stones mark the boundary between the estates of the Howard family, who lived at Dalemain, the imposing Elizabethan and Georgian hall built around an earlier pele tower near Pooley Bridge, and the Marshalls who lived at Patterdale Hall. The Marshalls bought Patterdale Hall in 1825 from the Mounsey family who were lords of the manor before them.

WALK 48: Aira Force and Gowbarrow Fell

Hollow trunk giving fun in Aira woods

SUMMARY: Aira Force is one of the tourist honey pots of Lakeland since it was immortalised by Wordsworth, and the National Trust have done a fine job in managing its well walked paths. At busy times there is a constant flow of people enjoying the paths through the woods along the streamside. Sightseers peer over the little bridge and picnic on the rocks at High Force. All this does not detract too much from the beauty of the place and a walk up the valley as a prelude to the quieter climb over Gowbarrow Fell is quite delightful. The summit is the highest point of an ice-shorn plateau, now a maze of heathery knolls. Return lies along an airy balcony path with glorious views across Ullswater and the surrounding fells.

It was on the lakeshore at Aira Point that Wordsworth gained his inspiration to write his well-loved piece on 'a host of golden daffodils', whilst the ravine at Aira Force is featured in his poem *The Somnambulist*.

HOW TO GET THERE AND PARKING:

On the A592 Patterdale road 2¹/₂ miles north of Glenridding, pay and display parking for Aira Force. Refreshments, toilets, information board.

Distance:	4 miles (6¹/₄km)
Grade:	Moderate
Height gain:	1085ft (331m)
Terrain:	Valley and low fell. Mainly on good paths.
Summit:	Gowbarrow Fell - 1577ft (481m)
Map:	OL5, HSW-EL

THE WALK: Start at the rear of the car park where the wall has been beautifully extended into an information area and archway giving access to the Aira Force walk. *The path runs by great oaks and the first glimpse into the wooded valley with the gurgling Riddings Beck shows what draws an international stream of visitors.*

Go through a gate by a hollow trunk, an instant attraction to children, and fork L where the pinetum saturates the air with fragrance and the Chilean pine (monkey puzzle tree) wears its bark like a wrinkled stocking. As the sound of the force grows louder mount the steps. Either keep on the path ahead or go down to the lower bridge for a fine view of the fall and continue up the other side to join the easier route which crosses the upper bridge. Ignore a gate on the left, leading to an upper parking on the A5091 at Park Brow. *Just beyond select your view of the waterfall which gives pleasure in the driest spell and awesome viewing in the wet.*

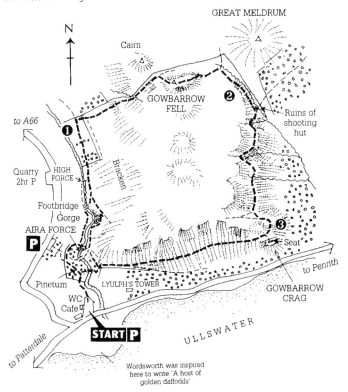

Wordsworth was inspired
here to write 'A host of
golden daffodils'

High Force

From the stone mem-orial bridge continue up either side of the beck. (If you choose the right-hand bank ignore steps right leading to the fell.) The paths climb leading to a wooden footbridge. Here gain the right-hand bank and con-tinue up-stream to High Force, another fine set of falls, then continue to a wall and gate. Ignore the path right, go through the gate and on through the wood which soon ends giving views over Dockray village to Great Dodd. Just before the next gate at a signpost, 'permissive path to Gowbarrow', turn R up the fell. Go over a stile in the wall and forge ahead up the side of the plantation. The path is steep but the scene up Patterdale to St Sunday Crag and Sheffield Pike compensates. Pass the corner of the plantation and continue by the wall. The cairn to the left is not the summit. Bend L with the wall then look back down to Dockray and see the Old Coach Road to Threlkeld winding up the hillside to the corner of the forest. The gradient gradually eases and the triangulation point on the summit of Gowbarrow Fell appears. Fork R to it where paths converge from all directions to enjoy the circular panorama. Leave to the north-east, opposite to the National Trust plaque on the pillar and heading for the end of Ullswater. The path descends in stages running parallel to the wall and from this side our ridge of Airy Crag appears a very impressive little summit. (Ignore the stile in the wall corner unless you intend to visit Great Meldrum, a rather fancy name for a shapeless hump, and return to this point.) Gradually bear R above the deepening Collierhagg Beck. Ignore a path left to a stile and continue ahead past the ruins of an old shooting hut, which has a lovely view of Hallin Fell from its empty door. This is now the popular balcony path, famed for its splendid views over the lake, (see Walk 38 pages185 and 186 for topographical drawings) which traverses the precipitous east slopes of Gowbarrow Park. Bend R and cross a deep ravine with a bridge where the path has fallen away. Ignore any paths branching right and uphill as you begin a gradual descent to round a corner at Yew Crag where a memorial seat looks out over Place Fell and High Street. Carry on for $^1/_2$ mile until Lyulph's Tower, a strange castellated folly, built in 1780 as a shooting lodge for the Duke of Norfolk (one of the Howards of Dalemain) can be seen below. Arrive at Aira Force woods and keep L to a stile then go ahead at a great dead stump to pass huge trees, go down to a bridge and up the steps beyond. Turn L and through the gate to the start.

WALK 49: Great Mell Fell

Great Mell Fell

SUMMARY: Great Mell Fell is a loner, a cone rising from rather uninspiring surroundings and unjustly dismissed in other guidebooks. Few people make the short climb to its summit, yet those who do are amply rewarded, especially if following

Distance:	2½ miles (4km)
Grade:	Easy
Height gain:	908ft (277m)
Terrain:	Low fell and woodland. Boggy in places. No path on the fell.
Summit:	Great Mell Fell - 1761ft (537m)
Map:	OL5, HSW-NL

our chosen route, for the stunning views unfold gradually, first to the Pennines, then the shapely northern fells with Blencathra's ridges. You reach the top to be captivated by the panorama from High Street to Helvellyn and beyond.

Paths are slight and in the woods you will need to cross some boggy patches, past which the climb is easy underfoot until rougher ground is reached near the summit. The return uses the 'tourist' route, which has a slight path in places.

The fell is covered with a natural mixed mature woodland and aged trees surrounded by their saplings give a special dimension and charm.

In Wainwright's day, the hill was out of bounds as it belonged to the Ministry of Defence with a rifle range on its northern slopes. Now owned by the National Trust one can roam anywhere. The last wild cat in Cumbria was killed here in the mid 19th century.

HOW TO GET THERE AND PARKING: Best approached from the A5091 which links the A66 to the Ullswater road near Aira Force. Turn east off this and park on the south-east side of Great Mell Fell just north of Brownrigg Farm where a lane leads to the fell wood; or from the A66, turn south signed Matterdale. The road runs below the eastern side of conical Great Mell Fell. Where the wood almost reaches the road park in a rough lane.

THE WALK: Go up the lane and turn R at the National Trust sign into the wood. Follow the path rightwards along the perimeter fence at the edge of the old broadleaf woodland. The path is taken over by a stream for a while then improves. *A boulder by the fence gives chance to examine the rock. Different from the usual angular Lakeland stone this is a fine conglomerate in an abrasive sandstone matrix. The uniform erosion of this rock has resulted in the conical shape of the fell.* Keep

Panorama from the summit of Great Mell Fell

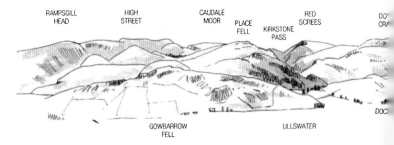

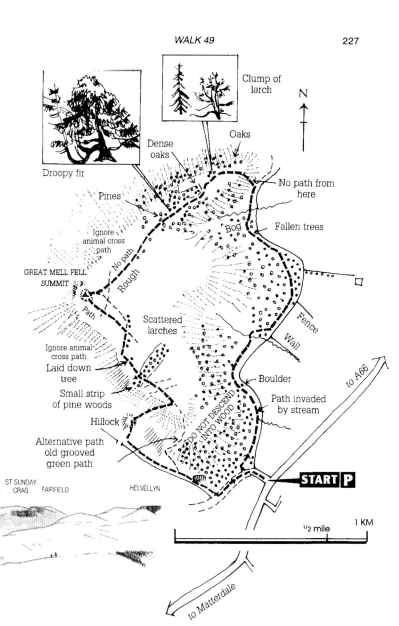

Clump of larch

N

Droopy fir

Dense oaks

Oaks

No path from here

Pines

Fallen trees

Bog

Ignore animal cross path

GREAT MELL FELL SUMMIT

No path

Rough

Scattered larches

Fence

Wall

Ignore animal cross path

Laid down tree

Small strip of pine woods

Boulder

Path invaded by stream

to A66

Hillock

DO NOT DESCEND INTO WOOD

Alternative path old grooved green path

ST SUNDAY CRAG   FAIRFIELD   HELVELLYN

START P

½ mile   1 KM

to Matterdale

on by the fence and look out over the pasture to the dome of Little Mell Fell (505m) and beyond, on the Pennine horizon, the table-top profile of Cross Fell and the radar station on Great Dun Fell, just a tasty sample of the viewing feast to come. Cross a stream and continue. The path moves away from the fence for a while and begins to climb gently as it turns around to the north-eastern side of the fell then runs along the line of the fence once more. There has been storm damage and short diversions have to be made. *The horizon is now occupied by the lower Border hills with the trench of the River Eden hidden at their feet.* Cross a boggy stream then in a few yards the fence bends away down the hill, the path descends and our DIY route to the summit begins.

Go diagonally L up the grass and onto the spur. *As soon as you can look over the turf in front to (left to right) Blencathra, Bannerdale Crags and Carrock Fell,* turn up the spur to the left of the first group of larch trees. (The rough aim is to follow the spur to the summit.) **Do not** go along the edge of the woodland as the north-western slope of the fell is very steep and densely thicketed. Look for a break through the densest trees ahead and slightly left uphill where you can make your way past a large droopy fir and some fragrant pines. *When you reach the fir you can sit on its curved branch to enjoy the scene back north-east to Penrith below its Beacon Hill.* Keep plodding up, pass the tree-line and continue over short heather. *Take care not to step in a narrow drainage ditch as you admire the shape of the bonsai-like weather-stunted pines.* Bend westward always heading for the highest point and join a path for the last 6ft of the climb to the summit tumulus and cairn (537m). *Oh! what a magnificent panorama, this must be one of the finest viewpoints in the northern Lakes. The vast upland moor between Mell Fell and the fells to the west is a massive deposit of boulder clay left behind by ice. A layer of blue clay was mined to make tiles, pipes and bricks.*

Return on the path south-east in the direction of Little Mell Fell towards a cluster of four larches to meet a cross path. Turn R heading towards the valley gap where Ullswater lies and keep on down the spur in the direction of the right edge of the wood. Pass through a corridor in a tongue of pines still descending gently. Emerge from the trees facing Little Mell Fell (SE) to head down the spur past a rush-ringed recumbant larch on the right. In 200yds the ridge flattens and a small cross-path is met. **Do not continue on this heading and enter the wood**. Turn R down the rushy slope where a vehicle track develops. Go down to a green hump. Pass red stones and go down to the fence. Turn L along the perimeter fence. Turn L to find a stile into the old sunken lane which you follow back to the parking.

CHAPTER 6
The Eastern Fells and Dales

Mardale, filled by Haweswater bites deep into the high fells of High Street, and is a justly popular starting point for some classic walks, mostly too long and strenuous for this book. Our selection visits the most interesting parts of the dale and gives breathtaking views. Many visitors to Mardale come to see the only eagles nesting in Lakeland, or in times of drought, as in 1995, to walk over the normally submerged village bridge.

Swindale is a quiet backwater, a deep cut valley where peregrines nest, well worth a visit.

The Lowther valley is broad and pastoral where the influence of the Lowther family is still much in evidence, and the walking quite different to the other areas in this book, for the underlying rock is sandstone and limestone.

Packhorse bridge, Cawdale,
with stream in spate

WALK 50: Circuit of Willdale

GREAT BIRKHOUSE HILL

Old Quarry   THE HAUSE

Nick of hollow way

WILLDALE

SUMMARY: For over 2000 years the now lonely hills above Haweswater have seen man's activity. Many old cairns, dykes and enclosures hint at its significance in prehistoric times, whilst the numerous sunken green tracks, or 'hollow ways' tell of its continued use in medieval times. Our walk uses some of these old paths to make an interesting circuit of Willdale, one of Lakeland's least visited dales, where you can still hear the skylark's song and curlew's call.

HOW TO GET THERE AND PARKING: Follow the minor road from Shap village through Bampton Grange to Bampton. Turn R then L at the telephone box up a steep surfaced lane leading through The Howes, an unfenced area of rocks and gorse, through Hullockhowe. Go over a cattle-grid and park on the verge just past an isolated stone barn where the left-hand wall turns left giving access to the open fell.

THE WALK: Turn L by the intake wall down towards the lower corner of a plantation which, at first, appears to be the only feature on the desolate spread of wild,

Distance:	5 miles (8km)
Grade:	Moderate
Height gain:	1082ft (330m)
Terrain:	Medium fell on grassy paths.
Summits:	Great Birkhouse Fell - 1603ft (489m)
	Low Kop - 1876ft (572m)
Map:	OL5, HSW-EL

The walk around Willdale

mountainous moorland which confronts you. An old path materialises leading towards the farmhouse of Stanegarth and Cawdale Beck emerging from its valley to the north-west (right). Cross a rush-filled dip and branch down R to the tree-lined gorge. Here Cawdale Beck descends in a series of lively cascades to rush under an elegant packhorse bridge and pause in the pool beyond before its confluence with Willdale Beck. There is a fan of paths leaving the bridge but go ahead (fractionally left) on the main one for 50yds through a pebbled stone edged section and branch L towards the valley of Willdale, with Great Birkhouse Hill to the south and Hause End to the north. Notice a fenced area on the left then keep your eyes on the stream to find its junction with the Intake Sike forming a triangular 'island' and a tiny clapper stone bridge spanning the beck. Cross L onto the island and after jumping Intake Sike follow it up its fold in the fell, with the intake wall bending to and fro away to the left, and cross the sike to the right bank then to the left. A large erratic boulder, deposited by the ice lies captive inside the wall while others like two fangs leer down on you as you go over the brow and meet a bigger cross path coming from Drybarrows Farm.

Turn R to the ford, well - peaty wallow, cross easily downstream and pull up the slope on a green path to the welcome song of the skylark, now becoming rare on the Lakeland hills, with a view of Little Birkhouse and Four Stones Hill to the south with the wooded far side of Haweswater beyond. Proceed until Selside shows through the gap ahead then fork R and in 50yds choose your onward route. (A stone pillar has appeared in the aforesaid gap.) Ahead a) is an old hollow path rising gently across the fell and the right fork b) which is described in detail and recommended makes the traverse of Great Birkhouse Fell (wrongly positioned on the OS map).

a) Keep straight on the hollow path which rises gently with ever expanding views of Haweswater and the head of Mardale until a prominent marker cairn is seen on the right.

b) Fork R on the path which mounts in sweeping curves towards the ridge of Great Birkhouse Fell with a long vista of the Lowther Valley to the east. At a ring of stones to the left turn L and continue. Do not cross an infant gill but

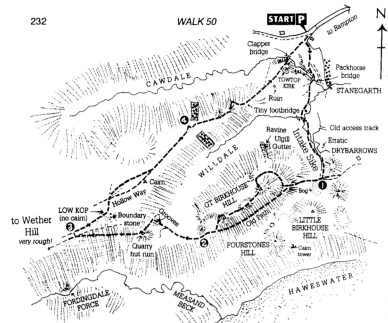

turn L up the grass to the cairn on the first top. *An ancient cairn, looking like an old ruin, stands in the gap between our mountain and Four Stones Hill.* Turn R (west) along the rising pathless knoll towards the summit cairn. *Suddenly encounter an unusual and very beautiful view of the head of Mardale with Harter Fell and the Nan Bield Pass over to Kentmere as the western horizon.* Carry on to the large cairn on

Haweswater from Great Birkhouse Hill

the summit where the nature of the terrain as far as the eye can see is so wild and desolate that it is hard to imagine communities living here. The next landmark is a marker cairn ahead (west) with Fordingdale, the valley of Measand Beck beyond and to the right our return ridge clamped on either side by a pair of plantations. Descend diagonally L to join the green hollow path and turn R along it. The marker cairn is prominent on its little rocky knob and as it is left behind take a bird's-eye view down into Fordingdale. Pass a huddle of stones to the left of the path then cross the head of Willdale. At a fork keep R on the hollow path and as you climb the zig-zag look back to see how significant the marker cairn would be to the quarry workers. Take care not to miss the left bend of the path to go through a cutting, past the remains of a quarry building (enough for a wind shelter) made of lovely grey mottled stone, which has the soapy fell of schist. *The reason for the quarry is evident in the easily cleaved stones which lie around.* Go through the overgrown quarry and along the path with the Force in Fordingdale echoing below. At the head of the dale is twin-cairned High Raise with Low Raise lapping in front to its left.

The hollow path which has mounted steady and straight takes a right curve and levels on a flat ridge crest. A prominent trod turns back sharp right, ignore it and in front (north) stretches the vast featureless moor and peat hags of Wether Hill and Load Pot Hill to its right. Turn R and go 25yds over the moor to the highest point of the flattish ridge to find another path and a scattering of eyelet pools. Turn R along it to begin the return. Approach the highest point Low Kop to find that the path becomes faint and there is no cairn. Before you cry 'lost' cast about and about 20yds to the right, south (towards Haweswater) you will discover a pool and a small boundary stone about a foot high to pinpoint your position. Go back to the highest point, continue slightly descending along the ridge for 100yds. A path reappears,

HIGH STREET

follow it to the junction and turn R along a hollow path. The groove quickly develops and a good flat path runs alongside. *The groove holds snow in the winter and its white ribbon provides a favoured tour for cross country skiers.* The paths divide but rejoin later and the turf path beside the right-hand groove makes for the best walking. *To the right is a fine profile of Great Birkhouse Hill with a view of the Lowther valley. Our return ridge can be seen ahead and left is the deep cut valley of Cawdale with Loadpot Hill beyond. Pass the plantations, now in the days of environmental planting, deemed to be ugly. However the left-hand one proved to be a welcome haven when we were caught by a sudden blizzard on a ski trip.* Pass a stick in a cairn on the ridge end and descend past a ruin across Towtop and just before making the dramatic drop into the bed of Cawdale Beck look right at the ancient circles of Towtop Kirk.

Cross the sturdy clapper bridge and go ahead to the lane at the start.

Towtop Kirk is a scheduled ancient monument. It is an early Christian enclosure 6th to 8th century which may have been an early chapel, a hermit's residence or used for burials. In the centre are the foundations of a horseshoe-shaped building. Nearby is a peat-drying platform. A rudely cut cross was found here.

The sturdy clapper bridge over Cawdale Beck

WALK 51:   Four Stones Hill and Haweswater

The two remaining stones on Four Stones Hill

SUMMARY: A delightful short walk which links the attractive small summits at the lower end of Haweswater. From this grassy balcony the views up the lake are superlative. Measand Beck, with its little ravine and cascades is visited before return along the stony path by the lakeshore.

HOW TO GET THERE AND PARKING: From the northern end of Shap village turn to Bampton Grange and Haweswater. Turn R just before the dam and park at Burnbanks just through the open gateway.

THE WALK: Set off R up the MCWW (Manchester Corporation Water Works) public footpath, a track zig-zagging through woodland to the fell gate. *Burnbanks was built to accommodate the workers on the dam above and has now mellowed into an attractive little backwater on the Coast to Coast Footpath.* Turn R on a rising green path. (Our aim is Burnbanks Hill, complete with aerial, up on the left using an easy way to

Distance:	4¹/₂ miles (7¹/₄km)
Grade:	Easy
Height gain:	721ft (220m)
Terrain:	Low fell and valley. Grassy paths. Some trackless walking.
Summit:	Four Stones Hill - 1361ft (415m)
Map:	OL5, HSW-EL

Haweswater from the TV aerial above Burnbanks

gain the height.) Ignore all paths branching down to the right and keep contouring around the end of the hill. *Note the deep scratches on the first boulder gouged by the ice which once covered the area.* Take the next L fork more steeply up the hillside. Just over the near brow an ancient sunken path brushes our way. Keep up L and arrive at the aerial hilltop taking an unneeded rest forced on you by the splendid view. *The sturdy dam and solemn water of the lake are softly enhanced by the delightful silhouettes of the woodland canopy.*

Descend west to the gap and up the path between the mine grubbings. (There are other workings up to the right but on investigation there is nothing to see and grassy hollows may hide danger.) Continue along the flat shelf. The stones passed on the right are the remains of an ancient cairn. *The strange iron stakes on the hilltop above are the remnants of an aerial, not historic phenomenon. The middle section of Haweswater gradually comes into view with the mountains of the High Street range along the western horizon.*

The next section is almost trackless and you may prefer to make your own way. We went as described.

At the end of the shelf, indicated by scraps of an old wall running up to the right, continue a short distance (100yds) to a stream runnel. Turn up R to what looks like a col. When level with a cairn, which is about 200yds to the right of the path, turn L and make your way up the slope of Little Birkhouse Hill.

From the summit there is a fine scene (see p238). To the east over the Lowther valley the grey line of Knipe Scar is dwarfed into insignificance by the dark horizon of the Pennines with Dufton Pike balancing its shiny ball beside the table-like Cross Fell.

Continue to progress west for 100yds across a dried up pool to gain a minor summit. Next in line is Four Stones Hill identified by the prominent pointed cairn down on its left shoulder. Amble down shelves to the gap occupied by a boggy tarn. Cross the outlet trickle and find the small path leading to the cairn. *This structure is so positioned that it will draw the eye of every walker passing through.* Turn R and climb to the summit. It is completely plain so go straight over and descend to a major right of way path at a prehistoric round cairn by

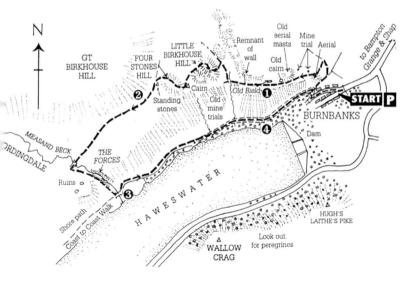

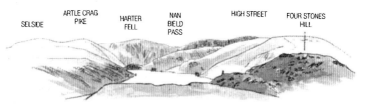

The head of Mardale from Little Birkhouse Hill

a pool which is often dried up. Turn L and you cannot miss the two standing stones but may wonder what has happened to the other two. Keep looking back at them as you stroll down the gently descending path towards Fordingdale Bottom and their piercing situation is impressive. *The cairns and stones hereabouts are remnants of the ancient tribes who lived above Mardale over 2000 years ago. There are exceptional views up Mardale to its valley head and the Nan Bield Pass over to Kentmere.* Choose one of the many vehicle tracks spreading from the ford to arrive at the Measand Beck and cross the footbridge. (The fellside ahead with the snaking path is the return route from Kidsty Pike.)

Turn L and keeping close to the beck, a lively stream lined with marsh marigolds, pass the ford in 100yds and, with the two standing stones still sentinels on the skyline, reach the top of the gorge marked by a small rowan. *The beck falls in an enchanting series of cascades, falls, spouts and pools through a gill decked with trees and flowers and set about with grassy arbours, so allow time to enjoy its delights as you descend to the main lakeside path.* Turn L and go over the bridge and along the gorse-lined path. *A plaque tells of the capture of Heltondale and Hawes Beck in 1959. Across the other side of the lake the outfall of water collected from Naddle Beck and Swindale splashes white into the reservoir.* Do not miss the R turn over the stile and gate at the outward track and go down through the woodland to Burnbanks and the start.

Great Birkhouse Hill

The Ordnance Survey do sometimes make mistakes! On their OL5 map Great Birkhouse Hill is shown adjacent to Little Birkhouse Hill but is in fact a lower summit of the same hill. Great Birkhouse Hill according to local farmers is the bigger, quite separate fell to the north-west, which is traversed by Walk 50, and is unnamed on the OS map.

WALK 52:
Naddle Ridge, Harper Hills and Haweswater Shore

Early winter snow on the path out of the Naddle valley

SUMMARY: A pleasant circuit which traverses the moorland rim of the quiet Naddle valley. Height is easily gained and walking is easy but can be wet in parts. Descent to Haweswater is exhilarating, along the line of a waterworks underground pipe. The mountains which surround the head of Mardale are seen at their best, whilst the path is interesting to follow, across the deep ravine of Guerness Gill and later through an area of fine juniper. The return along the lakeshore path, only opened to the public late 1995, is attractive although the views are totally one-sided.

HOW TO GET THERE AND PARKING: From Shap village take the lane to Bampton Grange and Haweswater. Pass the right turn to Burnbanks (alternative parking),

Distance:	7¹/₂ miles (12km)
Grade:	Moderate
Height gain:	787ft (240m)
Terrain:	Low fell and lakeshore. Grassy paths.
Summit:	Harper Hills - 1377ft (420m)
Map:	OL5, HSW-EL

WALK 52

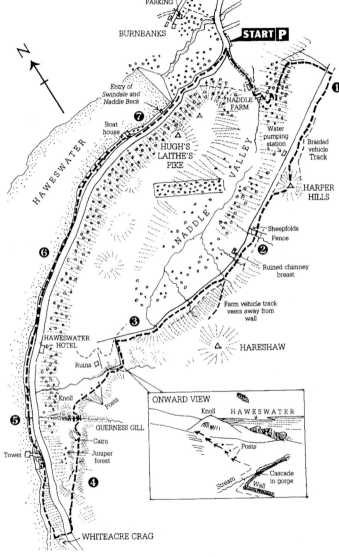

to Bampton

ALTERNATIVE PARKING

BURNBANKS

START **P**

①

Water pumping station

NADDLE FARM

Braided vehicle Track

Entry of Swindale and Naddle Beck

Boat house

⑦

HUGH'S LAITHE'S PIKE

HARPER HILLS

HAWESWATER

Sheepfolds

Fence

②

NADDLE VALLEY

Ruined chimney breast

Farm vehicle track veers away from wall

⑥

③

HARESHAW

HAWESWATER HOTEL

Ruins

Knoll

Posts

⑤

GUERNESS GILL

Cairn

Juniper forest

Tower

④

ONWARD VIEW

Knoll

HAWESWATER

Posts

Stream

Cascade in gorge

Wall

WHITEACRE CRAG

cross the Naddle Bridge and park on the spacious verges before the bend and drive to Naddle Farm.

THE WALK: Go along the drive, public bridleway, to Naddle Farm. *Across the pasture the remains of the Naddle stream runs in its wooded valley before joining the River Lowther.* Go straight through the farmyard then bend L to cross the stream above the concrete aqueduct at the deer fence gate.

Keep ahead on the rightward bending stony path to a stile, follow the path as it rises left through the wood and soon glimpses of views to come flit between the trees. At the wood end a gate leads onto the open fell with a fine view back over the dam to Four Stones Hill which we will see more intimately on the return route. Carry on, noticing the finger cairn on Friths' Crag backed by the Cross Fell Pennine horizon, to a gate in a cross wall.

Go through and turn R (the onward path goes over the moor to Swindale). Let the wall be your guide (for the next 2 miles) and choose one of the farmer's various ATV (all terrain vehicle) tracks to suit. The scene is one of wild moorland. Over the wall to the north a finger cairn on Hugh's Laithes Pike indicates the edge of Mardale and as height is gained Burnbanks is seen nestling in its surround of oak woodland. Sounds of rushing water seem somewhat incongruous as you approach the summit of Harper Hills but there is a waterworks installation perched nearby. The summit cairn has a splendid view (see sketch). To the south Swindale lies deeply hidden and the Old Corpse Road crosses the folds of the fells to the west before descending to Mardale. There is also an opportunity to spy out the onward route. Note the wall we accompany as it turns north across the head of the Naddle valley.

Descend the track towards the wall and keep along it to meet a cross fence and go through the gate. Cross Lower Goat Gill passing sheepfolds by a grassy mound then carry on along the wall again. Pass a lone chimney and go over the brow. The track forks and spreads to avoid boggy bits, then unites again and draws back to the wall. *Over the wall the old Naddle oakwood, stunted with the harsh conditions, still survives and the mountains of High Street can be seen ahead.*

Looking northward over the Naddle Valley from Harper Hills

MARDALE ILL BELL   HIGH STREET   KIDSTY PIKE   WETHER CRAGS   WETHER HILL

When the wall begins to bend right keep by the wall on a narrow path (the ATV tracks swing away left). Pass a fenced gap in the wall, which allows a stream through. There are two parallel paths, one near the wall the other 100yds uphill along the top of small rock bluffs which allow a view over a desert of Turk's head grass and down the Naddle valley. Pass an outcrop with a horn-shaped rock up to the left (ignore the gate in the wall). Carry on to the watershed where you can take a last retrospective look at the route so far before being stunned by the sudden dramatic spectacle of Mardale.

Approach the cross wall but do not go through the sliding gate. Carry on along the wall and turn R as the wall turns at the gill. After 50yds cross the gill and go down its left-hand bank to the first cascade where the water plunges into a mini-gorge. Go diagonally L to a gap above a prominent knoll (see map). There is a faint path with concrete posts, which mark the line of the water pipe. Go through the gap and cross Guerness Gill bridge. Keep ahead and slightly downhill to locate the next concrete post then make a short, steep climb to a gap with a metre of stone wall perched on a rock. Pass waymark cairns and walk into an impressive view of Mardale Head with Harter Fell rising into the western sky. Carry on along a shelf and at the next post keep level above the main juniper and yew to the gap at the next post where the cries of the gulls from the gullery island of Wood Howe can be heard. The onward path, which offers superb views, leads to the road and gate, seen below.

Cross the road and go through the gate opposite into the reservoir enclosure. Care is needed on the steep path winding down a rocky rib then diagonally R through the bracken to join the shore path.

The path progresses clearly along the southern side of the reservoir and needs no description but we give a few notes to indicate interest and progress.

When the tower is in sight keep R up to the corner of the wood by the wall to find the path running between the wall and the plantation. Pop out of the trees onto an elaborate staircase descending from the road to the water tower. Cross it and carry on to a stand of beeches where a track is crossed diagonally right down a few steps. (Signs will be erected.)

Cross a sloping ramp, the ongoing path being slightly uphill. Cross the Guerness Gill bridge and fork L beyond a wall, the right fork leading up to the road. Another bridge crosses a smaller gill and as the path passes through old woodland the Haweswater Hotel can be seen above right. The access stile to the road is a few yards past the hotel. Across the water is the valley of the Meathop Beck recognised by its plantations of larches. The path tucks close under the wall for a while and the aspect is somewhat lopsided but swings away from it again (road access). *The thundering fall on the opposite shore is the captured waters of Cawdale and Heltondale pouring into the reservoir.* The dam is now in sight. Pass a boathouse and make your way up the drive to the road. Turn L on the road and pass the plaque commemorating the diversion of the Naddle and Swindale becks into Haweswater in 1957 by the MCWW. A short way down the road arrive at the start.

FROM BURNBANKS ALTERNATIVE PARKING: Return along the road and turn R using the signed Coast-to-Coast footpath through the woodland to Naddle Bridge.

WALK 53:　The Tarns of High Street

Blea Water below High Street with Caspel Gate on the right

SUMMARY: The tarns are Small Water and Blea Water; both fine examples of glacially carved combes nestling in their deep craggy hollows, well worth visiting for their sombre mountain atmosphere. Approach to Small Water is by the old packhorse

Distance:	4¹/2 miles (7¹/4km)
Grade:	Strenuous
Height gain:	1266ft (386m)
Terrain:	Medium fell, some rough walking and stony paths.
Summit:	Rough Crag - 2059ft (628m)
Map:	OL5, HSW-EL

path to Nan Bield Pass which is still paved in places. The link to Blea Water is virtually pathless in places but straightforward, whilst the return along the sharp ridge of Rough Crag may hold rewards for eagle spotters.

HOW TO GET THERE AND PARKING: Car park at the head of Haweswater.

THE WALK: Leave the car park on the main bridleway up the valley as indicated by an old iron MCWW (Manchester Corporation Water Works) signpost, 'to the Gatescarth and Nan Bield Passes'. In 30yds the bridleways divide and we keep straight on uphill towards Kentmere walking into impressive mountain scenery. Cross a stream on its way down to Mardale Beck and go through a kissing gate in a cross wall. The path now passes

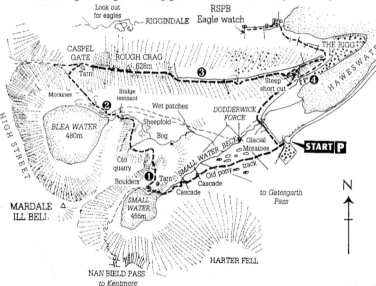

*Hardy fell pony in its
shaggy winter coat*

amongst smooth heaps of glacial debris dropped by retreating ice. *On the right a series of milky cascades highlight Blea Water Beck. Its tarn, which we visit later, lies hidden in its deep combe below High Street and the Long Stile Ridge.* Pass a wind-bent hawthorn to a gate in a wall. *The path begins to show features of its pony-road origin. Occasional pitched stones survive the erosion yet the line of the overgrown route, easing the gradient for the laden ponies, requires a generous imagination. In medieval times this was the shortest pony route between Penrith and Kendal.* Cross a clapper bridge by a waterfall, then pause in the crook of the zig-zag to look back down Mardale. From here you can look back and pick out Rowantreethwaite Beck, a deep gash on the southern flank of the reservoir, and the line of the Old Corpse Road winding up the fell on its way over to Wet Sleddale and Shap (Walk 54). The path approaches closer to the beck, and levels as you reach Small Water The beck chuckles from the tarn, its departure hastened by the wind which plunges down the bare slopes of Harter Fell and Mardale Ill Bell. Cross the stepping-stones then in 100yds leave the path to make its way to the top of the Nan Bield Pass ahead and branch R up a grassy bank to the largest of a group of boulders - a knobbly volcanic specimen - to find yourself on an upper shelf containing a small tarn and a rock outcrop with scree to the left. Make your way towards the tarn on a slight ridge where a trod develops. Bend L towards the scree following the trod which descends the slope keeping the scree to the left. The outcrop lowers to a spur just above a flat boggy basin. Go L round the toe of the spur and look ahead to identify an old quarry path which crosses the fell and leads to the stream. Note the tumbledown walls of a sheepfold; we are aiming just above this. Traverse the left-hand side of the bog on a sheeptrod which runs about 30ft above the bog and along the edge of the bracken to meet the old quarry path.

*Remains of miners' bridge
below Blea Water*

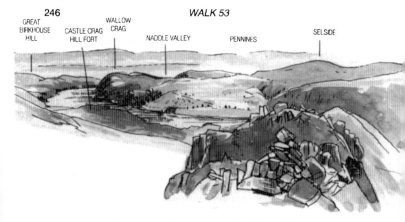

GREAT BIRKHOUSE HILL   CASTLE CRAG HILL FORT   WALLOW CRAG   NADDLE VALLEY   PENNINES   SELSIDE

Haweswater from the summit of Rough Crag

Keep R on it now rising through bracken above the sheepfold heading towards the stream. Go upstream for 50yds above the bracken where the old bridge still totters. Gain the footpath 30ft up the opposite bank. Turn L to the dam at Blea Water.

The deep cold tarn in its corrie is best seen from the onward path via Caspel Gate to Rough Crag but a pleasant rest can be had on the turf bank above its rocky shore if you choose to use the short return.

TO CASPEL GATE AND ROUGH CRAG: At the dam ignore the path round the tarn and turn diagonally R up the grass-covered moraine. On reaching the brow the path gradually becomes obvious and the tarn becomes a circular mirror reflecting the craggy walls of High Street. Caspel Gate, the pass to which we are heading, is the lowest point where the High Stile ridge meets the ridge of Rough Crag to the right. *Look up to where a scalloped necklace of stones was left by retreating ice.* Go up over the next moraine hump after which the path becomes intermittent, its line rising away from the tarn.

Plod upwards to a cairn, cross the stones of the 'necklace', head for the prominent path ahead only for 50yds to just beyond a small cairn where the gradient eases at a small hollow. Turn diagonally R across the grass to meet a major ridge path and a new outlook over Riggindale east to the Pennines. Turn R and pass the little tarn on Caspel Gate. *Observe the clues - a tarn hollow with lip beyond, a smooth gap with neighbouring rough ridges - where a tongue of debris-laden ice pushed over from the Riggindale glacier before depositing its weighty load as the moraines we have just ascended.*

Carry on along the path to the summit of Rough Crag, meanwhile keep glancing towards the smooth skyline on the far side of Riggindale. *You may see a golden eagle soaring against the peak of Kidsty Pike for this valley is a guarded* RSPB *reserve.* Go over the summit and along the descending ridge path which supplies continual reward, a rolling panorama scanned by each turn of the path. Descend a rocky step to a wall which runs by the path and after stepping over a crosswall and the next hump the car park can be seen below with the pony road over Gatesgarth to Longsleddale rising prominently up the far fellside. Stay by the wall choosing the most amiable footfall and reaching two small cairns, a few yards apart on opposite sides of the path. Look over lower Riggindale. *Above the plantation and intake wall is the knobbly spur of Castle Crag, site of an ancient fort and settlement.*

Go down the very steep end of the ridge amazingly easily to a green lawn (a steep short-cut branches right at a cairn), then on by the wall to meet the Haweswater north shore path at a plantation.

RETURN TO THE PARKING: Turn R.** Go along the foot of the ridge to the junction with the short return. Turn L over the bridge, up the rise and L to the parking area.

TO RIGGINDALE RSPB OBSERVATION POINT: Turn L, go through the wall gap and Riggindale is before you. The path leads through gentle pastures above the lake to a larch plantation where a few signs of the old settlement remain, the most interesting being an old potash pit incorporated into the wall beyond a small stone building. *Go behind the wall to see the remaining red sandstone lining of the kiln where bracken was burnt with birch twigs to create the potash which when boiled with tallow produced soft soap used in the cleaning of wool.*

Riggindale potash pit

The next crosswall is the limit of requested access for viewing in the nesting season. Return to ** for return to the parking.

Golden eagle

SHORT RETURN FROM BLEA TARN: Return down the valley on the left (east) side of the stream choosing one of the two paths available. the higher one is more clearly seen but the lower (the continuation of the approach route) is green underfoot. Both paths pass through a boggy patch and join to turn down into Mardale. Go through a kissing gate and past beautiful Dodderwick Force.

Turn R over the bridge, up the rise and L to the parking area.

Blea Water is 65m deep, gouged into the bedrock by the ice which formed on the lee side of High Street.

Eagles were present in the Lake District in the late 1950s and successfully nested in 1969. For many years their location was a closely guarded secret. Now there is a hide in Riggindale, manned during the nesting season, to prevent walkers inadvertently disturbing the birds and to guard against intrusion. In 1996 chicks were again successfully hatched, the first since 1992. More recently there has only been a male eagle present on site. He regularly displays come the breeding season hoping to attract another female into the valley. Riggindale is an RSPB bird reserve.

WALK 54: Old Corpse Road & Selside

SUMMARY: A sense of history pervades this walk. Think of the dalesfolk who toiled with their dead on the long trek to burial at Shap, the nearest consecrated church. The survey tower on the hilltops is a memory of the building of the

Distance:	5¹/₂ miles (9km)
Grade:	Strenuous
Height gain:	1798ft (548m)
Terrain:	High fell
Summit:	Selside - 2148ft (655m)
	Artle Crag Pike - 2338ft (713m)
Map:	OL5, HSW-EL

water pipeline to Manchester; the boundary stones, a reminder of the land-owning gentry. Your descent of the tight zig-zags of Gatesgarth Pass is a reminder of its importance as a vital pony route from Mardale to Kendal market.

HOW TO GET THERE AND PARKING: Drive along Haweswater past the Hotel until opposite the gullery island of Wood Howe near the head of the lake. A wider stretch of road allows parking on the left near the start of the Old Corpse Road.

Riggindale from the Old Corpse Road

THE WALK: Set off up the track signed Old Corpse Road to Swindale. At first the path climbs steeply and the scenery is immediately wonderful. The waterfall, a white blaze to the right, is in Hopgill Beck. The steepness soon eases into zig-zags, its turns showing various aspects of the lake. Pass a large cairn and at the next turn Rowantreethwaite Gill opens ahead, its many pretty falls hidden in summer by foliage. Go through a rock cutting then stop between the next two cairns and look straight across the valley to spot the site of the old hill fort above Castle Crag and Riggindale, home territory of eagles.

After the next cutting we arrive at some ruined buildings with stepped gables. *A welcome rest for the cortege but a sad moment as the corpse turned its back on its home valley for a final journey over the moor.*

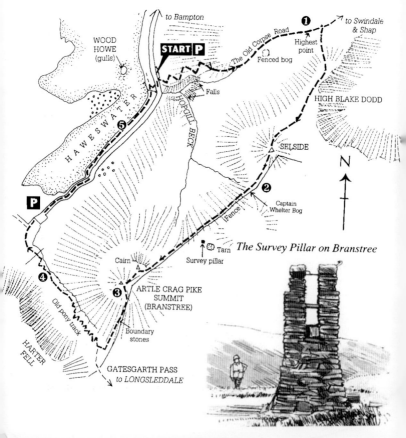

The Survey Pillar on Branstree

Posts indicate the road as it traverses the wide, shallow valley of Rowantreethwaite Beck, but from post no.3 look out for upstanding marker stones too. The rolling skyline on the right holds our onward route. A small fenced area to the right encloses nothing but a nasty boghole. Ignore trods which branch off, pass pole no.5 and carry on to the highest point where the road levels before beginning its descent into Swindale. At pole no.6 the ridge path crosses at right-angles.

WARNING: if adverse weather conditions threaten do not proceed beyond this point.

Turn R on a narrow path leading to the broad ridge. When you get near a 'construction' of stones on the left, look back for the eastern panorama across the Lowther valley to the Pennines 20 miles away. Carry on to the top of the near brow and the path is now clear ahead with the tilted table-top of High Blake Dodd near at hand and the cairn on Selside in the distance. Keep on the path until you can take a few steps to the left to recline on the tilted table and marvel at the intricate view of Swindale. Trace the Old Corpse Road with your eye as it descends to cross the Swindale Beck and picks its way along the southern daleside on its journey to Shap.

Continue along the path with tiny sprigs of bell heather showing pink through the grass and fluffs of cotton grass waving above the black peat. Pass through a break in a high bank of peat and on to the summit of Selside where you meet a fence corner and can sit inside the ring of the cairn and admire the view.

Keep the same south-westerly direction and follow the fence down to Captain Whelter Bog. This is far less dramatic than its name intimates. Keep on rising past purple thistles and a scattering of buttercups which brighten the turf.

Way down to the R a square sheepfold marks progress, but next look to the left where a pillar stands uncomfortably with its environment. *It is a survey pillar from the building of the Longsleddale aqueduct in the 1930s, the unequal weathering of the concrete capstones a vane to the prevailing winds. Its twin tops neighbouring Tarn Crag to the south above Longsleddale.*

If you want to examine it more closely stride over the fence and on arriving at the pillar the fold of the ground holds a little tarn where you may want to linger awhile then rejoin the fenceside path holding the height gained by traversing the moor.

After climbing the short steep section work R away from the fence through a natural slate field to the prominent cairn on Artle Crag from where there are a splendid views of the mountains of High Street. Now for the summit. No need to return to the fence, just cast your eye to confirm its direction and take an onward parallel path a short distance until opposite

The prominent cairn on Artle Crag

the end of a cross wall. Don't trip over the weary scattering of stones as this is the summit cairn of Artle Pike (or Branstree on some maps) but do take a closer look at the circular bird bath. *This is an unusual Ordnance Survey trig point, its three-pronged brass level often being underwater.*

Amble across L to the fence and descend noticing the boundary stones along its line, the division of the Lonsdale and Howard estates. Ahead the pony track over Gatesgarth Pass from Longsleddale to Mardale is clearly seen. An area of boggy ground blocks direct access to the pony road so turn R and join it where you choose.

The old road is well worn. Turn R to pick your way northwards down its winding course into the head of Mardale. Clapper stones still bridge the streams and some patches of the original pitched stones, set to give footing to the loaded ponies, remain in situ. This was a regular route for carts from Mardale to Kendal market. Go through a gate and down into the valley bottom. At the path junction turn R through a kissing gate to the car park.

At the far end of the car park join the lakeshore permissive path which

runs pleasantly below the wall giving serene views to the opposite shore. Keep on until you cross a little arched bridge over Rowantreethwaite Beck. Go through a gap in the old wall and turn R up the hill to a gate in the wall near the start.

Boundary stone on Branstree.
(Examine both sides.)

The Corpse Road was used to take the dead for burial at Shap, until the 18th century when a graveyard was made at Mardale Chapel.

Haweswater

The dam was started in 1929, the reservoir completed in 1940, drowning the Dun Bull Inn, renowned for its shepherds' meet. A famous early photograph of one of the shepherds forms the basis for a mural at the Westmorland M6 south-bound services. The water collection in eastern Lakeland covers a vast area for Haweswater is fed by underground pipes from Ullswater and the neighbouring valleys.

WALK 55:   Swindale and Seat Robert

Truss Gap and Gouther Crag, Swindale

Not to be undertaken in poor visibility

SUMMARY: Always quiet, Swindale is a remote spot, approached by very narrow lanes which demand care and consideration. The deep-set valley head is rugged and beautiful whilst the

Distance:	7¹/₂ miles (12km)
Grade:	Moderate
Height gain:	1016ft (310m)
Terrain:	Valley, medium fell, can be very wet on the moor. Some pathless walking.
Summit:	Seat Robert - 1688ft (515m)
Map:	OL5, HSW-EL

moorland above gives broad views and an isolated atmosphere. The valley makes an excellent short walk by the permissive path to Mosedale Force, with a return along the old pony trail and the surfaced lane. The full round includes the lonely conical summit of Seat Robert and some rough untracked fell country: not to be undertaken in mist.

HOW TO GET THERE AND PARKING: At the northern end of Shap village turn west to Bampton Grange. Over the river bridge turn L and follow the signs to Swindale.

Parking area at the permissive limit of vehicular traffic access. The walk is described from here (although walkers often drive a further ³/₄ mile to a small parking area on the left before Truss Gap Farm. On no account drive further).

THE WALK: Set off along the road which allows speedy walking, splendid views across the symmetrical slopes of the U-shaped valley and interesting observations to make. Pass two barns and Swindale Foot Farm. *An incongruous stone structure in the next field is one of the many waterworks traps for capturing a merry stream and transferring it to the Haweswater Reservoir.*

On approaching Truss Gap Farm stop and take note of the return route. Across the valley to the left of Gouther Crag is the deep ravine of Gouthercrag Gill where the waters of Askew Beck cascade to the valley. Our descent path is to the left of this ravine to cross either the footbridge or the stepping-stones (public footpath sign). (The prominent path slanting gently to the left is the Old Corpse Road to Shap.)

South side - THE FOOTPATH UNDER GOUTHER CRAG: Turn L, cross the bridge and go diagonally R to the wall corner bending round it on the permissive path below Gouther and Outlaw crags. *Peregrine falcons nest here and the RSPB mount a guard over them each year, so if the path is closed please cooperate.* Cross a bridge with a carved 'chain-gate' over Gouther Crag Gill. Ignore a more prominent onward path used by the rock climbers and where the wall on the right changes to a fence branch down R, keeping near the fence and on the lower side of the strip of woodland. Pass large boulders and along to a gateway in a crosswall. Go round the end of the next crosswall and eventually emerge from the trees to see the valley head. Do not gaze in wonder from here but continue through a gate in a crosswall. At the far corner of a high wall with a wire on the right you can look over the valley. A rock island, The Knott, rises from the valley floor and Hobgrumble Gill cuts the headwall behind. Keep on the contouring path between purple flowers of the scabious and insect-eating butterwort in their alternate dry and wet habitats, until abreast of the heaps of moraine and the Simon Stone, a glacial erratic,

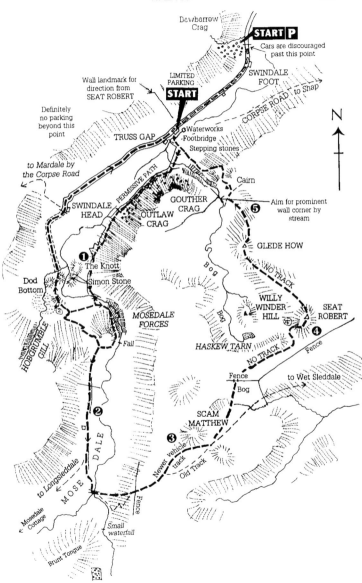

Dewbarrow Crag

START **P**
Cars are discouraged past this point

SWINDALE FOOT

Wall landmark for direction from SEAT ROBERT

LIMITED PARKING

START

Definitely no parking beyond this point

CORPSE ROAD to Shap

TRUSS GAP

Waterworks Footbridge
Stepping stones

N

to Mardale by the Corpse Road

SWINDALE HEAD

PERMISSIVE PATH

OUTLAW CRAG

GOUTHER CRAG

Cairn

Aim for prominent wall corner by stream

5

GLEDE HOW

1 The Knott

Simon Stone

Dod Bottom

MOSEDALE FORCES

Bog

WILLY WINDER HILL

SEAT ROBERT

4

HODGRUMBLE GILL

Fall

HASKEW TARN

NO TRACK

Fence

M O S E D A L E

to Longsleddale

2

NO TRACK

Fence

to Wet Sleddale

Bog

Fence

SCAM MATTHEW

Bog

3

Newer vehicle track

Old Track

Moosedale Cottage

Small waterfall

Brunt Tongue

lurking shyly under a group of trees on the valley floor. To the left is the tree-lined ravine of Mosedale Beck and soon our little path bends towards it. Go over a stile and footbridge then choose your onward route.

either a) THE MOSEDALE FORCES: Turn L and (* north side route joins here) find your own way up the grassy rakes between the rocks, pausing at intervals to peer into the gill for maximum pleasure. At the top turn R and cross the moor to meet the pony road by the perched boulder.

or b) THE PONY ROAD: Turn diagonally R and cross the slope until meeting the pony path. Turn L joining the north side route **.

or c) A SHORT RETURN BY REVERSING THE NORTH SIDE OUTWARD ROUTE

North side - THE ROAD AND FOOTPATH OVER THE GLACIAL MORAINE: Continue along the road behind the farm. *Gouther Crag contains several rock climbs but more importantly is a nesting place for peregrine falcons which have bred successfully under the watchful vigil of voluntary wardens.*

At Swindale Head go behind the farmhouse and on the public bridleway to Mosedale. (The Old Corpse Road joins here from Mardale.) The walled lane doubles as a sheepfold and restricts the view but soon we emerge into the valley head.

The cirque we are in is an excellent example of glaciated scenery. The valley floor contains glacial moraine and ice-shorn rocks and the sheer headwall, now cut by Hobgrumble Gill, towers over the scooped out corrie basin of Dodd Bottom, an old lake bed. From the hanging valley of Mosedale the beck pours down in spectacular waterfalls. The valley head is a worthwhile objective in itself.

Cross the bridge and continue on the path which traverses a moraine ridge between Dodd Bottom and Mosedale Beck. In the field over the beck is the lone Simon Stone with its surround of trees.

Either:

1. Climb steeply up to Mosedale by the main pony path (south side route joins here **) taking care to identify its zig-zagging line until reaching a perched boulder where the gradient eases.

or:

2.   Turn L to the waterfalls (join the south side route *) and thread your way up the right-hand side of the cascades enjoying the exquisite display.

The atmosphere has changed. Desolate moorland of faded wind-bent grasses, broken only by a trio of green patches and the glint of the beck, makes the line of the old wall, which we follow, a friendly feature. Go through a gate in a cross fence and pass two old sheepfolds. Keep on until the path and the valley bend right round the foot of Ash Knott on its way to Longsleddale. Down to the left a bridge stands proud above the beck. Follow the line of the old wall to the bridge.

From the bridge go straight up the fellside. (The old right of way path running to Wet Sleddale takes a loop right and is overgrown with rushes.) *A derelict plantation of fir survives on the slopes of Brunt Tongue and the upper Mosedale valley stretches on to the Gatesgarth Pass and Longsleddale. Mosedale Cottage nestles in a fold of the fellside and it takes little to imagine the storm-worn traveller's relief as he homed in on its friendly light.* Join the old path and go on to a fence. Go through and keep to the path on the crest of the ridge. (Note: There are many paths, trods, and vehicle tracks.) The sad old path to Wet Sleddale is intermittent. Aim for the hill ahead, Scam Matthew, then keep round to its right (S). (The hump to the far left is High Wether Howe.) You will soon merge with the old right of way path which seems to have recovered its dignity. *From here Wet Sleddale Reservoir can be seen and a mile ahead Seat Robert, our objective, stands out*

Swindale from High Blake Dodd, Selside Pike

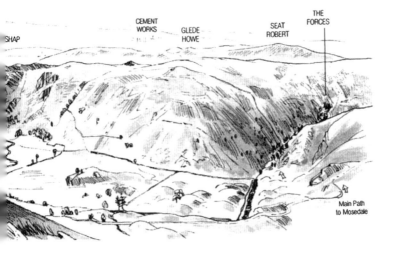

with distant Cross Fell and the Pennines behind.

Just over the watershed below Scam Matthew a grass track forks left. This leads to a gate in a fence and continues towards Seat Robert, keeping above the worst bogs. Cross the peat bog that defends Seat Robert and go for the summit cairn (1688ft) where there is an extensive view of the Lowther valley and the outstretched horizon of the Pennines beyond. *The summit is the site of a Bronze Age burial cairn.*

Check your direction and onward route before you leave the summit as it is untracked and rather featureless. Look to the north-west with the cairn to your left, the wind shelter to your right and your back to the fence/wall. Down to the left is Haskew Tarn which drains towards Swindale. The issuing stream Haskew Beck, forms a shallow valley, and plunges down the gorge of Gouthercrag Gill. Our path descends to the immediate right of this gorge. Ahead is a line of knolls which provides drier ground and aim for a prominent wall which drops into the valley on the opposite side of Swindale.

Descend towards the line of knolls and cross a vehicle track. A useful animal trod picks the driest way as you keep ahead with an eye on the developing beck which circles behind Willy Winder Hill over to the left (west). When you have reached a knoll with a pate of ice-smoothed rocks (1504ft) Swindale looks much nearer and we have a definite objective in sight with the cairn on Glede Howe. The final summit gives a previously hidden view of the mountains to the north-west of Swindale and the prominent triangular peak which catches the eye is Kidsty Pike.

Now make your way towards the wall corner by the stream choosing the easiest passage down Black Crag, only a series of tussocky shelves with the odd rock, and cross a vehicle track. On approaching the wall find a path and follow it R for 200yds then branch L to a marker cairn. (The Haskew Beck disappears as it enters the Gouthercrag Gill gorge.) An old green path leads from the cairn down the hillside. The path becomes stony and enters a trench. On reaching the valley floor cross the river by the stepping-stones or go downstream to the bridge. Turn R along the road to the parking.

WALK 56: Knipe Scar

Suspension bridge over the River Lowther below Knipe Scar

SUMMARY: A walk for the spring when the varied flora is at its best, both by the stream and on the limestone scars. Children will love the suspension bridge.

HOW TO GET THERE AND PARKING: From the northern end of Shap village turn west on a minor road towards Bampton. Park on the far side of the river bridge at Bampton Grange.

THE WALK: Cross back over the bridge to St Patrick's Church where a footpath sign points you onto the grass between the gravestones and walk under cherry blossom in spring to a kissing gate leading into the riverside meadows. Go to a ladder stile in the opposite wall and glance back to see the picturesque village with the white limestone edge of Knipe Scar behind.

Keep ahead aiming for a stone barn and nearer to the river. *The shallow water, an allowance from Swindale Beck and the Wet Sleddale Reservoir, is edged with golden marsh marigolds and hosts*

Distance:	6¼ miles (10km)
Grade:	Easy
Height gain:	557ft (170m)
Terrain:	Riverside and low fell. Grassy paths.
High point:	Knipe Scar stone circle - 1115ft (340m)
Map:	OL5

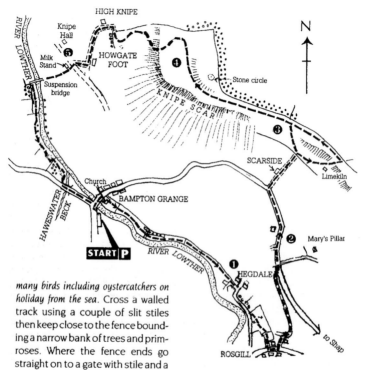

many birds including oystercatchers on holiday from the sea. Cross a walled track using a couple of slit stiles then keep close to the fence bounding a narrow bank of trees and primroses. Where the fence ends go straight on to a gate with stile and a footbridge over a stream. Go on to the next stile and then the buildings of Hegdale appear ahead. The gate is to the left of a long low barn giving access to a walled lane. Turn R on the surfaced road up a slight rise to leave the road L at a gate and stile. Cross the field diagonally passing under the wires and left of a wall remnant. From here is an extensive view over Haweswater and a slit stile can be seen ahead. Go over the stile, pass an erratic boulder and seek out a gate to the right of the houses at Rosgill.

Turn L up the road for 100yds then fork L by two magnificent redwood trees to a track junction. Turn R along an old walled lane with some of its set stones remaining to ease the climb to the Shap - Bampton

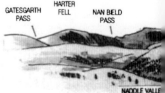

Grange road.

Turn L and on the eastern skyline stands Mary's Pillar. *This is a memorial to Mary Casterley, a talented landscape artist who died young. The memorial was erected by her family in 1854.* There is no public access. Pass an old bank barn and Lake View enjoying the vast panorama to a road junction. Here turn R to Scar Side Farm.

Daffodils border the lane up to the farm. Pass a stone barn, the new adjoining building hiding a 900ft bench mark and datestone of 1820 and an old pump with a stone trough, now retired to a garden feature. Go past the farm to a gate at the top of the lane and here make a choice of route.

a) Take the L fork and proceed up the common to the plantation wall and the top of the scar turn L.

b) Take the R fork and go along behind the limekiln and up the limestone shelves to the plantation wall then bend L along the top of the scar. This is a little longer than a) but the more extensive view is exhilarating.

Continue along parallel to the wall passing a small area of limestone pavement with erratic boulders. Do not stride along too fast but try to identify progress for a successful visit to the stone circle. Note where the path descends slightly, then is nipped between a larger area of limestone pavement and the rocks of a low knoll, next it becomes bordered with bracken to left and right. Here turn R on a trod to the stone circle which is not easy to see until approached and still not easy to see when you find it! Head for a break in the wall and a post marks the ancient stone circle about 50yds before the wall.

Return to the path and gently descend. *On the eastern horizon rolls the bulk of the Pennines with Cross Fell its highest point.* The path now descends in a curve away from the wall to avoid a rock step then veers back towards it descending through bracken, in zigzags, to High Knipe Farm. Go through the lowest gate on the left into a fenced track then through the farmyard to the access lane. Look over the wall to Knipe Hall in its hollow.

Pass Howgate Foot and continue to the road. Cross straight over by a milk churn platform and make your way down to the river bridge. The flood pipes and 'tide marks' reveal another mood to this gentle stream as it

View west from Knipe Scar

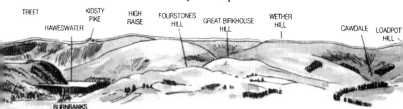

TREET KIDSTY PIKE HIGH RAISE FOURSTONES HILL GREAT BIRKHOUSE HILL WETHER HILL CAWDALE LOADPOT HILL

HAWESWATER

BURNBANKS

Knipe Scar from Bampton Grange

delivers its excess water to the Solway. Sway across the narrow suspension bridge and turn L over a stile and along the riverside path. From here Knipe Scar looks most impressive. At the end of the little plantation continue along the riverside, over a stile in a fence and the village of Bampton is in sight to the right. Go under power lines and bend L to a ladder stile. Continue beside Haweswater Beck to a wicket gate at the road. Turn L over the bridge and it is 200yds to the start.

The Stone Circle is a scheduled site. It may be a burial cairn.

WALK 57: Lowther Park

Lowther Castle

SUMMARY: A walk based on the River Lowther using footpaths on either side to examine the lovely parkland and buildings on the Lowther estate. Please respect the surroundings and keep entirely on the public paths.

Askham is an attractive village with extensive village greens and two pubs. You could enjoy a pub lunch then wear it off on the walk.

HOW TO GET THERE AND PARKING: Park near the river opposite St Peter's Church. Room for a few cars on the other side of the river bridge.

THE WALK: Walk up the hill to the village. Pass the Punchbowl Inn then turn R into a bridleway. *The solid wooden panelled gateways with iron studs give an immediate 'estate' atmosphere and the house to the right is the Askham Hall, now the*

Distance:	6 miles (9½km)
Grade:	Easy
Height gain:	Negligible
Terrain:	Parkland and riverside meadow. Good paths.
Map:	OL5

residence of the present Earl of Lonsdale.

Keep straight on between the buildings and through a gate into a walled lane. (Look back for a better view of the Hall.) At the second field gate turn R. The footpath sign is on the field side of the fence and not visible

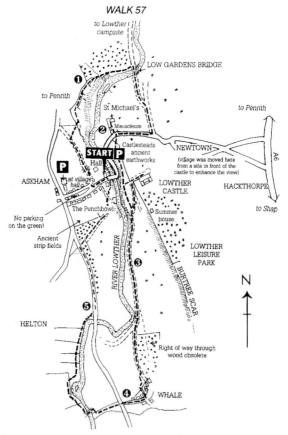

from the lane. Cross the field diagonally L to the corner noticing the erratic boulders strewn about as you go. Climb the substantial stile over the massive wall and go ahead into Heining Wood to reach a major path. Turn L through the pleasant old woodland gaining a little height while passing a fenced larch plantation. At the top of a rise the path narrows but when opposite Lowclose Farm (away left) it widens again and the River Lowther can be seen down through gaps in the trees on the right. Keep by the fence, cross a small stream then admire a stand of elegant old pines as you pass. Descend to a rather special iron gate with an unusual hinge and rising roller giving access to the road.

Turn R and cross one of the bridges over the river and continue up the road. As you progress through the parkland the impressive turrets and tower of Lowther Castle catch the eye. At a fork keep R, go over the cattle-grid and along the avenue towards the Gothick castle which, on reaching the road, brings disillusionment to see that it is merely a hollow shell. Turn R and walk down the road to the church.

It is an interesting diversion to visit the churchyard which contains the mausoleum of the "Yellow" Earl and William, Earl of Lonsdale and read an information sheet in the church porch describing the ancient Scandinavian hog back carved stones to be found in the churchyard. Below the church you can see some old cultivation terraces.

SHORT RETURN: Go straight down the road to the river bridge and start.

TO CONTINUE: Turn L on the public footpath opposite the church, enter the field at a gate and cross diagonally R to a stile into the wood. Follow a narrow indistinct path gradually bending L through the trees. The path improves and runs high above the river through banks of cellendine and bluebells. At a branch keep ahead to a curved seat then turn L to a major track and wall corner.

If you want to take a closer look at the castle turn L then bear R following the track along to the gatehouse. *It is a sad sight, hardly worth the extra walk, but by just looking round the wall corner an ornate "Sleeping Beauty" doorway testifies to its former glory.*

Return to the path. If not visiting the castle, turn R and ignoring a left fork descend through the plantation (replanted 1958). Emerge through a gateway to a fine view up Mardale to the mountains of High Street. Keep on for 100yds then look up to the left where the castle wall embraces Burtree Scar. The summerhouse was sited to enjoy the same view we have just experienced. Down the valley the River Lowther noisily enters its gorge as we continue to a gate. Pass the plantation then just past a gate where the track forks take the L track. Follow the track on the lower edge of the wood and on towards the farm. Look R for a stile and yellow waymark. Go into the field keeping the same direction and avoiding the farm to steps and a wicket gate in front of large barns. Go along the wallside to a stile and fingerpost at Whale. Turn R down to the road junction where you go straight across and on the public bridleway to Helton. Go down a track beside the stream and over a stile on the right to the footbridge over the river. Cross the Lowther and turn R. We now have a pleasant riverside walk through several fields complete with stiles and stream bridges (you cannot go wrong) until meeting a public footpath sign and stile out onto the road. Turn L ½ mile along the road, up a brow and when within earshot of the main road find a public footpath sign indicating a R turn over a stile to turn L into a fenced track which leads left towards a plantation. Ignore a stile left to the village but look through the gap to see a series of ancient narrow strip fields beside the village. Continue 25yds to a bend and go over the stile ahead (yellow waymark) to a public footpath sign pointing to a path L. Follow the right-hand fence down to cross a track. Keep along the fence to a wicket gate into the churchyard then hug the right wall which gives you chance to peer into the gorge. Keep to the right of way path which goes round the back of the church to a stile onto the road at the start.

The Earls of Lonsdale

The Lowther family acquired the Manor of St Bees and in 1643 Sir Christopher Lowther built a pier at Whitehaven and began to dig coal which outcropped on the coast nearby. His son Sir James expanded the work. He was a liberal employer and the ensuing mines became profitable. The 5th Earl was nicknamed the 'Yellow Earl' after his personal colours. He donated the Lonsdale belts for boxing, and as a founder of the Automobile Association, was responsible for its yellow livery.

Lowther Church in 1682 was surrounded by houses. Sir John Lowther disapproved of this clutter in his view and demolished the village, having it rebuilt a discrete distance away and named Newtown.

Lowther Castle has had a disastrous history. The early 13th-century castle was rebuilt by Sir John Lowther only to be destroyed by fire in 1720. Between 1806 and 1811 the present structure was built in the Gothic style. Now it is a haunting shell for it was mostly demolished in 1957. The park covers 600 acres and is a fine example of landscaping, begun in 1680 by Sir John. Oddities abound - notice the decorated walls, gates and doorways seen on our walk. From a distance the smooth parkland is seen as a contrast to the close walled fields to the west of the river.

Bringing the sheep in for shearing, Mungrisdale

SELECTED BIBLIOGRAPHY

W.G. Collingwood (Revised by William Rollinson)*T he Lake Counties* J.M. Dent & Sons 1988

Cumbria Amenity Trust Mining Heritage *Beneath the Lakeland Fells* Red Earth Publications 1992

Roy Millward and Adrian Robinson *The Lake District* Eyre Methuen 1970

W.R. Mitchell *The Lost Village of Mardale* Castleberg 1993

Norman Nicholson *The Lakers* Robert Hale 1955, Cicerone Press 1995

John and Anne Nuttall *The Tarns of Lakeland* Vol 1. *West* Cicerone Press 1995

John and Anne Nuttall *The Tarns of Lakeland* Vol 2 .*East* Cicerone Press 1996

John Parker *Cumbria - A guide to the Lake District and its County* John Bartholomew & Son Ltd 1977

W.H. Pearsall and W. Pennington (Collins New Naturalist series) *The Lake District* Bloomsbury Books 1989

John Postlethwaite *Mines and Mining in the English Lake District* 1887 Republished by Michael Moon 1975

Ian Tyler *Seathwaite Wad* Blue Rock Publications 1995

Ian Tyler *Honister Slate* Blue Rock Publications 1994

Ian Tyler *Greenside. A Tale of Lakeland Mines* Red Earth Publications 1992

Jim Watson *Lakeland Villages* Cicerone Press 1988

Jim Watson *Lakeland Towns* Cicerone Press 1992

LISTING OF CICERONE GUIDES

Short Walks in Lakeland
1 South Lakeland
2 North Lakeland
3 West Lakeland
The Cumbria Coastal Way
The Cumbria Way and the
Allerdale Ramble
Tour of the Lake District

DERBYSHIRE, PEAK DISTRICT AND MIDLANDS

High Peak Walks
Scrambles in the Dark Peak
The Star Family Walks
Walking in Derbyshire
White Peak Walks
The Northern Dales
The Southern Dales

SOUTHERN ENGLAND

Suffolk Coast & Heaths Walks
The Cotswold Way
The Great Stones Way
The North Downs Way
The Peddars Way and Norfolk
Coast Path
The Ridgeway National Trail
The South Downs Way
The South West Coast Path
The Thames Path
Walking in Essex
Walking in Kent
Walking in Norfolk
Walking in the Chilterns
Walking in the Cotswolds
Walking in the Isles of Scilly
Walking in the New Forest
Walking in the Thames Valley
Walking on Dartmoor
Walking on Guernsey
Walking on Jersey
Walking on the Isle of Wight
Walks in the South Downs
National Park

WALES AND WELSH BORDERS

Glyndwr's Way
Great Mountain Days
in Snowdonia
Hillwalking in Snowdonia
Hillwalking in Wales: 1&2
Offa's Dyke Path
Ridges of Snowdonia
Scrambles in Snowdonia
The Ascent of Snowdon

The Ceredigion and Snowdonia
Coast Paths
Lleyn Peninsula Coastal Path
Pembrokeshire Coastal Path
The Severn Way
The Shropshire Hills
The Wye Valley Walk
Walking in Pembrokeshire
Walking in the Forest of Dean
Walking in the South
Wales Valleys
Walking on Gower
Walking on the Brecon Beacons
Welsh Winter Climbs

INTERNATIONAL CHALLENGES, COLLECTIONS AND ACTIVITIES

Canyoning
Canyoning in the Alps
Europe's High Points
The Via Francigena: 1&2

EUROPEAN CYCLING

Cycle Touring in France
Cycle Touring in Ireland
Cycle Touring in Spain
Cycle Touring in Switzerland
Cycling in the French Alps
Cycling the Canal du Midi
Cycling the River Loire
The Danube Cycleway
The Grand Traverse of the
Massif Central
The Moselle Cycle Route
The Rhine Cycle Route
The Way of St James

AFRICA

Climbing in the Moroccan
Anti-Atlas
Kilimanjaro
Mountaineering in the Moroccan
High Atlas
The High Atlas
Trekking in the Atlas Mountains
Walking in the Drakensberg

ALPS – CROSS-BORDER ROUTES

100 Hut Walks in the Alps
Across the Eastern Alps: E5
Alpine Points of View
Alpine Ski Mountaineering
1 Western Alps
2 Central and Eastern Alps
Chamonix to Zermatt
Snowshoeing

Tour of Mont Blanc
Tour of Monte Rosa
Tour of the Matterhorn
Trekking in the Alps
Trekking in the Silvretta and
Rätikon Alps
Walking in the Alps
Walks and Treks in the
Maritime Alps

PYRENEES AND FRANCE/SPAIN CROSS-BORDER ROUTES

Rock Climbs in the Pyrenees
The GR10 Trail
The GR11 Trail – La Senda
The Mountains of Andorra
The Pyrenean Haute Route
The Pyrenees
The Way of St James:
France & Spain
Walks and Climbs in the Pyrenees

AUSTRIA

The Adlerweg
Trekking in Austria's Hohe Tauern
Trekking in the Stubai Alps
Trekking in the Zillertal Alps
Walking in Austria

BELGIUM AND LUXEMBOURG

Walking in the Ardennes

EASTERN EUROPE

The High Tatras
The Mountains of Romania
Walking in Bulgaria's
National Parks
Walking in Hungary

FRANCE

Chamonix Mountain Adventures
Ecrins National Park
Mont Blanc Walks
Mountain Adventures in
the Maurienne
The Cathar Way
The GR20 Corsica
The GR5 Trail
The Robert Louis Stevenson Trail
Tour of the Oisans: The GR54
Tour of the Queyras
Tour of the Vanoise
Trekking in the Vosges and Jura
Vanoise Ski Touring
Via Ferratas of the French Alps
Walking in Corsica

For full information on all our
guides, books and eBooks,
visit our website:
www.cicerone.co.uk.

Walking – Trekking – Mountaineering – Climbing – Cycling

Over 40 years, Cicerone have built up an outstanding collection of 300 guides, inspiring all sorts of amazing adventures.

Every guide comes from extensive exploration and research by our expert authors, all with a passion for their subjects. They are frequently praised, endorsed and used by clubs, instructors and outdoor organisations.

All our titles can now be bought as **e-books** and many as iPad and Kindle files and we will continue to make all our guides available for these and many other devices.

Our website shows any **new information** we've received since a book was published. Please do let us know if you find anything has changed, so that we can pass on the latest details. On our **website** you'll also find some great ideas and lots of information, including sample chapters, contents lists, reviews, articles and a photo gallery.

It's easy to keep in touch with what's going on at Cicerone, by getting our monthly **free e-newsletter**, which is full of offers, competitions, up-to-date information and topical articles. You can subscribe on our home page and also follow us on **Facebook** and **Twitter**, as well as our **blog**.

Cicerone – the very best guides for exploring the world.

CICERONE

2 Police Square Milnthorpe Cumbria LA7 7PY
Tel: 015395 62069 info@cicerone.co.uk
www.cicerone.co.uk